Praise for *The Big, Bad Bo*

"When I was a kid, the plant world was a narrow and ɩ
only weeding (yuck) or soppy love poems (double yuck). ... *The Big, Bad Book
of Botany* had come my way, I would have giggled and goggled at its showy display
of wacky plant lore."
—*Wall Street Journal*

"This combination of history, mythology, lore, science, and sheer entertainment
takes us on a tour of the world's most unusual plants."
—*Sacramento Bee*

"A fascinating summary of some of the most famous and important plants grown
around the world."
—Dr. F.G. (Eric) Hochberg, Curator Emeritus, Santa Barbara Museum of
Natural History

"[A]n entertaining compendium of unusual plants. Full of history and intriguing
cultural tidbits."
—*Miami Herald*

"This gracefully written book will appeal to general readers interested in botany,
who will enjoy browsing information on a wide variety of strange and/or useful
plants."
—*Library Journal*

"A literary walk through an amazing botanical garden. Full of fun facts and surprising legends, the book is a great read for both plant-lovers and novices alike. I
thoroughly enjoyed it and learned a lot—broccoli will never look the same!"
—Dr. Ellen Prager, marine scientist and Safina Center Fellow at Stony Brook
University

"In a quirky, alphabetical collection of folklore, traditional botany, growing sug-
gestions, and modern science and nutrition, Largo shares delight in the weird and
wonderful corners of the plant world. . . . Colorful. . . . Largo's palpable enthusiasm means every page yields something to catch the reader's interest."
—*Publishers Weekly*

"Largo has the gift of transforming a nerdy catalog of facts into an apothecary of
invigorating information. His encyclopedic knowledge is never an end in itself,
but it is always an engine for historical insight and reflection on human nature."
—*BookPage*

"Not your standard reference book. . . . Written with an eye for humor and
cocktail-party-friendly trivia, this botanical exploration can serve as a coffee-table
piece or conversation starter."
—Shelf Awareness

ALSO BY MICHAEL LARGO

The World's

Most Fascinating

Flora

The
BIG, BAD BOOK
of
BOTANY

MICHAEL LARGO

Illustrations by
Margie Bauer, Kristi Bettendorf, Beverly Borland,
Silvia Bota, Marge Brown, Marie Chaney,
Susan Cumins, Jeanie Duck, Julio Figueroa,
Bobbi Garber, Pauline Goldsmith, Leo Hernandez,
Andres Kelich, Carol Ann Lane, Elsa Nadal,
Carol Onstad, Joe Pullen, and Donna Torres

WILLIAM MORROW
wm *An Imprint of* HarperCollins*Publishers*

FIRST EDITION

Based on a design by Joy O'Meara

Library of Congress Cataloging-in-Publication Data has been applied for.

ISBN 978-0-06-228275-0

23 24 25 26 27 LBC 17 16 15 14 13

To Joe Largo.
Thank you for your help and for being a son who makes a father proud.

What is a weed?
A plant whose virtues have never been discovered.

—Ralph Waldo Emerson

CONTENTS

Introduction

What is green and allows you to breathe? That life-sustaining lungful of air you just took had to come from somewhere. Without plants, and the oxygen they produce, there could be no animal life on earth. These were our planet's pioneering organisms, who first learned the tricks of adaptation to survive on our once-sterile rock, and who turned it into the vibrant, blue-green home we know today. They are both our forerunners and our contemporaries in life—but what do we really know about plants?

No one has cracked the encrypted language of plants. Insects chirp, bees buzz, animals growl, hiss, hum, and even transmit low-frequency sound waves. But plants, as far as we know, never say a thing. Fields of tall summer grasses waft without agency, moving whichever way the wind blows. Roots stay where their seeds originally sprouted. A rose makes no announcement when its bud opens in full-petal bloom. Pine trees in a forest stand like silent sentries. A bent coconut palm owes its haphazard arc to the ocean winds and sea mist; it is silent on the changes its species needed to learn in order to survive where it does. There are trees living today that are estimated to be eight thousand years old, and nearly microscopic phytoplankton that live and die within an hour—but neither will divulge their history or the secrets they contain unless we look. Without plants, we would simply not be here.

Plants have no brains. We can be certain they have absolutely no way to perceive this world in any way remotely similar to our view. But is there another level of "consciousness" we have yet to understand? Plants do everything possible to survive and to reproduce toward the continuation of their species. This is no easy feat, particularly as disadvantaged as plants are to alter the environment in which they find themselves. The seemingly magical biochemistry these entirely stationary organisms acquired to survive and thrive is astonishing. Much has come from looking at the chemistry within; for example, we now understand how a plant produces oxygen via photosynthesis—an amazing process we would never be able to duplicate—and there are countless other techniques plants employ that even the smartest computer could not match.

The primary goal of every living organism is individual survival and the preservation of its species. As more complex plants arose, new ways to procreate came into play. Plants had to find a way to attract "helpers" to transfer male pollen to a female ovary in order to make a "baby"—what botanically we call fruits, or seeds. The collection of means they devised to accomplish this all-important process was and still is diverse. What we admire as a flower is basically a billboard, grown with the sole purpose of saying "Hey, check me out" to bees, beetles, or birds. Some enticed with sweet nectar, others chose toxins and traps, yet all methods proved to be marvelously diverse and interesting.

Most of what our earliest ancestors knew of plants has been forgotten. The first attempt to catalog plants is found in sacred Indian texts from 1100 B.C., known as the *Avestan Writings*. Aristotle's student Theophrastus compiled a book, *Historia Plantarum,* sometime during the second and third century B.C. that included information on 500 different species. The most important book about plants was written by first-century A.D. Greek physician Pedanius Dioscorides, titled (when later translated into Latin) *De Materia Medica,* which remained the standard and most extensive book about plants for nearly sixteen centuries. These books treated botany more like herbalism, and were meant to reveal the best plants for medical purposes. There was no science, no medicine, no pharmacology for early peoples; the kinds of things we depend on from science were found in plants, and survival depended upon knowing the properties and secrets each species held.

In this book, I try to combine the reference-like quality of these early texts and the most fascinating folklore of the past, with descriptions, life cycles, advice on cultivation, and the benefits these plants provide. But more important, I hope to capture the incredible diversity of plants and marvel at the vast plant kingdom's many wonders. We need to look at the amazing greenness about us in a new way—with not only awe and respect, but also renewed curiosity. Likewise, we must protect the incredible flora we are fortunate to still have among us, lest our own actions cause them to disappear forever.

ABSINTHE
Artemisia absinthium
Green Madness

Along ancient dirt roads and on the hillsides of England, in most of Europe, the Middle East, and in fact all the way to the edge of Asia, a brilliantly green, pointed-leaf plant once grew in abundance. It flourished in bushy clusters, reaching about three feet in height with a thin, nonwoody stem. From early summer until the last days of autumn, its yellow, button-size flowers bloomed up and down its stalks like miniature strobe lights, creating an inviting, colorful landscape.

Absinthe, commonly called *wormwood,* is a perennial plant. Like other perennials, absinthe loses its flowers, leaves, and stems each winter, withering to nothing. However, its sturdy, fibrous roots remain dormant in the soil, springing to life each year when the snow and cold weather cease. It grows rapidly, and because it relies on the simplest method of seed disbursement—allowing gravity to simply spread its seeds around the base of the parent plant—wormwood once dominated landscapes for miles. Due to its speedy germination and quick growth, it killed (often smothering with its shade) all other plants that attempted to occupy its ground.

A common practice in early civilizations was to "field-test" every plant people found, including absinthe, in order to discover what use it might have in aiding survival. Absinthe, despite its vast availability, was thought to be rubbish, particularly after it was deemed inedible. Extremely bitter in both taste and odor, wormwood became such a widely recognized synonym for something nasty, unpleasant, and even poisonous that the Bible refers to it that way more than a dozen times. For example, in the book of Revelation: "A third of the waters became wormwood, and many people died from the water."

Still, despite its reputation, people did eventually find uses for absinthe. The ancient Greeks named the plant *apsinthos,* sometimes referring to it as "Artemisia" after the goddess of medicine, Artemis. They believed the plant could be used in an elixir to kill intestinal worms. In medieval times, doctors and alchemists recommended it as a last-ditch cure for tapeworms and other stomach aliments—although it was likely to poison the patient as well—a practice that would lead to the nickname wormwood. Looking to the plants around them almost as we would a vast supermarket or drugstore, early civilizations believed every plant was put on earth with a purpose, that often being to help humankind. Wormwood's sap found use as a salve to repel fleas and ticks, and the ancient Egyptians even used it as an additive to certain wines as early as 1500 B.C.

Absinthe's real heyday would eventually derive from our unceasing desire to find new intoxicants. Historians have even argued that human beings moved from a nomadic species to one that stayed put—ultimately creating cities and civilizations—primarily out of a desire to guard and nurture the plants that made wine and other inebriating tonics or ale. In the mid-1600s, after naturalist Nicholas Culpeper included a recipe for a drink made from wormwood in his book *The English Physician,* people began eyeing the plant anew. Culpeper described the end result as a bitter drink, although one that when sipped "with prudence" brought on a "stream-of-conscious . . . unlike anything else in the herbal world." Subsequently, many tried to make the absinthe concoction in their cottage kitchens—though far from tripping pleasurably, most ended up fatally poisoning themselves.

The true origin of the liquor absinthe—known also as the "Green Fairy" and all the rage for the latter half of the nineteenth century—is clouded in mystery. While a refined formula for the spirit (which primarily is made of sugar, fennel, anise, and leaves and flowers of the absinthe plant) appears in *The Complete Body of Distilling* (G. Smith, 1731), a pair of Swedish sisters is rumored to have perfected the recipe years before. The pair used it as a "medicine" before selling the formula to another doctor. Whatever the real story, a nonfatal recipe for a wormwood-based alcohol eventually landed in the hands of a professional distiller, Henri-Louis Pernod, who would go on to establish the first commercial absinthe distillery in 1798. The finished product, called "Pernod Fils," was a leprechaun-green liquor at a super-potent proof of 136 (for comparison, a bottle of beer might be 8 to 12 proof, a measuring of its ratio of water and other ingredients to its alcohol content). Pernod's drink also contained *thujone,* a chemical found in some species of the plant and eventually discovered to be the source of absinthe's infamous hallucinogenic qualities.

Surprisingly, it was the strength of the alcohol and mixture of other herbs—rather than the trace amounts of *thujone*—that transformed this once-bitter plant into the rapidly soothing and ultimately very popular drink it became. By 1900, 36 million liters of absinthe were sold annually in France alone, the high sales continuing until it was outlawed in 1915. The drink, if taken in excess, can cause blindness, cramps, nerve damage, and mental disturbances. Absinthe was actually the main catalyst behind the American temperance movement, which brought about the Volstead Act, otherwise known as Prohibition, banning the production and sale of alcohol in the United States.

Wormwood belongs to a large genus of plants, along with nearly 400 different species cataloged in the daisy family of Asteraceae. The first variety of this plant appeared on earth approximately forty million years ago.

AGAVE
Agave tequilana
The Tequila Weed

This succulent, bluish green plant with long, swollen, spiky leaves was once in such high demand it caused wars and invasions, even as far back as ten thousand years ago. Wandering tribes of the semi-arid regions of Mexico, the Mesoamerican highlands, and parts of South America saw animals eating agave and using the plant's naturally sweet leaves to sustain themselves. Prehistoric tribes used all parts of the plant, for everything from clothing and shelter to food and drink. Historians believe this multifaceted plant was instrumental in the rise of both the Mayan and the Aztec civilizations. The Florentine Codex of 1580, a Spanish catalog of the region's assets, cited the agave plant as an essential food and fiber for the Aztecs and other natives of the region. Fossil remains of human feces from that period and earlier confirm that agave was an important dietary staple, enabling survival in an often inhospitable land.

Mexico is a unique mosaic of varying terrains, including deserts, rain forests, coastal areas, and mountains. In the botanical sense, Mesoamerica is frequently noted as an important "center of origin and biodiversity" for many species of flora. *Blue agave, Weber's blue agave,* and *tequila weed* are some of the common names given to one of the plants in the Agava-ceae family, the plant known scientifically as *Agave tequilana*. There are as many as 200 types of agave plants, but all are succulents, meaning they've adapted a way to store moisture in their leaves and survive prolonged droughts and climatic shifts. The blue agave favors higher altitudes, flourishing at 5,000 feet above sea level. The tequila agave's leaves can grow as thick as a human thigh at its base and become as long as a man is tall, ending in a sharp point at the tip. It has a turnip-like root, or heart, called a *piña,* which can weigh hundreds of pounds on its own. Having run through the last of their supply of brandy, the sixteenth-century explorers known as the Spanish Conquistadors soon discovered more than just gold on arriving in the Americas; they found, after heating the agave's bulbous root, that the syrupy sap could be fermented and distilled, making a uniquely potent alcoholic drink.

One Flower Before Death

The tequila agave is able to ensure its pollination through a unique relationship it has developed with a particular mammal. Some species live anywhere from ten to one hundred years, with the plant producing just a single flower in its lifetime; decades of storing sugars, waters, and nutrients are geared toward this goal. If pollinated, one flower will produce thousands of seeds. The flower rises on a stalk as tall and straight as a flag-

A Worm in the Story

Devotees of tequila remain in disagreement concerning the true origin of the drink (even if the Aztecs made a brew similar to it, called *ogli,* a thousand years before). Nevertheless, legend has it that the first full-scale production of this type of "mescal wine" began in 1608 near the town of Jalisco, Mexico. Don Pedro Sanchez, a shrewd Spanish aristocrat dubbed "the Father of Tequila," took advantage of the king of Spain's ban on the production of wine in Mexico (revenue from Spanish wine exports had dwindled), planting thousands of acres of tequila agave and declaring it a liquor rather than a wine. Though the don was thrown in jail for breaking the king's law, he was released only two years later, and the Don Pedro brand of tequila (although likely not the original formula) exists to this day. Beginning in 1950, several commercial distilleries began placing actual worms in their tequila bottles—a famous marketing ploy. The worm is a butterfly larva, and while they do bore into certain agave roots, today commercial distilleries add them on purpose to give the spirit a home-brewed, natural character. Eating it doesn't prevent hangovers, as some believe, but it does provide a wee bit of protein.

*In science, a species that has only a single reproductive event employs a breeding strategy called **semelparity**. Its entire life, its years of storing nutrients, is geared to fulfilling this singular and ultimate act. The Pacific salmon is another species that practices reproductive semelparity; the fish forges upstream against all odds, knowing that death is the outcome, but does so to ensure the future of its species. As for the agave, its one brilliant flower comprises many short, tubular blossoms—an ultimate celebration of its life and funeral wreath as well.*

pole, reaching a height of 20 feet or more. After it blooms, the mother plant dies. In addition to its all-or-nothing style of blossoming, the tequila agave must attract a particular long-nose species of bat (*Leptonycteris curasoae*) to its nectar to achieve pollination. A migratory species, *curasoae* eats primarily nectar from the agaves, cacti, and certain rain forest flowering species. The agave opens up its petals in the darkest of night in an attempt to offer an inviting nest. When the bat rests among the petals its fur gathers the pollen. The mammal will then disperse it to another agave. If the plant happens to bloom while no bats are passing through its area, it will not propagate, and its one bloom will be for naught.

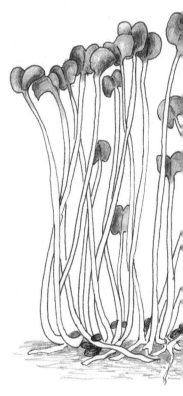

ALFALFA
Medicago sativa
A Match Made in Nature

Alfalfa is not a grass, as it might appear to be, but is actually a member of the pea family. Like other peas, its seeds are actually protein-filled legumes. Many believed the plant originated in Iran—when the region was a temperate "Garden of Eden"—and for centuries farmers cultivated the plant, which could grow nearly anywhere, to maximize grazing pastures, giving their livestock the most nutritional value per acreage.

Alfalfa's resilience lies in the chemistry of its roots. Plants of this family, and many others, need nitrogen found in soil to grow. For most plants, if a seed happens to germinate in nitrogen-depleted terrain, its chances of survival dwindle, and it will likely achieve lackluster growth and fail to proliferate. Alfalfa, however, enjoys a special relation with a bacterium that lives in its root nodules and provides in return the extra nitrogen the plant needs to thrive. The root hairs of the alfalfa secrete certain chemicals, predominantly known as flavonoids, which create an inviting chemical concoction that attracts the bacteria. Alfalfa and many other legumes depend on this bacteria (*Sinorhizobium meliloti*), which is cited as nature's minuscule nitrogen "fixer," in order to survive in otherwise inhospitable soil. Alfalfa counts on *meliloti* to turn the depleted soil that surrounds the plant's roots into a home-brewed fertilizer of sorts.

Behind the Sprouts

Alfalfa is a perennial and can live in the wild for twenty years and grow to about 3 feet in height. In the last few decades, many people have touted the nutritional value of eating alfalfa sprouts, which continues to reign as one of the totems of "health food." Many of the commercially grown alfalfa crops have been genetically modified, however. In 2005, scientists managed to splice the genes of certain alfalfa plants with a chemical compound found in the weed killer known especially under the brand name Roundup. This allows farmers to spray herbicide to kill surrounding weeds without affecting the crop. While alfalfa seeds and sprouts do contain proteins, amino acids, and vitamin D, in some cases they can cause people to develop a disease similar to lupus if consumed in excess. The best alfalfa sprouts to eat are those of the unmodified stock, germinated in only purified water.

ALOE VERA
Aloe barbadensis
Medicine in a Leaf

The succulent aloe vera plant that we know today is a derivative of a wild species now extinct. What grows today is a product of four thousand or more years of cultivation. We know this from numerous medical texts that specifically mention the plant for its multiple health benefits. Egyptian papyruses dated to 2000 B.C. contain formulas for aloe vera's use as a remedy for any number of external and internal aliments. Alexander the Great supposedly made sure to conquer the small island of Socotra for its abundant crops of aloe vera, which he needed to heal the wounds of his soldiers. So essential was aloe to medicine, Western explorers nearly always took it with them, beginning in the 1500s and throughout the era of colonization, spreading it around the globe. Since its leaves can be stuck in soil and will easily take root on their own, aloe vera grows outdoors in temperate and tropical climates throughout the world, from the Caribbean islands and the Indian countryside, to gardens in Australia and the windowsills of many urban apartments.

Aloe is a large group, with more than 500 varieties, all of which have fleshy leaves for storing water and nutrients. The aloe group traces its territorial origins to Africa and the Arabian Peninsula. There are many succulents—12,000 different species—and the group evolved rapidly, appearing first in the late Paleocene and early Eocene climatological epochs of about fifty-five to fifty million years ago. The period was marked by dramatic warming, such that tropical alligators, for example, could live in regions of what we now call Greenland. Numerous plants went extinct but those that did survive the epochs' haphazard shifts from abundant rain to prolonged months of drought really thrived. To achieve this feat, however, these succulents had to practically reinvent the biological systems plants had employed for countless eons. Instead of growing roots deeper into the soil to search for water, the succulents went up, making their leaves their canteens and storehouses.

Succulent comes from the Latin word *succos,* meaning "juice." The waxy leaves of succulents developed what are called stomata, or surface pores, which help reduce water loss. Opposite to how they work in deciduous leaves, in succulents these pores close during the day and open up at night. In simpler terms, succulents began working the night shift to capture needed carbon dioxide, using the cooler temperatures to prevent too much water from escaping. The plant stores the essential gas until the following day, when it's combined with sunlight and water to create carbohydrates and sugars.

Medical studies over the last fifty years have regularly attested to aloe vera's ability to aid in healing wounds, impeding skin fungal growth,

More than three hundred pharmaceutical drugs now in use mimic the chemical composition of certain plants long known to possess healing properties. Aloe products have spawned a multibillion-dollar industry that employs the plants' "juices" in numerous first aid products and skin care lotions.

reducing inflammation, and even correcting the side effects of hypoglycemia, some gastrointestinal ailments, and certain types of diabetes. It all comes down to the predominant type of chemical found in the plant, classified as polysaccharides. Many plants have these complex carbohydrates. Even though aloe's pulp is nearly 99 percent water, aloe contains in its other 1 percent a special blend of enzymes, minerals, water-soluble and fat-soluble vitamins, polysaccharides, and organic acids. The chemicals found in this small percentage of the plant's makeup are diverse and wide-ranging. They include enzymes such as alkaline phosphatase, inorganic compounds such as calcium, chlorine, chromium, and zinc, and amino acids, including leucine and lysine, to name but a few, as well as vitamins B_1, B_2, B_6, C, and folic acid. Aloe vera's medicinal formula is one that only nature's grandest chemist could have devised.

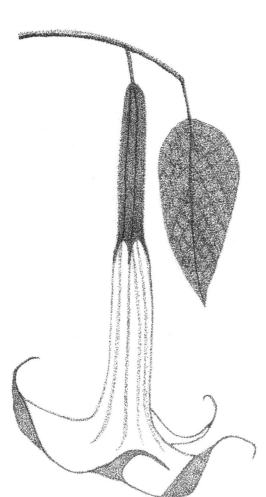

ANGEL TRUMPET
Brugmansia sauveolens
Temptress in D Flat

Beauty is often deceptive, and sometimes the prettiest things prove the most deadly. The angel trumpet is one such tropical, exotic plant. It blooms with gorgeous, dangling flowers shaped like a horn—such as the trumpet—in vibrant shades ranging from yellow, white, pink, and orange to cream. It likes hot weather, 80 degrees or more, and cool nights. It is an annual plant, its life span roughly only one season long. But in that short time, the angel trumpet can grow into a woody, stalky shrub with a height of nearly 6 feet and a girth of 20 yards. A shrub can produce hundreds of dangling flowers, each as beautiful as the next. Though a native of the tropics, it's planted during the summer in northern climates as a border shrub, often used to define landscaping perimeters. Many herbivores, such as deer, somehow can detect that the plants are poisonous and know not to eat them. Hummingbirds particularly enjoy angel trumpet nectar, and the plant is adept at attracting a wide array of pollinators, such as honeybees and other insects.

The scientific name of the angel trumpet is *Brugmansia,* and it belongs to a genus of only seven similar flowering plants grouped in the Solanaceae family. Most of the shrubs in this family contain strong and highly toxic alkaloids. *Brugsmania* is one plant that decided it was better off not relying on other organisms for propagation, instead producing bright flowers to attract the much gentler insect world to ensure pollination and survival. All parts of the angel trumpet, from the roots, stalks, stems, and leaves to the flowers, are extremely poisonous. As a result, even planting the angel trumpet is illegal in some communities.

Paths of Survival

Paleobotany is the study of prehistoric plants and, just as is the case for dinosaur hunters and paleontologists, most of what we know of what plants were like and how they evolved we've surmised piecemeal; understanding what life was truly like on earth in the distant past is a jigsaw puzzle without a guide, and one with countless pieces of information to fit in place. Nevertheless, the consensus is that the first land plants appeared an incredibly long time ago, about 450 million years. It took another 250 million years before the first flower bloomed, during the Triassic period. Angiosperms, or flowering plants as we know them, came into wider disbursement approximately a hundred million years ago. This event was a major contribution to the development of terrestrial animal life; flowering plants, of course, were crucial to the evolutionary rise of insects, which in turn created a food chain allowing larger animals to evolve. Some plants adapted to find a useful way to employ the services of insects and animals, while others developed drastic means to dissuade animals from causing them harm. The angel trumpet is an example of the latter. With such attractive flowers and a short life span, the angel trumpet had no choice but to turn its entire cellular composition into a toxin deadly to any animal that tried to nibble it.

ANT PLANT

Acacia
If You Can't Beat 'em, Join 'em

The ant plant, one of 100 genera of plants known as myrmecophytes, has adapted to allow entire colonies of ants to inhabit it, and both plant and ant coexist beneficially from the arrangement. The plant went the bed-and-breakfast route to ensure protection from other insects, fungi, parasites, hungry herbivores, and even encroaching vines, making itself so inviting to its guests, they would never check out. Voracious and territorial denizens, the ants never want to leave, and thus they retain a vested interest in the plants' survival. The plants count on the ants not only for protection, but for housekeeping and pollination. In return, the ants have a ready-made colony, which provides irresistible food sources and even specialized plant secretions that stimulate better ant communication via the ants' pheromones. Ants are so numerous on the planet, estimated to account for nearly 15 percent of the entire animal biomass, that it was a smart evolutionary move by the plant to utilize the services of these widespread and powerful little creatures, rather than wasting energy fighting them off.

*In science, this type of union is called **obligate mutualism**, meaning that both species, as different as they may be, need each other for survival. In laboratory tests, when worker ants were removed from the colony of ant plants, they could find no other way to live, and so died. Likewise, the plants quickly succumbed to an array of harmful parasites and diseases.*

The distinctive feature of these ant plants is their internal composition, with inviting hollow or tubular spaces in their swollen stems, leaves, and spines. The nectar of the plant's flowers feeds the ants. Other types produce special buds, high in fat and protein, as a means of enticement. In general, while ants are not considered the best pollinators, since they clean themselves frequently or dust off the pollen, in this case, while gathering and feeding on the nectar of the plant, they are able to do the job efficiently. In addition, the ants then take the plant's seeds into the colonies—within the plant itself, which serves an almost womblike function—until the seeds mature. The ants eat only the outer crust of the seed, doing no other damage to it, and then remove it from the colony and plant or disperse it. What guests!

There are 100 or more variations of ant plants, some only growing above altitudes of 3,000 feet, others finding homes in grassy areas and swamplands. In any case, in addition to its ingenious method of survival, the ant plant surely offers a lesson on the concept of peaceful coexistence between the unlikeliest of partners.

ARTICHOKE
Cynara scolymus
A Thorny Delicacy

There are as many as 140 different types of artichokes, all belonging to a group of plants known as flowering thistles, though about only 40 varieties are now grown commercially today. All thistle plants have spiky leaves and thorny stems, some as sharp as barbed wire, and nearly all are tailored to dissuade herbivores. The artichoke and other thistles are cataloged in the Asteraceae family, which contains 23,000 species, including daisies and sunflowers. The artichoke is native to North Africa and the Mediterranean regions, and still grows wild there. The ancient Greeks treated it as a good food source and the Romans cultivated it both as a delicacy and an aphrodisiac. In Greece, if a woman wished to bear a boy, she was told to eat a steady supply of the vegetable.

The Fate of a Mistress

Greek mythology explains how the artichoke came to be. One day Zeus came down to earth to speak with his brother Poseidon, God of the Sea, when Zeus spotted a very attractive young woman by the name of Cynara near the shoreline. He was surprised the girl seemed unafraid and slightly aloof at meeting a god. This apparently stirred Zeus's interest in the woman even more, and he invited her to come

Although some recipes utilize artichoke leaves, the most edible portions are the parts of its annual bud. The bulbous bud has clusters of thick petals that, if not harvested, produce a purplish flower. The plant is a perennial, although usually it produces the edible bud only after the second year, dying off altogether after seven or eight years. It grows to about 4 to 6 feet in height, with the bud perched at the tip of its stem, which rises on a hefty stalk above its thorn-riddled leaves.

Today, California cultivates all the artichokes consumed in the United States, while the rest of the world's supply comes from Spain, France, and Italy. As for the plant's aphrodisiac properties, the ancient Romans weren't entirely wrong. If you come across an artichoke that hasn't been soaked with insecticide, the buds will contain more antioxidants than any other vegetable, which can make people who eat them healthy and possibly more vibrant. Some studies have found that the plant aids in digestion, and some have made the claim it can reduce the risk of coronary disease.

with him up to Olympus. Their secret affair became a regular thing whenever Zeus's wife, Hera, was out of town, and Zeus became so pleased with Cynara that he transformed her into a goddess. Cynara got so fed up with getting attention only when Hera was out of sight that she went back down to earth to see her mother. When she returned to Olympus and Zeus learned of her unauthorized visit among the mortals, he became so enraged that he cast her out of the heavens forever and transformed her into a thistly artichoke plant.

AVOCADO

Persea americana
A Pit for a Sloth

That slice of avocado in your salad is not a vegetable, but actually a berry.

The fruit of the avocado tree, or alligator pear (nicknamed as such for the fruit's leathery skin), houses a huge, single pit or seed. The most familiar type of avocado plant we know today is a very ancient tree species, having originated in Mexico about ten million years ago. Cave drawings in Coxcatlán, Mexico, from ten thousand years ago that display an image of an avocado, along with fossil evidence, prove it was an important food source among aborigines.

Avocado trees can grow to 60 feet in height, with a wide outshoot of branches. The tree itself belongs to an even older family of plants known as Lauraceae, or the laurel family, consisting of as many as 3,000 different species. These plants originated when the supercontinent Gondwana comprised nearly half of the Southern Hemisphere. As the landmass shifted and eventually became today's South America, Africa, and Australia, varieties of avocado-like plants moved with it, and as a result now appear in far-reaching semi-tropical climates around the world.

It's the Shape of What?

The English word *avocado* stems from the Spanish word *aguacate.* Actually, this was merely the Spanish pronunciation of what the Aztecs had been calling the fruit long before the Spaniards arrived. The Aztecs referred to it as an *âhuacatl,* which translates to "testicle," since they compared the avocado's pear shape, especially hanging as it did from trees, to part of the male anatomy. The fruit represented such a potent symbol of fertility, the Aztecs gave it a sort of X rating. Virgins were not allowed to leave their huts to see the dangling fruits amid harvesting; it was believed the fruit would make them lustful and unable to wait for a sanctioned marriage.

Self-Sufficiency

Many of the avocado's characteristics contain hints of how ancient plants lived during that period. Avocados are evergreen; they may lose leaves, but newer ones replace the fallen leaves immediately. It is also a flowering plant, although the yellow-greenish blossoms are small at only about ¼ inch. Unlike most flowering plants, which need to pollinate (that is, transport pollen from a male flower to a female bloom), the avocado is a hermaphrodite; the flower of this plant has both male and female parts. In the ancient world, when insects were scarcer than in later eons, plants could count on nothing but themselves to propagate. This led to the process that goes by the sophisticated botanical phrase "dichogamic protogyny." In simpler terms, this means the flower is a hermaphrodite that has a female part that opens one day, closes at night, then opens again the next day with male characteristics, allowing it to achieve true self-pollination. Nevertheless, only relatively few species in both the plant and the animal kingdoms still boast this method of reproduction, which was much more prevalent among the earth's earlier organisms.

Why Such a Large Seed?

The seed of the avocado is exceptionally large, and so paleobotanists have long wondered how the plant achieved disbursement. Surely such a rock-size seed wouldn't be carried by the wind. The fruit, although not poisonous to us, is toxic to most animals alive today (including cats and dogs), causing death within hours. Even birds avoid poking their beaks into the fruit. In fact, its large pit is an example of what's called an "evolutionary anachronism," meaning the tree had most likely formed a relationship with some large, now-extinct animal to help scatter its seeds. Perhaps it was a large sloth or some creature with a giant mouth to eat the big avocado pits, as we would do peanuts. Dispersal of the seed, so the theory goes, was then achieved by defecation.

AYAHUASCA

Banisteriopsis caapi
The Door of Perception

Ayahuasca is an Amazonian vine that contains a chemical known as DMT, a psychedelic compound belonging to the tryptamine group. DMT is an alkaloid substance that occurs naturally in many plants and animals, including humans, where it's found in the neurotransmitter regions of the brain. *Ayahuasca* means "Vine of the Soul" or "Vine of the Dead." The name comes from aborigines of the Amazon region and is a Spanish translation from the Quechua language. Natives used the plant for centuries in both religious ceremonies and for medicine. When brewed, the bark makes a bitter-tasting tea, a mere sip of which can induce long-lasting and far-reaching hallucinations. Shamans believed DMT allowed one to visit the astral plane and garner insights unattainable in ordinary sensory perception, such as visiting and talking with dead ancestors to gain otherworldly knowledge.

The plant grows as a thick, woody stem and a twisting ropy vine in the Amazon Basin of Peru, Ecuador, Colombia, and Brazil, clinging to trees and attempting to find pockets of sunlight through the dense foliage. Its oval leaves with pointed ends are about 10 inches long. It blooms flowers of both white and pink petals at irregular intervals. The vine itself can reach 100 feet or more in length. It belongs to the Malpighiaceae family of plants, which has approximately 1,300 species, all of which are found in tropical and subtropical climates.

How a Hallucinogen Might Help

Plants, like all life on earth, evolved methods to aid survival and propagation. Some entice with sweet nectar, or grow thorns to keep attackers away. Many, however, either by chance or on purpose—a question no botanist can fully answer—have evolved an internal composition that, if consumed, causes animals to hallucinate. This adaptation may have developed totally by chance as a by-product of some other favorable mutation or survival mechanism. Mushrooms and cacti are other examples of plants with similar properties. How the plant could "know" it would have this effect on animals was surely unclear at first and obviously involved a long process of trial and error.

How does ayahuasca's unique bio-arsenal benefit the plant? In some cases, this defense method might cause animals that ate the plant to lose their sense of purpose and wander away before destroying it more. As for enhancing disbursement, animals, and early humanoids in particular, found the hallucinogenic properties appealing and might thus have protected and cultivated the plant. A significant number of archeological findings indicate early humans frequently sought flora with psychedelic properties; even Neanderthals added hallucinogenic flowers to their burial sites. Another benefit may be the chemicals' effect on insects, the primary enemy of early and modern-day plant life. It is not uncommon to find plants that have developed compounds, like DMT, effective in fending off harmful pests.

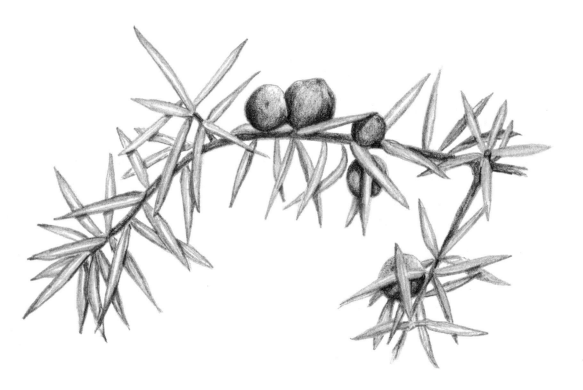

The intoxicating qualities of many plants have worked wonders for their survival. For example, for numerous berry-bearing plants, if the fruit was not dispersed and instead was allowed to ferment on the vine, more birds were attracted. Robins, among other birds, have been known to seek out and gorge themselves on fermented blackberries or juniper berries, which results in their flying into trees or smashing into windows. From the plant's perspective, this is a brilliant way to get its seeds dispersed. If the bird dies, all the better, since the seeds in the belly will have even more fertilizer to germinate in as the avian's carcass decays.

In the case of ayahuasca, its chemical composition ultimately proved a boon. Today the plant is treated like gold; travelers seeking psychedelic experiences have engendered a booming tourism industry in the regions where it grows.

BAD WOMAN
Cnidoscolus angustidens
Bites like a Cobra

This nettle plant, nicknamed *mala mujer,* or bad woman, by the Spanish, is dangerous to the touch, but like most nettles, its chemistry holds some very beneficial qualities. Nettles, also sometimes called *laurels,* are grouped in the family known as Urticaceae, which has 45 genera of shrubs, trees, herbs, and vines. Most of these feature stinging hairs on their stems and leaves. Nettles grow all over the world, with the exception of the Arctic, Antarctica, and South Africa. The scientific name for nettle derives from the Latin *uro,* meaning "to burn." *Nettle,* in English, comes from the Anglo-Saxon word *naedl,* meaning "needle." The *mala mujer* exists in the highlands of the American Southwest and has one of the deadlier bites in the family. A mere touch of its spiky hairs causes a stinging sensation, as if one has been bitten by a snake, and the pain can last for hours. The relentless itchy rash it leaves will persist for days, giving way to months of purplish, discolored skin near the site of the sting.

Stinging nettles have hairs that, when touched, come loose and act as mini hypodermic needles. These hairs contain a concoction of chemicals, including the catalyst serotonin, bicarbonate of ammonia, acetylcholine (which affects the nervous system), leukotriene (an immune response compound), histamine, and folic acid, to name a few. The combination produces a toxic pool, visible as a small white dot at the base of the hair. Upon contact with a predator, the mixture shoots up through

Mythology around the prickly nettle plant abounds. The Vikings believed nettles were especially important to the god Thor, and that burning one in a fire could prevent lightning strikes. Germanic cultures used nettles in medicinal rituals, believing that sickness could be cured by grabbing the plant by the roots and waving it over a patient while reciting his (and his parents') names. According to Greek mythology, these stinging plants arose after a watchful father transformed his beautiful daughter into a prickly plant to prevent the god Apollo from seducing her.

the hollowed center of these specialized defensive hairs, much like the way venom travels through the biting fangs of poisonous snakes.

However, early civilizations were not easily persuaded into avoiding the plant. Many pagan cultures, for example, believed there was a spirit in every living thing (including plants), and so the nettle's sting was a way for the plant to dissuade those unworthy of its secrets.

In fact, some early civilizations used the needles' secretions as a remedy to alleviate the more painful effects of arthritis and rheumatism. In medieval times, people prepared the nettle as a drink, purportedly to rid the body of excess water; they would also grind the plant into a paste to treat joint pain. Centuries before the introduction of hemp and cotton, people used the strong fibers in the plant's stems, reportedly as soft as silk, to make garments.

Stinging nettles are perennials and grow in size from 2 to 6 feet. Today the plant has many purposes, from green dyes producible from its chlorophyll, to herbal supplements meant to aid the immune, urinary, respiratory, and circulatory systems. This latter use taps into the secret the bad woman and other nettles seem to guard with their caustic hairs—a rich internal mix of health-stimulating vitamins, including A, B_1 (thiamine), B_2 (riboflavin), B_3 (niacin), B_5 (pantothenic acid), C, D, K, E, potassium, calcium, manganese, acetylcholine, serotonin, sulfur, iron, selenium, magnesium, chromium, and zinc.

A Formula for Magic

Medieval Europe was a hotbed for death by poisoning. It was the most popular form of stealth murder in the period, aided in popularity and ease by the proliferation of apothecaries, which made many poisons available, including deadly herb extracts. This was also a time when many gravitated toward a belief in magic and mysticism. Such was the influence of the occult that people often presented themselves as sorcerers, magicians, spiritualists, and healers, all boasting a wide spectrum of "magical plants." Birch, hawthorn, elder, and hazel were among the most prevalent. Poplar, for example, was useful if you wanted to fly; linden would make you immortal, while lovage would provide you with prophetic abilities. Rowan would allow you to see the future, one of many plants to which magicians ascribed psychic powers, along with wormwood, yarrow, rose, borage, peppermint, flax, elecampane, and many, many more, including, of course, the nettles.

BAMBOO
Bambusa oldhamii
The Grass of Giants

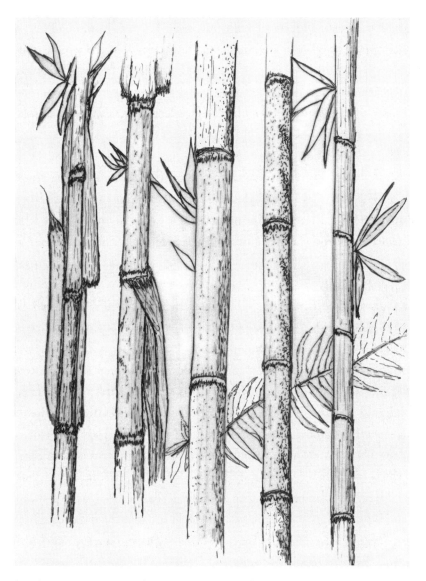

The distant ancestors of bamboo evolved from the early grass family of wheat, barley, and rice, and scientists still classify modern bamboo in the Poaceae family of true grasses. Bamboo developed into its own genera about forty-five million years ago, giving rise to as many as 14,500 different bamboo species, from nonwoody types to what we call Old World woody bamboo, the variety with which we are most familiar. Though we primarily associate bamboo with tropical climates, some species are hardy enough to withstand freezing temperatures. The giant bamboo of China, which grows to 60 feet, is actually the tallest grass in the world. Many species have incredibly long life spans of hundreds of years, and have served as an important aspect of religious symbolism in many cultures. Additionally, bamboo is still a plant of great commercial value to this day, used primarily as timber.

Unlike trees that start as tender seedlings, the stalks or stems of the bamboo, called culms, break from the ground at their birth, or germination, with a wide diameter. It's the fastest-growing species in the plant world; some are able to increase their height by more than 3 feet within twenty-four hours. Bamboos are perennials and never shed all their leaves at once. They are also a flowering plant, but their blooming cycle is atypically long and irregular. Most bamboo will bloom only at intervals of 65 or 120 years. When they do produce flowers (as well as a massive amount of seeds), bamboo can cause a sort of ecological havoc. Rats become suddenly abundant, and cities or towns close to native bamboo forests become overrun with rodents and, as a result, disease. Scientists are still at a loss to explain this strange pattern of blooming. Some hypothesize that the evolution of such abundant seed dispersal was directly related to rodents—although the extra seeds may cause a sudden boom in rat populations, the rats are hardly ever able to eat all of the seeds. The bamboo only flowers again when time has thinned out the rat population, ensuring that the seeds retain a good chance of germinating. The only "enemies" of the bamboo are pandas of China, which eat its leaves; lemurs that favor Madagascan bamboo; and gorillas and chimpanzees in Rwanda and Uganda. The primates both enjoy the bamboo species of their regions as a good food source, and even break off the stalks to let the sap ferment into a special alcoholic cocktail.

Giant bamboo (*Bambusa oldhamii*) and its close Asian relatives originated in Taiwan and produce a very strong wood. Used to build structures in the South Pacific, South America, Asia, and even parts of Australia, bamboo is even strong enough to hold up small suspension bridges that have survived for decades. Builders still use it for scaffolding while erecting skyscrapers in Hong Kong, and it supports the weight of numerous workers and building materials. In addition to its strong composite fiber, bamboo has featured in the best longbows, spears, and all sorts of weapons throughout history. In fact, the first "rifle" was made of bamboo. The Chinese, as early as the tenth century, placed gunpowder in a hollowed bamboo stalk, allowing them to fire rock projectiles with considerable accuracy.

Bamboo Symbolism

In China, bamboo is a symbol of longevity, while in India a gift of a potted stalk is a sign of friendship. Depending on the number of stalks, the gift can mean different things: a whole cluster in a pot brings a healthy and prosperous life; only two stalks symbolizes love and a way to double your luck; three stalks gives long life, happiness, and wealth. However, in Chinese culture, four bring bad fortune and negative energy.

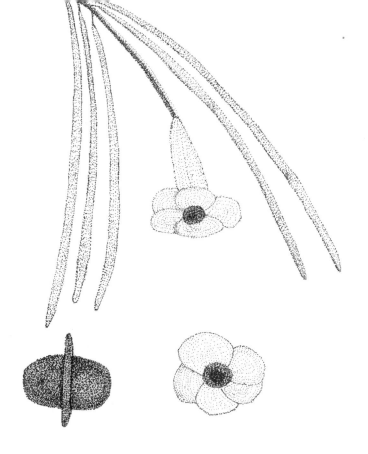

BE-STILL TREE

Thevetia peruviana
A Warning in a Name

Oleanders are beautiful bushes. Their lance-shaped, dark green leaves have a waxy finish, and when in bloom the plants have large, whorled pink, white, red, and yellow flowers, which smell similar to apricots. The plant originated in the Mediterranean region, and because it grows quickly in a burst of color, early settlers transported it around the world to beautify and give "hostile" lands what they considered a civilized look. Oleanders thrive primarily in warmer climates, and are often found growing in vacant lots in California and Florida. Some varieties can survive the summers of slightly cooler regions and are used frequently by gardeners and landscapers to add a quick-growing burst of color.

Be-still tree and *lucky nut* are common names of a few oleander species, but each is extremely deadly. Just a nibble of a few of its leaves, or just a sampling of its black nuts, can cause vomiting and quite often a rapid death. Oleanders contain a chemical classified as a cardiac glycoside. These deadly chemicals affect the heart, causing wildly erratic beats and irregular constrictions and contractions; the human nervous system begins freaking out, as it were, which quickly proves fatal unless vomiting is induced or a stomach pump is employed within minutes. Oleander ranks in the top five ornamental plants that cause fatalities. Ancient societies were well aware of its fast-acting poison, and because even a small amount can be deadly, it was often the food additive of choice for would-be assassins.

A Deadly Trend

Though it's important to be aware of plants and their more dangerous qualities, sometimes informing the public can bring unintended consequences. In Sri Lanka, for example, a television program designed to raise awareness of the oleander's poisonous nature led to a string of suicides among young women in 2006; from just 2 the number jumped to nearly 200 in only three years. Among the elderly, the more botanically savvy have been known to select the oleander to be part of their exit plan, since the lovely plant adorns the grounds of many nursing homes. Hence the nickname "be-still" for this swift killer.

Oleanders' toxins are in all parts of the plant, such that a few leaves that might fall into a dog's water bowl are enough to kill the animal. Even campfires mistakenly built from oleander wood can cause deadly fumes, and urban legends tell of a whole troop of scouts who died, or fell seriously ill, after using the sticks of oleander to roast hot dogs. Oleander nectar gathered by bees and transformed into honey also contains toxins. Just 100 grams of any part of the plant could cause a horse to keel over within minutes.

> *In Christian mythology, the oleander was understood to be a nonflowering bush that miraculously bloomed flowers after the archangel Gabriel announced the Virgin Mary's immaculate conception. In Tuscany the oleander is still called St. Joseph's staff.*

BEECH

Fagus grandifolia
Copy Paper

There are seven types of beech trees found in Europe, North America, and Asia, and all are deciduous, meaning they lose their leaves in winter. Beeches produce a hairy, spiky nut casing, which contains one to a half dozen edible seeds, though they're quite bitter if consumed raw. The leaves have softly pointed tips running their entire length. Beech bark is a grayish silver color, and soft, and thus often provides a forestry blackboard of sorts for lovers, who etch their names in hearts on the bark, and for trappers, who will often leave notes in the bark, either with directions or merely to tag the site. As such beech bark was the world's first canvas for graffiti artists; in fact, the word *beech* derives from the German *buch,* meaning "book," as the tree's bark was often used as a writing parchment in Europe prior to the invention of paper.

Some beech trees can grow as tall as 90 feet and have a 4-foot diameter. They are magnificent-looking trees, and their wide-spreading branches grow in the shape of a crown. Their wrinkly bark is often mistaken for old skin, faces, or other anthropomorphic features, giving these trees an eerie quality, particularly at night. Some even call them "ghost trees," since they so often appear in spooky stories. The most outlandish tales claim that beech trees actually talk when the moon is full.

Talking Trees?

The idea of plants communicating with humans and other plants isn't exactly new (there are many urban legends), but the notion of a kind of botanical telepathy has gained such traction with certain scientists that a new field—psychobotany—has even begun to take shape. Some early theories suggest that plants substitute a kind of biosynthesis for standard, observable communication. Psychobotanists are currently investigating whether plants are able to employ a kind of biochemical messaging to interact with their environment on a level not yet intelligible to human beings.

Beech wood has a few commercial uses, particularly for flooring, but loggers consider it worthless. Many commercial lumber enterprises develop their acreage by ridding the land of beech trees, saying their wood is good for firewood and nothing more. That said, hollowed-out beech trees provide abundant habitat for wildlife and a bountiful supply of nuts for numerous animals. Some American beech trees, if left undisturbed, have lived for three hundred years.

BEER PLANT
Humulus lupulus
Buds and Suds

Ale has long been a staple of our diet. Abundant archeological evidence proves that the beer-making enterprise goes back at least seven thousand years. Fermenting vases, barrels, recipes, and mugs and drinking vessels date to pre-Sumerian times, show up in Mesopotamian and Egyptian writings, and have been discovered in both Neolithic Europe and Asia. Past civilizations tried to ferment all kinds of plants into ale but found that the natural sugars in many species of grasses, particularly wheat and barley, produced the best-tasting and most potent lagers. Indeed, much of the human race's first attempts at complex problem-solving and biological engineering centered around making the best beer. It was a matter of such importance that certain early societies even worshipped gods and goddesses of brewing. At times in history, fermented beverages have been safer to drink than the water supply; although water usually looks clear, it's impossible to guess at the bacteria within. Ale was the favored drink of many civilizations throughout the centuries, and consumed by all age groups. Even babies and toddlers drank it on a daily basis.

The first ales were primarily made from grain, water, and yeast. Ale engineers solved the problem of how to get enzymes out of the grain's sugar, found in its seeds, by mashing and boiling the grain at a particular temperature and then allowing yeast to transform it. Yeast, classified as a single-cell fungus, interacts with the grains through an anaerobic process (meaning it doesn't use oxygen) in order to ferment the grain's sugars into alcohol. In clusters, yeast looks like a mold, as on old bread. Ancient brewers thought the appearance of yeast on barley, rye, or wheat after harvesting was a miracle, and though they didn't know what it was, they knew ale couldn't be made without it. It wasn't until 1866 that Louis Pasteur demonstrated that yeast was the primary cause of beer fermentation.

Nowadays most beer is made from barley, hops, yeast, and water. The discovery of hops and their use as an additive seem to date to the Middle Ages in Germany. Hops not only act as a tremendous preservative, but serve as an important flavor enhancer. The hop plant (*Humulus lupulus*) also contains chemical sedatives. Hops are in the Cannabaceae family of flowering plants, as is marijuana. The "hop" is actually the female part of the plant's cone-shaped flowers, though the entire plant is commonly referred to as "hops." It grows naturally in North America, Europe, and parts of Asia. As a vine, hops use other plants for support, growing around a host to achieve their height and search for sunlight.

BELLADONNA
Atropa belladonna
Deadly with Benefits

Atropa belladonna is a Eurasian perennial, with reddish bell-shaped flowers that bear glossy black berries. Other names for the plant include *belladonna, deadly nightshade, devil's berries, naughty man's cherries, death cherries, beautiful death,* and *devil's herb.* The plant earns its sinister nicknames from the extreme toxicity of its foliage and berries, which contain potent dosages of tropane alkaloids. Its most common name, *belladonna,* derives from Italian, meaning "beautiful woman." Historically, women have used the herb's oil to dilate and enlarge the pupils for seductive effect. Although it's grouped in the nightshade or Solanaceae family of flowering plants, belladonna has a number of less deadly cousins, including potatoes, tomatoes, eggplant, jimsonweed, tobacco, and chili peppers.

A native to Europe, North Africa, and western Africa, the herb grows wildly in many parts of the United States, mostly in dumps and quarries, near old ruins, under shade trees, or atop wooded hills. Belladonna is a branching plant that often grows to resemble a shrub of about 4 feet in height within a single growing season. Its leaves are long, extending 7 inches, and its bell-shaped flowers are purple with green tinges, about 1 inch long. The fruit and berries appear green when growing, but as the toxins get stronger in the ripening stage, they turn a shiny black color. Belladonna blooms in midsummer through early fall, and its roots are thick, fleshy, and white, growing to about 6 inches or more in length.

Nightshade is one of the most toxic plants in the Eastern Hemisphere. While the roots are the most deadly part, the poisonous alkaloids run through the entirety of the plant. Scopolamine and hyoscyamine are among these toxins, both of which cause delirium and hallucinations. Nightshade berries pose the greatest danger to children, since they are attractive and look deceptively sweet. Just two berries can kill a child who eats them, and it only takes ten or twenty to kill an adult. Likewise, even consuming a single leaf can prove fatal to humans. Cattle, horses, rabbits, goats, and sheep can eat nightshade without ill or lethal effects, though many pets are vulnerable. Symptoms of nightshade poisoning present quickly, so if medical aid is far off, drink a large glass of warm vinegar or a mixture of mustard and water, which may dilute and neutralize the plant's toxicity.

Though today we understand that the risks involved in using nightshade outweigh any potential benefits, it has a long history of being used in medicine, in cosmetics, and as a weapon. Ancient Romans harnessed the effects of the plant to make poison-tipped arrows guaranteed to kill, and still others found it an effective anesthetic for surgery since numbness and drowsiness are side effects.

According to the National Cancer Institute in Milan, Italy, nightshade can provide relief from the discomfort, warmth, and swelling associated with radiotherapy used to treat breast cancer. People have used the plant as a pain reliever for centuries, as well as a muscle relaxer and anti-inflammatory, and to treat peptic ulcers, histaminic reactions, and even motion sickness. A sedative effective in stopping bronchial spasms from asthma and whooping cough, colds, and hay fever, belladonna has also found use as a narcotic, diuretic, antispasmodic, and hydriatic. Despite the risk of toxicity, many use it as a recreational drug for the delirium and vivid hallucinations it can cause.

Belladonna spreads rapidly, and farmers consider it a major pest. Since the berries are sweet, animals and birds eat them, and their droppings provide the plant's primary mode of seed disbursement. The seeds' hard coat makes germination a difficult feat, but after they have passed through an animal's digestive tract the chances of procreation increase. Even under the right conditions, the seeds still take several weeks to germinate.

If you wish to grow your own crop of the herb, soak the seeds in refrigerated cold water for two weeks, replacing the water daily. Plant the seeds immediately after two weeks. The young seeds will need sufficient moisture if they're to germinate successfully, so choose a plot outdoors in May, when there is no fear of frost, and after a strong rain, when the soil is fairly moist. Place the seeds 18 inches apart from one another and make sure to keep them free of weeds or other plants. First-year plants should be thinned out to about 2½ to 3 feet to avoid overcrowding in the next year.

Because it's so difficult to grow, belladonna rarely appears in gardens. Though it's cultivated for medicinal purposes in England, France, and North America, the herb has no major value as food. Some home gardeners plant it for its large, colorful display of berries, but remember: this beauty blooms with no printed warning signs, and it's a risky and deadly choice to grow haphazardly.

BETEL PALM
Areca catechu
A Nut with a Kick

Betel palm is a tropical tree abundant throughout much of the tropical Pacific as well as in Asia and parts of eastern Africa. The palm has scarlet or orange-colored fruits called betel nuts. Probably originating in either Indonesia or the Philippines, the tree has inspired religious and other symbolism in numerous cultures, and often figures in sacrificial rituals. In India, a bunch of betel leaves given between a couple formed an actual legal "document" signifying they had married.

The betel is a medium-sized palm tree. It has a long trunk that grows straight up, reaching 40 to 50 feet in height, though it's

also very slender, reaching only 4 to 6 inches in diameter. Its leaves are usually less than an inch in length, and are long and pinnate with numerous leaflets.

Throughout Indonesia, the leaves and nuts of the betel palm represent love and are treated much the way roses are treated in the United States on Valentine's Day.

In Bangladesh, India, Indonesia, Malaysia, and Taiwan, people grow the palm commercially for its seeds, known there as areca nuts. Sold fresh, cured, or dried throughout these countries, the nuts are often chewed, either whole or wrapped in betel leaves (like a quid of chewing tobacco), which gives the nut a fresh, peppery taste. Chewed betel nuts can act as a mild stimulant, inducing a warm, energized sensation. The effect is similar to that of a cup of coffee, though the nuts are decidedly more addictive. In fact, the nuts contain a chemical called arecoline, which, when combined with the leaves and some lime juice, produces a substance similar to cocaine. It acts on the nervous system and causes the release of dopamine. People can easily become addicted to betel quids.

Nevertheless, the plant is customarily believed to be beneficial, helping to kill bad breath, remove phlegm, and help "expel wind." It does turn teeth black, however, and grinds them down, and it can stain lips with a reddish dye. It causes the production of large amounts of bright red saliva, so a betel chewer will spit frequently. Ground into a powder, the nut can be ingested as a remedy to treat tapeworms and other intestinal parasites. Despite some health benefits, however, research shows that frequent use is linked to oral cancers and gastrointestinal problems such as stomach cancer and ulcers.

BIRCH
Betula pendula
Making Faces

Birch is a hardwood tree that bears a close relation to the oak. Silver birch is native to Europe and Asia and is commonly called the *Watchful Tree*. Its bark has crevices and grooves that look like tiny eyes—the birch held great spiritual importance as a goddess spirit in Celtic cultures, where it was said to keep evil away and bolster courage. For centuries afterward, these cultures constructed baby cradles only from birch wood, believing it a vital protection for infants.

Capable of growing 40 to 70 feet tall, a birch is usually small or medium-sized in comparison to others in its area. It usually grows in temperate climates and thrives in direct sunlight. The birch tree competes against other, taller trees, since it has adapted to thrive in soils with higher acidity.

Birches have simple leaves on which veins emanate from a single midrib. The leaves often appear in pairs and are about an inch long. The plant has small fruit with seeds that have learned to ride the winds like mini helicopters, similar to those found on maple trees. All birch buds grow early and fully mature by midsummer. The flowers on the tree open up as or just before the leaves emerge. These flowers are unique in that birches are monoecious, meaning they produce both male and female flowers.

In flowers, the male, pollen-producing part is called the stamen, consisting of what's known as a filament and an anther. They can take multiple shapes, but are usually more numerous than the pistil—the flower's female structure. More often than not, a flower will have only one pistil. Pollen is effectively the plant's sperm, while the pistil acts as an ovary, ultimately producing the plant's seeds or fruit. In most flowering plants, pollinators such as bees or other insects must transfer the pollen from the anther to the pistil. When a plant is monoecious, pollination can be achieved more easily, even by wind brushing flowers together, making the plant far less dependent on attracting pollinators.

Survival Technique

If you break a leg or a bone in the wilderness, have someone soak some birch bark until moist to make a fairly sturdy temporary cast.

Birch trees are oddly resistant to decay, due mostly to the many natural oils that occur in its wood. These oils give the fine-grained wood a satiny texture, making it ideal for polishing. This, with the ripples that occur naturally within the wood, make it a favorite among furniture makers.

Lightweight but flexible, birch wood is often used to make skateboards, as well as model airplanes. Birchwood's versatility makes it a sought-after lumber, often bringing in a higher dollar value per board than many other hardwoods.

The birch has other uses apart from its lumber. Birch oil extracts are useful in flavoring and in the production of leather oils, soaps, and shampoos. Tar extracted from birch bark is thermoplastic and waterproof, so it was used as a glue to fasten arrowheads to arrow shafts. Native Americans loved birch trees for this reason and because they could use the bark to make lightweight canoes, wigwams, and bowls. Birch leaves are used to make a medicinal tea with supposedly calming and diuretic effects, as well as an extract for dyes. Birch wood is also a favorite firewood because it burns without popping and ignites with the slightest spark. Even the bark burns well, bolstered by its natural oils. Birch sap makes a good sweetener, almost like maple syrup. Some choose to drink it straight, and fermenting it produces birch sap wine. Given all these wonderful characteristics, it's no wonder the Celts believed birch trees contained the benevolent spirit of a goddess.

BIRD OF PARADISE
Strelitzia
Looking like a Bird

Bird of paradise plants, also known as *crane flowers,* are a genus of five species of perennials native to southern Africa. The bird of paradise produces unique flowers, some of the most beautiful in the plant kingdom. The name comes from the flower's resemblance to the crest of a bird's head. The exotic flower makes this plant a popular ornamental piece. Its scientific name (*Strelitzia*) was chosen by English naturalist and explorer Sir Joseph Banks, who named it in honor of Queen Charlotte, wife of George III, and who also held the title of Duchess of Mecklenburg-Strelitz.

In Africa, birds of paradise represent joy and paradise itself. In the United States and throughout the world, they symbolize liberty and freedom.

> Birds of paradise are often planted by people who have close family in the military. In some cultures, a woman's giving the plant to a man is taken as a symbol of her faithfulness.

In addition to their desirable resemblance to birds, *Strelitzia* often finds its way into exotic floral displays. These flower arrangements are quite valuable, as they last about a week before wilting. Africans, though, are content to admire birds of paradise from afar and will not harvest or touch one in any way, believing it bad luck to disturb such beauty.

Birds of paradise are quite large as plants go. If grown to maturity, certain species can reach 30 feet tall and 15 feet wide. Their leaves are quite large, too, getting up to 28 inches long and 12 feet wide. They are a fierce competitor for sunlight, and their rapid growth allows them to quickly tower over others.

The bird of paradise's uniqueness lies in the shaping of its grayish green leaves, which are elongated and curved on the tips. They look a lot like banana leaves, though the bird of paradise's leaves often have a longer petiole. The leaves form a fanlike crown of foliage that can stay green all year long, given the right location and climate. The leaves are tough and durable. The flowers are the most stunning part of the plant, and it requires almost no imagination to envision one as a bird in flight. The colors of the flowers vary greatly, including mixtures of blue, orange, white, red, and yellow.

Even though its natural habitat is Africa, bird of paradise can survive summers in more temperate climates. The plant prefers loose, well-drained soil and needs full shade if it's to bloom at all (though it will still grow foliage in semi-direct sunlight). Birds of paradise can withstand gentle, salty winds and seem to produce the most spectacular colors when exposed to ocean breezes.

Grown indoors in a pot, bird of paradise must be transplanted often to avoid becoming rootbound. The plant should get a mixture of loamy potting soil and mulch, allowing it to stay moist but well drained. Even an indoor plant will need to sit outside to soak up some of the summer's light, though always shaded from full exposure. Sow seeds at least 6 feet apart to allow the plant to flower and bush out properly. Birds of paradise are big plants and must be treated as such; give each ample room to spread "its wings." Fertilizer, a good idea for these plants, is best applied in spring before new growth starts, as well as once per month during the summer.

Sunbirds are the plants' primary pollinators in Africa; when landing on the flower, the weight of the birds spreads the leaves apart and opens the flower top; the pollen sticks to the bird's feet. The bird is then able to deposit it on the next flower it visits. No one is sure whether the birds are lured by the plant's very birdlike flowers. Nevertheless, it's just another of nature's surprising coincidences that a bird-shaped flower depends chiefly on birds for pollination.

BLACK-EYED SUSAN
Rudbeckia hirta
Strength in Numbers

The black-eyed Susan is native to the eastern and central United States. Other common names for the plant include *brown-eyed Susan, brown Betty, poorland daisy, yellow daisy,* and *gloriosa daisy.*

Black-eyed Susan is a medium-sized plant, growing 12 to 29 inches tall and spreading out to more than 15 inches wide. Its oval leaves are 10 to 18 inches long and are covered with coarse hair. It boasts one noticeably large flower about 4 inches in diameter. These flowers, very rich and bright in color, have a "black eye," comprising two hundred to three hundred smaller brown pistil florets, or clusters of flowers, each one producing a seed. Ten to fourteen yellow florets surround the center. Since it looks very similar (though smaller) to the sunflower, it's unsurprising the black-eyed Susan is in the same family.

People have bred and domesticated this plant for centuries, and so the flowers now come in an extensive range of colors, including orange, red, and brown. These varied hybrids appear widely in parks and gardens and often feature on summer bedding schemes, in wildflower gardens, as cut flowers, and on borders and in containers.

Black-eyed Susan can grow in sand, loam, or clay, and in all types of soil in full sun. It is very competitive and will push other plants out of the way in order to support its own growth. Likewise, the plant can tolerate a lot of water, as its root system has evolved to maximize absorption. After the roots take in the water, it's drawn up to the main part of the plant, where the hairy leaves and stems help to keep it inside and prevent loss of moisture.

Black-eyed Susan has a short life, only two years. In its second year, the plant produces flower stalks, which bloom from May to October, depending on the variety. Butterflies, bees, and flies drink the nectar of this plant, thus pollinating it and creating seeds.

Snails and slugs tend to eat the leaves voraciously though they are not black-eyed Susans' worst adversary. Deer and rabbits love to eat the

In the 1800s it was popular to bestow a symbolic quality to flowers, and lists of a plant's symbolism appeared in various farmers' almanacs. The black-eyed Susan was given the attribute of "justice," perhaps because it appeared to bloom without prejudice in all sorts of terrains. Maryland voted to name the black-eyed Susan its state flower in 1918.

Xylem and phloem, put simply, are the tubelike structures in vascular plants that disperse water, nutrients, and sugars. Water and nutrients from the soil must be pulled up by the xylem, allowing the leaves to produce sugar, which can travel down via phloem to keep the roots healthy. Although it's not a steadfast rule in the botanical world, you can think of xylem as the upward ladder and phloem as the downward chute.

whole plant. Luckily, since they produce such an abundance of seeds, black-eyed Susan's population does not suffer for its many predators. It is probably the most widespread of all American wildflowers, a testament to its resilience and survival techniques.

Black-eyed Susan also has many uses to humans. Its roots provide a soothing wash for sores and swelling, and the Ojibwa tribe found it effective in treating snakebites and colds, as well as for the ridding of intestinal worms. The Menominee and Potawatomi people used the juice from the roots as drops to treat earaches. And many Native Americans put the vivid yellow florets to use as a dye to color rugs.

BLEEDING HEART
Dicentra
Love Tester

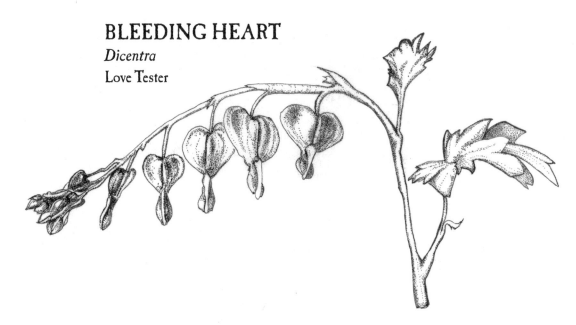

Bleeding heart, or *Dicentra,* is a perennial herbaceous plant in the family of Fumariaceae, which consists of 8 different species. It gets its name from its heart-shaped flower, each of whose petals looks like a scarlet drop of blood dangling downward. The name *bleeding heart* usually refers to *Dicentra spectabilis*, but *Dicentra* itself has many species, including *Dicentra eximia* and *Dicentra formosa*. The leaves have a fernlike look. Bleeding heart is a native of Asia and North America, but it grows anywhere with favorable heat conditions and good soil, from either a seed or stem cuttings. It's usually one of the most beautiful—and quirky—plants found in any garden.

Bleeding heart grows best in a soil that drains water well. However, the soil should be watered daily during summers, and in winters sparingly enough to avoid overmoist soil. It tends to grow well in partial to fully shaded areas—direct sunlight will wither it. The bloom period is during spring and early summer. The flower remains in full bloom for many weeks.

Bleeding hearts grow to a height of 2 to 3 feet and may spread horizontally to 2½ feet across. It is important to keep the plant away from intense sun—they cannot grow to full potential in too much heat. The leaves of the plant may also develop leaf spots or dark blemishes, though this is easily solved by pruning the affected leaf.

Medicinal Use

The Pacific variety of the bleeding heart plant has known medicinal uses. It can help allay pain and aches from sprains if added to a hot compress.

As an herbal remedy, roots of the bleeding heart, particularly if

She Loves Me Not

The heart shape of the flowers is so clearly defined that romantic legends and folklore about its origin abound. The most prevalent tale goes like this: Once a young man pursued a maiden, but she shunned his repeated advances. He bore gift after gift to persuade her to change her mind, but she refused to return his love. Alas, the hopeless young lover pulled out his dagger and stabbed himself in the heart. Where his body fell, the first bleeding heart flower bloomed. Another legend says the plant can tell you if your love truly has feelings for you—supposedly, if you step on a bleeding heart and red juice comes out, then you have true love. If white fluid comes from the crushed flower, then your lover's intentions are false.

Decorative Use

Bleeding heart is usually used as a bordering plant that when grown in clusters serves as a fence or to mark a perimeter and adds color in doing so. It can be planted as an indoor potted plant as well. It comes in varieties of red, white, and pink shades depending on the *Cleroden drum* species. The dangling red "blood drop" is most stunning on the white flowers.

harvested in summer, reportedly reduce anxiety and induce calmness. People in India make a tincture for asthma by placing the roots in a jar filled with alcohol for about six weeks. Some Native American tribes used the herb in tea to cure abdominal pain, diarrhea, and even bee stings.

Amateurs should proceed with caution, since the roots can be poisonous if not collected and combined properly. Parts of the plant often cause skin irritation, so it's best to look but not touch this beautiful plant.

BLUE ALGAE
Cyanobacteria
Plant or Beast?

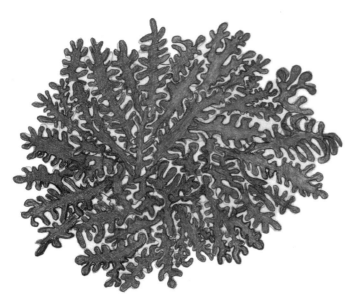

Algae, the glutinous, rootless, bloblike greenish mass we see in lakes, is actually a member of the plant kingdom. As science advanced, though, we discovered that some of the organisms we thought were algae were not plants at all, despite their green color and apparent use of chlorophyll and photosynthesis. *Cyanobacteria,* popularly known as "blue-green algae," is one of the oldest forms of bacteria that still exists on earth. It has been around for 3.5 billion years—yes, billion! *Cyanobacteria,* though microscopic in nature, are visible to the naked eye, as they commonly form clusters or colonies, particularly on the edges of warm lakes, streams, and canals, and at the shores of the ocean, or any body of water receiving enough light for production of food.

Cyanobacteria, therefore, are aquatic microorganisms that are photosynthetic in nature—but they are not technically plants! In fact, they could be an example of a prehistoric link between plant and animal. Although a kind of bacteria, their similarity to the plant has allowed them to retain the name "blue-green algae." Having perfected their method of survival despite eons of countless climatic shifts, these amazing plantlike creatures could reveal much of our planet's history.

Cyanobacteria are mostly bluish green in color, but in salty lakes may appear red or brown. All forms are gooey, smooth, and slippery, and soft to touch.

What's the Harm?

Not all species of blue-green algae are poisonous, but some may contain nerve and liver toxins that pose serious health risks to humans and sometimes even to other plants. People who swim in lakes and ponds with a higher concentration of toxic blue-green algae can fall ill; there have been cases where nerve or liver damage manifests after prolonged exposure to *Cyanobacteria*-rich water. Those infected will quickly endure stomachaches, vomiting, diarrhea, and skin rashes.

Bacteria Bloom

In places where conditions are favorable for *Cyanobacteria,* such as the shores of warm lakes, it can enjoy explosive growth. The phenomenon of their mass, clumping congregation is referred to as a "bloom," even though no flowers are produced. As a result, the clear water turns cloudy and opaque, like large cauldrons of pea soup. *Cyanobacteria* tend to die off within a week or two, causing the bloom to disappear. But if the ideal conditions remain static, more blooms, or new blue-green algae, will form in quick succession, replacing the previous colonies.

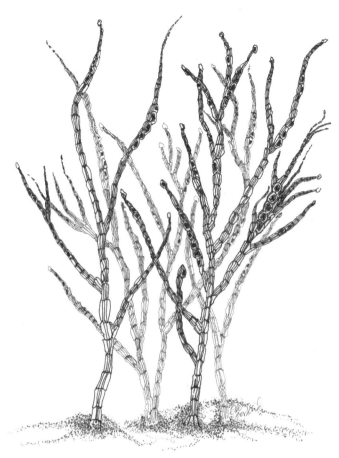

Oxygen Machine

Like plants, *Cyanobacteria* also contain chlorophyll, a pigment that traps sunlight for photosynthesis, which means this bacteria is autotrophic. Chloroplast organelles within any plant contain chlorophyll, and are themselves like a kind of cyanobacterium. Hence we believe they played a pivotal role in making plants green. Considered to be the first photosynthesizers on earth, *Cyanobacteria* were likely instrumental in the rise of the multicellular life form that would follow their arrival—plants.

Cyanobacteria perform the crucial function of converting atmospheric nitrogen into usable forms, such as nitrates that enrich soils. These nutrients, vital to most plants, are absorbed by the roots and then utilized by the plant body. All plants contain this bacterium and its chloroplasts, having eons ago forged a symbiotic relationship to enable photosynthesis. Anaerobic bacteria existed prior to this, but they couldn't produce oxygen. Without this monumental bacterium, *Cyanobacteria,* the earth would not have enough oxygen to sustain life as we know it. To observe this organism's terrestrial cousin, look at lichen, the mat-like plant growing on trees or rocks, and at other fungi.

Edible?

A kind of *Cyanobacteria* called *Spirulina* is a high source of protein and is an important food source for many people.

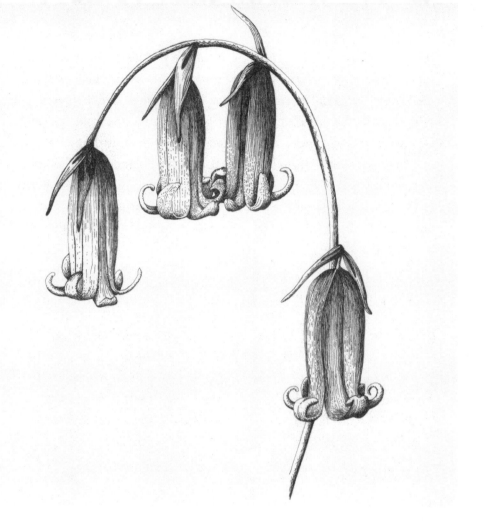

BLUE BELL
Hyacinthoides non-scripta
Endangered Beauty

The beautiful blue bell spreads out over large landscapes, adding a panoramic splendor to hills and fields. The way its flowers seem to look down toward the earth, it seems almost as if it is admiring its own work, like Narcissus unable to turn away from his own reflection.

Hyacinthoides non-scripta, known as *blue bell,* grows in large numbers in the United Kingdom and a few other areas in Europe. Britain supposedly has more than 50 percent of the world's blue bell population. Three other species are related to the common blue bell, growing mostly in Spain and Portugal and in certain parts of North Africa. Long ago, before England split off as an island, the cold, glacier-covered northern regions nearly wiped the species out; however, the blue bell somehow managed to migrate southward and survive eons of freezing temperatures. After the glacier retreated, and the formation of the English Channel separated Britain from the rest of Europe, blue bells once again made their way back up to the beloved English countryside.

The blue bell grows better in areas with high numbers of oak trees. This is due to the falling of oak tree leaves, which give the soil an acidic quality. To survive the lowered pH, the plant formed a symbiotic relationship with fungi growing on the oaks' roots; these are the Arbuscular mycorrhizal *fungi, which aid in the nutrient cycling of the soil.*

The common blue bell is now considered an indigenous species in Britain. The plant is protected—it's actually illegal to uproot blue bell bulbs. However, after centuries of cultivation, numerous hybrid varieties (many crossed with other species from Spain) have begun to pose a natural threat to the original, indigenous species. They grow quicker and are more aggressive, spreading out in huge numbers and overpowering the native blue bell; thus there is mounting concern the plant could go extinct.

The blue bell grows in spring, during the month of April. Blue bells try to accumulate as much sunlight as they can before the oak trees grow leaves, since the dense cover of the large trees allows little light to filter through. Blue bells in such areas display a necessary growth spurt, reaching full height in as little as a month. Because of the plant's beauty, some people have seen to it that outsized oaks are cut down periodically in order to increase the blue bell population. The growth of blue bells generally indicates the historical presence of oak trees in the area, even if none remain today. Blue bells are popular in home gardens. The plant relies on insects for pollination, which it attracts with its sweet nectar. The plant is perennial, and new growth sprouts from dormant bulbs; or it can reproduce from seeds.

A few legends surround the blue bell. For example, it's said that if a child walks into a forest of blue bells and plucks a bloom, the child will never be seen again. Even during the Middle Ages, people marveled its beauty and created superstitions to discourage unwanted plucking of these pretty flowers.

The bulb is poisonous, containing as many as fifteen biologically active compounds, so animals know not to eat it. As for its benefits, its bulbs are filled with starch and used as an adhesive. In recent studies, the plant's compounds have shown promise in combatting certain cancers and HIV. It is also used as a local medicine for the treatment for leukorrhea.

Even if the blue bell seems entranced by its own beauty—like Narcissus, who was so in love with his own image he died staring at his reflection in a pool of water—the blue bell's extinction would be a greater loss, not only for its beauty, but for its vast and still untapped potential to fight disease.

BLISTER BUSH

Notobubon galbanum
Tag, You're Scorched

Who'd have thought a plant in the same family as carrot and dill could be so dangerous? The aptly named blister bush is a perennial shrub that originated in Africa, growing in areas of high to middle altitudes with temperate climates. It can survive on only a bit of moisture as well as in cold climates—the plant thrives on winter showers—though the temperature must not go below freezing. Its leaves look similar to celery or parsley, but do not be fooled; they are certainly not edible. Blister bush has yellow flowers, which yield winged, flat seeds. The flowers grow from a huge, rounded, globe-shaped cluster called a green umbel, which can be 3 feet or more wide.

True to its name, the plant can cause blisters and irritation to the skin. Blister bush wields a soup of biochemicals, including bergapten, psoralen, xanthotoxin, and imperatorin. If skin comes in contact with or even close to this toxic concoction, what look like wounds and open rashes appear within one to two days. These chemicals interact with the skin and literally combust when exposed to sunlight. This mixture uses ultraviolet rays as a type of catalyst, which in science is referred to as phototoxicity. Phototoxicity takes place when chemicals use light's photons or energy to cause changes in molecules. You might not even immediately know you encountered the plant, especially if it happened close to nightfall. But as the days pass and you spend more time in the sun, the blister bush's irritants will manifest with a vengeance, and you'll think you've been hit by a plague.

However, despite this nasty defense mechanism, blister bush offers some gifts and a number of beneficial medicinal properties. People in rural areas of Africa use the plant in a solution (inserted in the rectum or taken by mouth) to dissolve kidney stones or to heal bladder problems. Some cures call for boiling the bush and making the patient inhale the fumes. As a traditional remedy, blister bush has found use in preventing miscarriage, suppressing menses, and in assuring retained placenta is fully dissolved after a woman gives birth. Some pharmaceutical companies are experimenting with the plant's potential use as a diuretic, and still others have used it (in combination with other medicines) to treat rheumatism—proving this tough, prickly warrior has more to offer than meets the eye.

Antidote? Not So Much . . .

The best way to limit rashes is washing off the area with soap and water immediately. If no water is at hand, apply suntan lotion if available. If irritation appears, rubbing alcohol will help dehydrate the blisters. But don't pop them to rid them of their water; it's best to leave them alone. The blisters will eventually wilt and heal after a couple of days, though they sometimes leave a scar.

BROCCOLI
Brassica oleracea
Born to Be Food

All parts of the broccoli plant are edible. Small and green with a large flower head, *Brassica oleracea* belongs to the cabbage family. It is native to Italy. However, the bunches we see banded together in supermarkets did not occur this way in nature. The Etruscans, a civilization that thrived in Italy around 800 B.C., were masters of horticultural engineering. They experimented with a variety of wild cabbage plants, eventually "inventing" the broccoli plant we know today. An instant hit, it remained a staple of the Italian diet for years thereafter. When introduced in the late 1600s throughout Europe, it even went by the name *Italian asparagus*. It wasn't until the 1920s that broccoli really took hold in the United States.

Rich in phytonutrients, broccoli can be boiled, steamed, roasted, or eaten raw. A cool season crop, it is similar to cauliflower, although it belongs to a different cultivar group of the same species. Broccoli leaves, stalks, and flowers all contain lots of health-promoting properties—it is rich in vitamin C, in addition to vitamins A, B_6, and E, calcium, zinc, selenium, magnesium, chlorine, folate, and other antioxidants that protect against cancer and stroke risks.

Superfood

The more we learn of broccoli, the more scientists and nutrition experts sing its many praises. If you can't seem to get past the distinctive taste, consider this long list of benefits: Broccoli promotes eye health, since it is packed with fat-soluble vitamin A and has the ability to prevent cataracts, blindness, and other age-related macular degeneration of the eyes. Its vitamin C content has a powerful antioxidant that empowers the immune system and protects cells from the damaging effects of free radicals. Its wealth of zinc acts as a cofactor in its numerous defensive actions against bacterial and viral attacks. Its rich store of iron promotes oxygenation, which will help you in the formation of hemoglobin. It also has benefits related to pregnancy and healthy babies since it is rich in folate. Folic acid in pregnant women helps in fetal brain development and prevents neural tube defects. Broccoli also contains sulforaphane, which enhances cardio-vascular and gastrointestinal health. It is rich in potassium, which in turn helps in the prevention of hypertension. Broccoli protects skin from sun damage and the carcinogenic effects of ultraviolet rays. Its sulforaphane content boosts the liver. Its calcium and phosphorus package strengthens the bones, especially for women prone to bone loss and osteoporosis. It is a powerhouse of phytonutrients, which detoxify the cells and cleanse the toxins, cancer-causing carcinogens, and free-radical residues. It is per-fect for weight loss since its fiber content lowers the levels of fat-causing cholesterol in the blood. Its magical phytochemical nutrients play a very important role in protection against cancer by boosting the detoxification enzymes of the body, which in turn promotes apoptosis of leukemia and melanoma cancer cells. It contains indoles, which are compounds that prevent breast cancer.

Wow! Broccoli's nutritional benefits are astonishing, and the science is there to support its inclusion in just about anyone's daily diet.

CALLA LILY
Zantedeschia aethiopica
Too Beautiful to Bear

As Albert Camus said, "Beauty is unbearable, drives us to despair, offering us for a minute the glimpse of an eternity." These are fitting words to describe the radiance of the calla lily. Its splash of vibrant color and uniquely delicate trumpet shape make the calla lily a symbol of beauty, not to mention adorable to nearly all who come across it. In ancient times, people worshipped the flower as a symbol of purity and chastity and treasured it as a celebration of light. Christians saw it as a symbol of the Resurrection, and it's still a fixture of Easter services. For most of its history, humans have used the lily at funerals, but in recent times it's become a popular guest at wedding ceremonies, too. The lily even prompted Henry Ward Beecher to write: "Flowers are the sweetest things God ever made and forgot to put into a soul."

Calla lilies originated in southern Africa, blooming near marshlands and riverbeds all year round. The calla lily was first scientifically catalogued in the mid-1700s and misnamed by the famous "Father of Taxonomy," Carl Linnaeus. The German botanist Karl Koch corrected the mistake a half century later. Linnaeus had grouped it with a characteristically different flowering genus, and Koch recategorized the calla lily under a new genus, *Zantedeschia* (Araceae family), in honor of the famous Italian botanist Giovanni Zantedeschi (1773–1846).

Most of the species of calla lily are native to southern Africa, growing predominantly in marshy areas. The calla lily plants thrive in a variety of soil and enjoy dappled shade as well as sunlight. The calla lily can grow continuously in watered conditions, even surviving mild frost. However, when water is sparse, the calla lily can adopt a deciduous nature, causing leaves to fall off at maturity. Most calla lily species are also rhizomatous, meaning they have underground stems that spread outward, blooming new stalks and flowers. *Zantedeschia* is a perennial, usually reaching 3 feet in height, and its shimmering flowers can rise 2 feet above its arrowhead-shaped leaves. The flower of the plant is called a spadix, which actually consists of mini-flowers gathered tightly around an axis point. The inflorescence, or pattern, of these tiny flowers can be showy white, yellow, or pink and forms a funnel shape around a central finger-shaped stalk, or thicker spadix. The larger spadix comprises a phallic flower stalk carrying several male (pistillate) and female flowers.

On the calla lily, the spathe or petal is actually a modified leaf, which can sometimes reach up to 10 inches long. The actual leaves are dusky green in color, ornamented with transparent speckles. The calla lily mixes well with other plants and can readily displace native wetland species. In this regard, it is also an acknowledged super "weed" suppressor, often eliminating plants considered less beautiful. The clump-forming habits of the calla lily easily overwhelm and crowd out other species, especially due to their underground stem system.

The Romans considered the calla lily an erotic flower, viewing it as a symbol of lust and sexuality. Giving the flower to a woman sent an explicit message of a man's intentions. The Victorians viewed it in much the same way, though considered it a sign of desire in "pure" love.

Despite this, the lily is not considered an invasive plant, and its impact on its natural environments is minor.

- The calla lily has often been used in paintings and was a favorite theme of the painter Georgia O'Keeffe. Her *Calla Lilies with Red Anemone*, painted in 1928, sold for $6.2 million at a Christie's auction in New York in 2001. Artist Diego Rivera also favored calla lilies.
- In India, calla lilies are sacred flowers and have been viewed as a symbol of death, cleanliness, truth and brilliance, purity, holiness, and marriage.
- In the Roman era, calla lilies were forced to bloom indoors during the darkest time of year to celebrate the preservation of the light and were said to make winter end sooner.

CANNABIS
Cannabis indica
Stone Age Stoner

For most of recorded history, "traditional" medicines have played an essential role in human health care. These remedies relied solely on the curative powers of plants; through trial and error, we discovered scores of effective treatments for a myriad of problems and diseases. Cannabis, popularly known as marijuana, is one mainstay of traditional medicine, completely apart from its psychoactive and physiological effects. The plant belongs to the Cannabaceae family of flowering plants and is native to Central and South Asia. The genus *Cannabis* comprises three varieties: *Cannabis indica, Cannabis sativa,* and *Cannabis ruderalis.* Colloquially referred to as *hemp, Mexican Spanish Marihuana, pot,* or *weed* (depending on the context), cannabis is one of the oldest plants cultivated purposefully for its fiber and seed oil, the latter of which is useful in medicinal remedies. These uses all predate its infamy as a recreational drug.

Archeological studies furnish evidence of cannabis cultivation dating back twelve thousand years. The first written record of cannabis use comes from the oldest Chinese book of traditional medicine, *Shen Nung's Pharmacopoeia.* The plant's mystic fame led to China's renown as the "Land of Mulberry and Hemp." Asian cultures regarded the plant as a "source of happiness," "joy giver," and "liberator." Cannabis also shows

The first documented cannabis craze occurred during the eighteenth century, when "life, liberty and the pursuit of happiness" were very popular ideals. A century later, cannabis began its steady descent into bad reputation, and a steep, nearly prohibitive tax was put on its sale. In 1937, the United States made the use, sale, and possession of marijuana illegal, though it remained legal (if heavily regulated) for certain medical uses. Currently, the scientifically proven benefits of marijuana have broken through the politically motivated hysteria surrounding the plant. It is currently in the process of being removed from the list of banned narcotics to being legalized. Supporters of its recreational use point to the statistic that no known deaths have occurred directly from marijuana use (although statistics of mortalities while under its influence are inconclusive). In contrast, alcohol, for example, is definitively proven to cause approximately 100,000 deaths per year in the United States.

up as a "sacred grass," or holy plant, in the Atharva-Veda, a collection of Hindu magic spells.

Hash and Assassins

The word *assassin* is derived from the Arabic *hashshashin*. This was a group of assassins founded by Hassan-i Sabbah who were active from the eighth to fourteenth centuries and targeted Persian rulers. The name of the group came about because assassins were given hashish before each assignment, supposedly to calm their nerves.

The term *cannabis,* or, more often today, *marijuana,* actually refers to the dried leaves, stems, and heads of the female flower (which is the only part that contains 1 to 10 percent THC, or tetrahydrocannabinol, the compound that gives marijuana its psychoactive effects). Hash, or hashish, is a compressed block of the resin found in the female buds of the plant, and contains 26 percent THC. THC becomes activated when it interacts with the proteins on brain receptors.

Cannabis is native to tropical and

temperate climates and grows well in a temperature range of 74 to 80 degrees Fahrenheit. Cannabis is a short-day plant, meaning it blooms best in spring and autumn, when days are shorter. It's an annually flowering herb, with light green leaves, reddish buds, and a sweet, fruity smell. The flowers of cannabis are dioecious, which means individual plants will bear either male or female flowers exclusively. Leaves of cannabis plants are compound palmately lobed (or arranged like fingers on a hand) and have notched leaflets. Initially, pairs of leaves will usually have a single leaflet, which gradually increases to a maximum of seven to thirteen per leaf. The peculiar diagonal venation, or protruding veinlike pattern, of the cannabis leaf distinguishes it readily from other superficially similar leaves. The male flowers are often borne in loose clusters termed a panicle, while female flowers are borne on racemes—a peculiar type of inflorescence, or cluster of stalked flowers arranged along an elongated, unbranched, and indeterminate axis. The fruit of the cannabis plant is called an achene, which is a simple, indehiscent (meaning it does not open at maturity) monocarpellate (formed from one carpel, or female and seed-bearing part of the flower).

Microscopic examination of mature cannabis plants reveals the presence of many glistening, translucent resin glands protruding from the buds, leaves, and, most abundantly, the floral calyxes, or leaflike envelopes that shield the developing buds and bracts of female plants. These glandular outgrowths, known as trichomes, are what secrete the compound delta 9–tetrahydrocannabinol (THC), as well as cannabidiol (CBD) and other cannabinoids.

Multipurposed

The cannabis plant is also commonly called "hemp," a name particularly used in reference to the soft fiber that comes from its stalk. Hemp is stronger and more durable than cotton and is used to make thousands of commercial products, most notably rope, paper, textiles, and construction materials. Hemp is also a popular food (such as hemp seed, hemp milk, and hemp oil) and a useful biofuel.

Marijuana and Religion

Cannabis first grew naturally throughout the Central Asian steppes, from as far south as Iran to the northern tundra and Siberia. Archeological evidence records its use in religious ceremonies as early as 6000 B.C. The nomadic Scythians smoked it and used it as incense. Many Bronze Age sites have been found to contain ceremonial pipes and cannabis seeds. The Assyrians referred to the plant as a "fumigant" and a sacred incense, and believed that smoking it could relieve one's soul of sorrow and grief. Biblical sources indicate cannabis was an ingredient in the holy anointing oils once used by Jews. In China, Taoists sought its hallucinogenic properties. Sufis and whirling dervishes claimed it was particularly helpful in improving one's balance while dancing and spinning. Rastafarians believe the herb (which they call *ganja*) was the first plant to grow on Solomon's grave, and that the mythical "Tree of Life" was actually a nod to marijuana. Rastas treat cannabis use as a sacrament and point to the Book of Psalms as an indication of its importance: "He causeth the grass to grow for the cattle, and *herb* for the service of man" (Psalm 104:14).

From the era of ancient man to modern day, the mind-altering psychoactive qualities of cannabis have proved quite as popular as its medicinal ones. Cannabis is classified as a minor hallucinogen with depressant qualities. The immediate psychoactive effects of cannabis consist of a state of relaxation and mild euphoria, while dreamy thinking, introspection, and metacognition are secondary. THC content provides a useful measure of a cannabis plant's potency.

Medical Uses

Cannabis can be used to treat a wide range of medical conditions, such as nausea and vomiting, to stimulate hunger in chemotherapy and AIDS patients, for glaucoma, movement disorders, asthma, neuropathic pain, and spasticity associated with multiple sclerosis. Synthetic forms of THC have also found their way into certain prescription drugs, including Marinol, also known as dronabinol in the United States and Germany, and Cesamet, or nabilone in Canada, Mexico, the United States, and the United Kingdom. In addition, people have used cannabis to treat bipolar and anxiety disorders, inflammation, infection, epilepsy, allergies, depression, and autoimmune diseases.

CARROT
Daucus carota
The Night-Vision Root

Carrots are a popular root vegetable, typically orange in color, although red, white, purple, and yellow varieties also exist. The word *carrot* derives from the Indo-European root *ker* (horn), due to its hornlike appearance. The carrot belongs to the family Umbelliferae, also known as Apiaceae. It is closely related to celeriac, celery, coriander, fennel, parsnip, and parsley, also categorized in the Umbelliferae family. The name *Umbelliferae* signifies the often umbrella-like flower clusters of the plants categorized within.

The crispy root (taproot) of the carrot is the most common edible part; however, the upper green part, or carrot top, which includes the leaves, stems, and umbels of flowers, can be eaten as well. Carrot roots have a sweet and minty aromatic taste, and appear both cooked and raw in many regional cuisines. In ancient times, carrots were actually favored for their aromatic leaves and seeds, and not for their roots, though the close relatives of the carrot—dill, fennel, parsley, and cumin—are still grown for this purpose. The edible variety of the carrot is a domesticated form of the wild carrot, a native of Europe and southwestern Asia. The wild carrot is known scientifically as *Daucus carota, carota,* while the cultivated domestic carrot is called *Daucus carota, sativus.* The domestic carrot is actually a highly selected-for variety, bred to reduce the bitterness and to minimize the woody texture of the taproot so evident on wild carrots. The ancestors of wild carrot supposedly originated in regions between Iran and Afghanistan, which remain the center of diversity for *Daucus carota.* It's not until fourteenth-century China that we see the first notations of carrots as a product of agriculture. Gardeners will find it grows easily even if they lack a so-called green thumb.

The carrot plant is a biennial, which means it takes two years to reach maturity to produce seeds. In the first season it grows vegetatively, flowering in its second year of growth to produce seed. However, when cultivated for the root, carrots are actually treated as annuals. The plants usually achieve a height of up to 2 feet and blossom during the months of June to August. The umbel, or the part that consists of a number of short flower stalks, and

Green Thumbs or Green Fingers

A person with a "green thumb" of course has a natural talent for gardening. However, the origin of the phrase is hard to pin down. In Britain, the idiom for such a person was one with "green fingers." Some believe the name originated with King Edward I, who had a great passion for gardening. According to legend, the king enjoyed fresh green peas so much that he engaged several serfs to keep him supplied. The serf who had the "greenest fingers" from many hours of shelling was always given a prize. In the United States, the phrase "green thumb" seems to date to colonial times, when tobacco provided a major cash crop for early Americans. Farmers handpicked the flowers from the crops to increase the size and weight of tobacco, using their thumbnails to simply cut the stem, which after some time could turn their thumbs green.

which together spread from a common top, gives its stems an appearance of umbrella ribs. Carrot plants like full sunlight and grow well in sandy soil, free of lumps and stones. The optimal growth temperature for carrot plants is between 50 and 75 degrees Fahrenheit. Low temperatures, changes in weather conditions, and various stress factors make carrots bolt, or go into an accelerated species-survival mode. A sudden cold snap can cause carrots to swiftly produce flowers and go to seed before the root reaches full length. The resulting roots prove more useful as animal fodder, and will likely not wind up as supermarket "baby carrots."

Carrot seeds are small (0.03 inches in diameter) and germinate quite well under cool conditions. The seedlings are very spongy and delicate and therefore cannot penetrate through a deep covering of soil. It is advisable to sow the seeds to a depth of about ½ inch and keep the soil moist. The plants achieve maturity within 12 to 16 weeks and therefore should be sown, depending on the region, from mid-February to July.

Baby Carrots

What we market today as "baby carrots" are actually regular-size carrots that are sculpted, shaved, and placed in tumbling devices to give them a soft rounded shape, before being soaked in a solution of water and chlorine.

The principal components of a carrot are water (88 percent), sugar (7 percent), protein (1 percent), fiber (1 percent), and fat (0.2 percent). The fibers are composed predominantly of cellulose and trace amounts of hemi-cellulose and lignin, but no starch. The presence of glutamic and other amino acids gives carrots their sweet taste and aroma. The characteristic bright orange color of a carrot is principally due to the presence of beta-carotene, and to some extent of gamma-carotene and alpha-carotene. The alpha- and beta-carotenes (also known as pro–vitamin A) are further converted into vitamin A in the liver (in humans). Scarcity of vitamin A in the body causes poor night vision, which explains the folk belief that eating carrots is good for your vision. Vitamin A is transformed in the retina to rhodopsin, a pigment necessary for night vision. Studies have also shown the protective effect of beta-carotenes against macular degeneration and senile cataracts.

What Protects Them, Helps Us

To protect itself from fungal diseases, the carrot root produces natural phytochemicals, or organic pesticides, called polyacetylenes, namely falcarinol and falcarindiol. Studies suggested that falcarinol and fal-carindiol have anticancer properties and thus reduce the risk of lung, breast, and colon cancers. Apart from their anticancer properties, falcarinol and falcarindiol have been shown to possess anti-inflammatory and anti-aggregatory or helpful blood circulation properties. Carrots are also rich in antioxidants and minerals, which help prevent cellular damage and slow down cellular aging. Additionally, carrots can prevent heart disease and reduce the risk of stroke. In short, carrots offer a rich supply of beta-carotene, a wide variety of antioxidants, and other health-supporting nutrients—a true "whole food" if ever there was one.

The main antioxidants in carrots are carotenoids, alpha- and beta-carotenes, lutein, ferulic acid, coumaric acid, hydroxycinnamic acid, caffeic acid, cyanidins, anthocyanins, and malvidins. They make carrots useful in preventing cancer and heart disease, and particularly beneficial to improving vision. The beta-carotenes are converted into vitamin A in the liver and are then transformed again in the retina to rhodopsin, a purple pigment the eye needs for good night vision.

CASHEW
Anacardium occidentale
The World's Nut

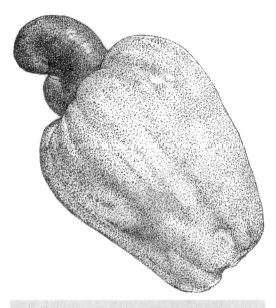

The cashew is a tasty nut and fleshy fruit of the Anacardiaceae family. The family comprises 73 genera and about 600 species, including mango, poison oak, poison ivy, pistachio, spondias, varnish tree, tannin, and Brazilian pepper. The cashew is a native of tropical South America (northeastern Brazil) in the region between the Amazon and Atlantic rain forests.

From There to Everywhere

Domestic cultivation of the cashew began well before the end of fifteenth century along the coast of northeastern Brazil. However, European traders and explorers didn't record its discovery until 1578. Also in the sixteenth century, the Portuguese introduced the cashew to the west coast of India and

The English word cashew *originally derived from Brazil's native Tupi tribe, who called it* caju, *meaning "a nut that forms on its own." Other common names for cashew include* merey *in Venezuela,* acaju *in Brazil,* cajuil *in Spain, and* noix de cajou *in France.*

southeast Africa. They first brought the plant to Goa and then spread it along western India and to Southeast Asia. Ranked as the number one tree nut crop in the world, cashews are commercially produced in thirty-two countries, on more than 7.5 million acres, particularly in tropical areas like Southeast Asia, Vietnam, Indonesia, India, East Africa (Mozambique, Tanzania, Kenya), and Australia. India, Vietnam, Brazil, and Nigeria are the world's leading cashew producers.

An Orgy of Flowers and Nuts

Well adapted to tropical climates, the cashew tree can achieve heights of between 32 and 40 feet in favorable conditions. The tree is evergreen with a dense, symmetrical, spreading canopy and irregularly shaped trunk. The leaves are green and spirally arranged, with a short stalk termed a petiole. Leaves are elliptical, leathery, and generally 6 to 7 inches long with a rounded or notched tip. The tree's flowers appear at the head of new batches of leaves, a flowering that occurs the most in tropical climates that are wet on and off throughout the year. Cashew flowers grow in a panicle format, appearing on stalks that branch out from numerous points of the main stem. Each of these panicles has a mix of bisexual flowers, containing both male and female parts, as well as strictly gendered flowers. Small and pale green in color at first (made of five yellowish green sepals and five slender, acute petals), the flower will eventually turn a reddish color. Both male and bisexual flowers have a single large stamen and five to nine smaller stamens. The flowers at the ends of the panicles bloom at a rate of 200 to 1,400 during one season. The bisexual flowers are self-fertilizing, though their pollination still depends on the transporting movements of either insects or the wind.

The actual, botanically distinct cashew fruit is a kidney-shaped nut that grows externally in a double-walled shell, surrounding an edible kernel more colloquially known as "the cashew nut." Initially, proper cashew nuts are pinkish in color, subsequently changing to green, greenish gray, and finally a grayish brown. Cashews are usually roasted or boiled before consumption, important for removing the toxic oil cardol, which occurs naturally within. At the time of maturity, the stalk or pedicle above the nut becomes swollen and fleshy, to form the pear-shaped accessory fruit, which precedes the actual nut or cashew fruit. This swollen peduncle, or pear-like structure, grows behind the real fruit, eventually yielding the cashew nut. The pulpy, juicy pseudo-fruit, usually called the "cashew apple" or "cashew fruit," has a strong, sweet flavor and is also edible.

Fresh or frozen cashew fruits are eaten raw or used as concentrates in beverages.

Benefits from Head to Toe and in Between

Cashew nuts are rich in calories and filled with soluble dietary fiber, health-promoting phytochemicals, vitamins, pantothenic acid (vitamin B_5), riboflavin, pyridoxine (vitamin B_6), and thiamin (vitamin B_1). They boast a laundry list of minerals, including manganese, zinc, potassium, copper, iron, selenium, and magnesium, all known to help promote health in various ways. The seeds are also enriched in monounsaturated fatty acids like palmitoleic and oleic acids, which enhance a healthy blood lipid profile. Apart from this, the nuts also carry trace amounts of a flavonoid antioxidant (zeaxanthin), which protects against macular degeneration in the elderly. The fruit juice of the cashew is medicinally useful in fighting influenza, while the tree's leaves, brewed as tea, make a potent diarrhea remedy. The bark, seeds, and leaves have also found use as an antiseptic vaginal douche, an antifungal agent for sores and rashes, and as an antipyretic agent or fever reducer—they're even effective in treating worms, and can be formulated to kill botfly larvae growing under human skin. In the history of traditional medicine, some used the cashew plant to treat snakebites, cracked heels, eczema, venereal diseases, psoriasis, scrofula, dyspepsia, intestinal colic, leishmaniasis, and syphilis-related skin disorders.

Even beyond its pharmacy of medical applications, cashew seed oil has industrial applications as well, proving a useful material in wood preservatives and plastics, and as a protective resin or coating agent applied to fishing nets.

CASTOR OIL BUSH
Ricinus communis
Nature's Night-Light

The history of sedentary human civilization is directly connected to cultivation—transforming wild plants into useful domestic species. Humankind roamed the earth chasing meat, but it was the plant kingdom that allowed us to settle down, all the while nurturing the expansion of culture and our planetary dominance every step of the way. None would deny the critical role plants have played in the development of our species. Not just a renewable form of sustenance for us (as well as our all-important livestock), plants are also crucial ingredients in many life-saving medicines and have given us the raw materials that fostered industrialization and made modern-day society and technology possible. The castor oil bush is one such example. We owe the course of our species's history to this amazing plant, indigenous and economically important to India, the Mediterranean basin, and eastern Africa.

Long Before Edison

The castor oil bush plant, botanically named *Ricinus communis,* belongs to the flowering spurge family, Euphorbiaceae. *Ricinus* (Latin for "tick") comes from the morphological appearance of castor oil seeds, which resemble certain Mediterranean ticks, particularly when engorged with blood. The use of the castor oil bush dates back to 4000 B.C., which we know from evidence of the seeds in Egyptian tombs to fuel oil lamps. This first fuel allowed humans to continue indoor activities when night fell, inevitably expanding social contacts and culture. Herodotus, Theophrastus, Dioscorides, and other Greek travelers documented the use of castor seed oil for body ointments, lighting, and as a purgative. In India, castor bean oil, called *eranda,* has been in use since 2000 B.C., often for burning in lamps or in open bowls with a wick, as well as being used as an unguent, laxative, and purgative. In traditional ethnomedical systems such as Ayurved, Unani, and Chinese medicine, castor oil is renowned as a cathartic and is often prescribed for arthritic diseases.

The castor oil bush plant is a robust, suckering perennial shrub that may grow to the size of a small tree, as high as 39 feet, when treated to full sunlight, heat, and adequate moisture. It favors sandy soil but can vary greatly and adapt its growth habit and appearance to meet a number of different environmental conditions. Most often, people cultivate castor oil in tropical and temperate regions.

The leaves or foliage are large, glossy, and palmately lobed, placed alternately on the stem with a long stalk. The lobes of the leaves are generally 6 to 8 inches across. Cultivated varieties have their own characteristic colorations, including black-purplish, off-dark reddish purple or bronze, reddish, dark red-metallic, bronze-green, maroon, bright green with white veins, and just plain green. This vastly expanded range of colors gives castor plants a beautiful ornamental look. The flowers occur throughout the year and are monoecious (separated male and female flowers on the same plant), oriented in dense terminal clusters. The male flowers grow on the under portion of the spike and are yellowish green in color, with numerous branched, prominent, creamy stamens. The female flowers appear at the upper part of the spike and have prominent red stigmata, the sticky parts of the flower where the pollen is deposited for fertilization.

Not for Raw Munching

The castor fruit is a spiny, greenish, deeply grooved capsule full of large, oval, laterally compressed beanlike seeds. Despite the name castor bean for its seed, the castor seed is not a true bean. At maturity, the seedpod, or capsule, dries and splits into three slices called carpels; upon splitting the seeds are forcibly ejected. The shiny castor beans have very beautiful, intricate external markings, with a small warty appendage at one end called a caruncle. The caruncle aids both in the dispersal of seeds and the absorption of water during planting. The caruncles are like small warts but they contain lipids and proteins, in addition to absorbing water rapidly. The caruncle oozes a gooey, oily substance that attracts ants, which then help in seed dispersal. Castor beans contain a highly poisonous and toxic substance called ricin, one of the most potent cytotoxins in nature. Ricin is known as a ribosome-inactivating protein, which means it kills off organelle sites of protein synthesis, called ribosomes. The reaction to toxic castor seeds is quite complicated and includes the clumping and breakdown (hemolysis) of red blood cells, and hemorrhaging in the digestive tract, which causes irreparable damage to vital organs such as the liver and kidneys. A dosage the size of only a few grains of sand will kill an adult within a few days.

From Light to Flight

Despite its toxicity, the castor oil bush has several medicinal benefits and numerous other applications when prepared correctly. The alcoholic extract of the castor leaf is known to protect the liver from damage against certain poisons. The root bark extracts of castor show analgesic, antihistamine, and anti-inflammatory properties. The bush can also act as a host plant for insects like the castor butterfly and silk moth, and other species in the Lepidoptera order even use it as a source of food for their larvae. For humans, the most important use of the castor plant has been the thick, almost colorless oil obtained from pressing the seeds. Though ancient man used it mostly to light up dark nights, there are an astonishing number of contemporary applications for the oil. It is found in cosmetics, soaps, dyes, coatings, lubricants, hydraulics, paints, inks, cold-resistant plastics, brake fluids, waxes, polishes, nylon, perfumes, and many pharmaceuticals. The U.S. Food and Drug Administration even approves castor oil as a "generally recognized as safe and effective" over-the-counter laxative. Castor oil and its derivatives (such as Kolliphor EL, a polyethoxylated castor oil) are added to many modern drugs, such as miconazole (antifungal agent), paclitaxel (anticancer drug), Sandimmune (immunosuppressant agent), and nelfinavir mesylate (HIV protease inhibitor). Due to its viscosity at low temperatures and effectiveness at higher heats, castor oil makes a good lubricant for race car and jet engines.

CELERY

Apium graveolens
The Green Wealth

Celery is one of the most popular vegetables in the world, and its reputation only continues to grow as more and more people discover its many nutritional assets. Celery stalks are a common food, but its leaves, fresh or dried, are also used as a flavoring. Its spectrum of green colors starts as a lime-like whitish color just above the roots, getting light green as its stalk grows upward, where it sprouts deep green leaves. The darker the leaves, the richer the nutritional value. Celery seeds are dark brown, have a flavorful and spicy taste, and produce an essential oil that people combine with salt (sodium nitrate) and market as a spice called "celery salt." A favorite among chefs, celery salt enhances the flavor of the famous Bloody Mary cocktail and is a distinctive ingredient of Chicago-style hot dogs. The French are known to specifically use celery as an ingredient for *mirepoix,* a base for soups and sauces.

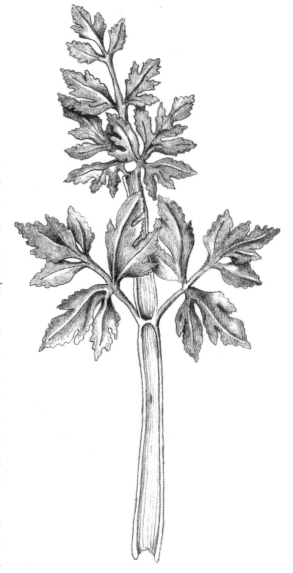

Carl Linnaeus gives the first scientific description celery in his *Species Plantarum,* but the valuable plant was long known to ancient civilizations. Tutankhamen's tomb contained celery leaves, and evidence of their use has even been discovered among the ruins of the Greek city known as the

Heraion of Samos, dating back to the seventh century B.C. Homer's *Iliad* mentions Myrmidons' horses running over wild celery around Troy, while in the *Odyssey,* the plant appears surrounding Calypso's cave. Alexander the Great always deviated from his path of conquest when he learned of nearby celery fields; he ate celery for its healing properties more than as a food source. In A.D. 30, Aulus Celsus, a Roman encyclopedist known for his tome *De Medicina,* mentions a formula using celery seeds for pain relief.

Celery belongs to the family of Apiceae and grows up to 3 feet tall. Its leaves are pinnate, resembling a feather, and reach approximately 3 inches long and about half as wide. Its creamy white flowers bloom in dense umbels and have a diameter of one inch. The seeds are brown, ball shaped, and tiny. Celery has a long growing season of about 125 days, which does not make it the easiest plant to bring to maturity. It re-quires rich soil with neutral pH, prefers moderate and cool temperatures, constant moisture, and full or partial sun exposure. It doesn't tolerate extreme heat, preferring cool nights, and will wither at the hint of frost.

The word celery *was first used in English in 1664 and comes from the Italian* seleri, *which derives from the Latin* selinon *and the Mycenaean Greek word* serino.

Celery cultivation varies in method; its seeds are typically sown in pro-tected greenhouses. Once the new sprouts reach about six inches, farmers plant them in deep trenches requiring intense irrigation during the entire growing season. For summer gardens, the temperature needs to be about 55 to 70 degrees Fahrenheit before outdoor planting will be effective. In commercial fields, the celery harvest starts when the average size is uni-form at about 12 to 14 inches tall, after which the crop must be stored in temperatures of 32 to 36 degrees Fahrenheit. The quality and subsequent packing of celery are determined by size, color, shape, thickness, and straightness. If it is cultivated correctly, much of the plant's nutritional value remains, though it's best to eat celery stalks within seven days after picking to get the full spectrum of health benefits. The plant contains at least a dozen beneficial antioxidants and has a super-low caloric content. A three-pound bunch of celery has only 3 grams of carbohydrates, 1.6 grams of fiber, and 0.7 grams of protein, and six calories per stalk. Its list of vitamins looks like a shelf in a supplement store, and includes vitamins A, B$_1$, B$_2$, B$_6$, C, E, and K; celery's other nutrients include thiamin, niacin, folate, calcium, iron, phosphorus, magnesium, sodium, potassium, and zinc.

CHINESE JUNIPER
Juniperus chinensis
Elegance in Nature

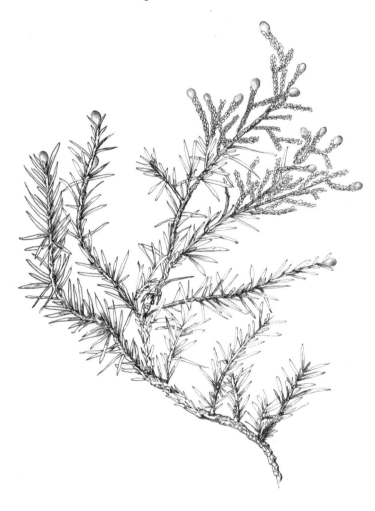

As its name indicates, this evergreen tree (or shrub) grows primarily in China, but it can also be found throughout Northeast Asia, including Japan, Mongolia, and Korea, as well as southeastern Russia. A fixation for many artists, the juniper frequently appears in ancient Chinese drawings and in minimalistic Japanese Zen paintings. Bonsai gardeners also favor the plant, and many cultures admire it for its aesthetic value.

The Chinese juniper grows in the wild to varying heights, 3 to 60 feet tall. However, none seems to have the exact same shape as the next; each forms a unique, individualistic swirl of branches in some variation of an oval or pyramid. Juniper is a green coniferous shrub with needlelike leaves growing only ¼ inch long and sharp to the touch. The plant blooms brown and yellow in spring, bringing forth beautifully soft, medium-green fragrant foliage, all of which shape the environment into a noble sight.

Chinese juniper prefers partial or full sun exposure and sandy or clay-rich soul with an alkaline pH. Planting shouldn't be too deep, yet the hole should be dug to a size that is twice the width of the root ball, or even wider, and no soil should be placed over it, though some organic matter will allow it to take root faster. Place about 3 inches of a thick layer of fertilizer on the area around the plant to maximize growth, keeping it 10 inches from the trunk. This way, rainwater and air can easily reach the root, though the trunk stays dry. Regular irrigation in the first growth season can speed up the process, though overall, the juniper matures very slowly.

Juniperus chinensis has more than 100 cultivars, each displaying different ornamental effects. The most common are Tremonia and Aurea, which have fabulous yellow foliage, followed by the Shoosmith, with its permanent juvenile foliage; there are also the columnar crown shape variation named Columnaris, the Kazuka with abundant cones, the golden Chinese juniper or Aurea, then Blaauw, Pyramidalis, Grey Owl, and Plumosa aurea. *Juniperus pfitzeriana* is a popular hybrid between *Juniperus sabina* and *Juniperus chinensis,* though it never grows beyond a shrub, making it best for smaller gardens.

Like an exquisite, pensive sculpture, the juniper tree is much beloved, as well as hardy and resistant to blight. Its most common enemies are leaf miners, scale insects, bark beetles, caterpillars, mites, and aphids.

Bonsai Juniper

Because of its beauty, Chinese juniper is often used as a decorative bonsai plant, the Shimpaku being the most commonly cultivated variety. As such, it is used both as an individual potted tree and planted in a group. The most famous individual bonsai is the 250-year-old miniature in England's Birmingham Botanical Gardens, known as the Omiya tree, after the city of that name in Japan. One of the most appreciated group bonsai, or forest-setting bonsai, is Goshin, a display located at the U.S. National Arboretum. That miniature forest took root in 1948 and contains eleven junipers. *Bonsai* is a Japanese word derived from the Chinese *penzai,* meaning tray planting. When certain plants are pruned to stay diminutive, they provide minimalistic elegance and give botanical life to the famous Zen saying "an ocean in a drop of water."

COCA
Erythroxylum coca
Of Coke and Coke

The contentious coca plant is a tropical shrub, or a blackthorn bush, originating from western parts of South America and belonging to the family Erythroxylaceae. Known best for its vivid green leaves, oval, thin, and opaque—and the source of the infamous psychoactive alkaloid cocaine—*Erythroxylum coca* has straight branches and can grow up to 6 feet tall. Coca flowers are small and posted in small clusters with short stalks; the corolla has five white-yellowish petals; the anthers have a heartlike shape, while the pistil has three carpels inside an ovary with three chambers. In the later phase of growth, red berries appear to replace the flowers.

Where It Grows
Coca grows best in damp, hot environments, such as forest clearings. However, cultivators prefer leaves grown in drier areas, mostly on the sides of hills, which help the plant produce more potent alkaloids. When brittle enough to break manually, the leaves are ready for picking. Rather than a single harvest, coca leaves can be picked throughout a single plant's life span, which can range from two to a whopping forty years. Typically, farmers will only harvest the newest leaves, allowing the older ones to remain, ensuring the plant can continue to produce food. Coca grows fast,

providing multiple opportunities in quick succession to gather new leaves. The first and richest batches of fresh foliage usually appear in March, after the tropical rains; the second harvest from the same plant occurs again in June, and a third occurs in October or November. The leaves are called *matu* when first harvested, at which point growers dry them in the sun, spread them about in thin layers, and pack them into sacks.

Coca seeds sow best in small plots during December or January. These plots, or *almacigas,* provide important shelter from the sun. When the young plants grow to 6 inches tall, they are placed in their final planting holes, called *aspi,* or possibly (if the ground is level) into furrows, or *uachos,* designed to keep the plot free of any invasive weeds.

There are two main species of cultivated coca, each with two varieties. The *Erythroxylum coca* has variations, *Erythroxylum coca* var. *coca,* also known as *Huánuco* or *Bolivian coca,* and *Erythroxylum coca* var. *ipadu,* known as *Amazonian coca.* The former is grown on the eastern Andes of Bolivia and Peru, in tropical, humid mountain forests, while the other variety is grown across the Colombian and Peruvian sections of the Amazon Basin.

A Longtime Favorite

Historical evidence indicates that natives of coca-growing regions used the leaves regularly. Analysis of mummies nearly three thousand years old found coca in their stomachs. The chewing of coca leaves, along with limes, was once a popular way to boost stamina. Coca also found use as an anesthetic in some cultures. The Incas considered it a divine plant, and all levels of society chewed it regularly, if not daily.

Coca was introduced to Europe during the sixteenth century but it never gained widespread popularity until the nineteenth century, when coca tonics, medicines, and even a coca wine arrived to popular embrace. The original formula for the soda Coca-Cola actually contained cocaine. It was removed in 1903 when public outcries for antinarcotic legislation began. The creators did not want the soda brand to come under controversy. The real Pandora's box of narcotic abuse, which would come to define the plant's reputation, had been opened in 1859 by Albert Niemann, who first isolated the main alkaloid of coca, which he named *cocaine.* The rest of the story is well-known, namely its swift rise as a popular and publicly consumed narcotic from the 1880s until 1920, when it was banned in the United States. However, nowadays, some governments in South America—Bolivia, Peru,

Medical Benefits of Coca

Coca is known as a very effective remedy to combat altitude sickness, and is a noted analgesic for rheumatism, headaches, sores, and wounds. It is also traditionally used for broken bones (it has a high calcium content) and during operations on the nose, and is used as a localized anesthetic. Coca improves blood vessel function and can slow or stop a bleeding wound—even its seeds work well to curb nosebleeds. Some Latin American natives reportedly use coca as a cure for asthma, malaria, and ulcers, to prevent bowel laxity, to improve digestion, and last but certainly not least, as an aphrodisiac. Its obvious addictiveness notwithstanding, most of coca's wide-ranging medical benefits have been confirmed by modern science.

and Venezuela, for example—have taken to defending more traditional uses of the coca plant, from tea to toothpaste. A few years ago, the Bolivian president Evo Morales publicly chewed coca leaves, campaigning to rehabilitate the plant's battered image.

COCONUT
Cocos nucifera
A Heavenly Archetype

If there were a contest to name the most amazing tree on the planet, it's likely that this beautiful plant would rank high, not only because of its appearance, which has an arching, wind-sculpted grace, and for its spectacular fruits, but also for the sheer life-sustaining force it provides for humans and animals.

The coconut belongs to the palm family of Arecaceae. It has a slender trunk that grows on average more than 60 feet in height. Its only leaves appear at the crown, and consist of featherlike, 12-foot-long fronds of intense green. Its hard, brown, and hairy-looking seed is round, ellipsoidal, or ovoid. It is interesting that botanically, the coconut is considered a *drupe,* not a nut, while the term *coconut* refers to the entire tree, including seeds and fruits. Its name comes from sixteenth-century Spanish and Portuguese explorers; *coco* means "skull" or "head"—three small holes in the shells of the seeds (actually germination pores) give them the appearance of a human face. However, it was Marco Polo in 1280 who first described coconut trees, having seen them in Sumatra during his travels.

Like other drupe fruits, the coconut seed consists of three layers: *exocarp,* or husk; *mesocarp,* composed of a fiber named *coir* that boasts many commercial and traditional uses; and *endocarp*—the core of the fruit surrounding the seeds. A mature coconut fruit can weigh up to one and a half pounds. One tree can produce thousands of coconuts during its average life span of seventy years. The coconut palm is generally classified into two types: the *tall,* which can give 75 to 100 fruits per year if planted on fertile soil, and the *dwarf,* which usually gives about 30 fruits. Usually, it takes around 6,000 mature fruits to produce one ton of *copra,* which is the kernel or dried meat of the coconut.

Coconut needs sandy soil, abundant sunlight, regular rains, constant temperature above 55 degrees Fahrenheit (the optimum temperature being 80 degrees), and humidity above 70 to 80 percent. Tropical and subtropical coastlines are ideal for coconut growth, since ocean currents will naturally dispense its seeds. This marks another spectacular characteristic of this tree—its seeds float!

Commercially cultivated seedlings take four to ten months to be tall enough to transplant to their final fields, where the palms are placed about 30 feet apart. After five to six years, the tree finally starts bearing coconuts, though it will not reach peak productivity until fifteen years old. Yields can last for fifty years, and sometimes longer. The copra meat is the prime target for harvest, used to produce coconut oil, one of the most valuable (not to mention healthy) vegetable oils in the world. Mixed with water, the copra makes coconut milk, a great substitution for cow's milk. Indonesia and the Philippines lead the world in copra production, but it is also one of the South Pacific's most exported products.

The inflorescence of *Cocos nucifera* is monoecious; female flowers are significantly larger than male ones. It flowers constantly, with some types of coconuts cross-pollinating, while some of the dwarf varieties self-pollinate.

What Else Is Coconut Good For?

Coconuts contain a lot more water than most fruits, and it can be consumed immediately or used in other recipes. Coconut "meat," or the white, pithy part of the interior of the seed, is also very popular in certain diets. The coconut water is used for oil production, mixed with the hard shell's charcoal and the fibrous husk's coir. Many use coconut milk and oil, which are considered healthy alternatives to dairy and other vegetable products, for frying and cooking, and the oil is often used in soaps and cosmetics. Traditionally, the leaves and husks are a fiber for making garments and parts of tools. In some cultures, coconut even has a kind of religious significance.

COFFEE
Coffea
And Now, a Coffee Break!

Although many believe coffee has been consumed since ancient times, the first documented evidence that coffee was prepared as a beverage similar to what we drink today dates to the fifteenth century. The monks at a Sufi monastery in Yemen wrote recipes for brewing and instantly praised the first hot cup of coffee as a gift from Allah. The whirling dervish sect of the Sufis also blessed it as something that helped them to keep dancing and whirling, giving them a boost of energy after longer periods of dancing and worship. By the sixteenth century, the Sufis' praise of coffee helped make it a common drink in Arabia, Persia, Turkey, and North Africa. It took longer to take hold as a fashionable beverage in Europe, but was considered a medicine in 1583, when German physician Leonhard Rauwolf described it after his trip to the Near East: "It is useful for illness," he wrote, "among all; particularly those of the stomach."

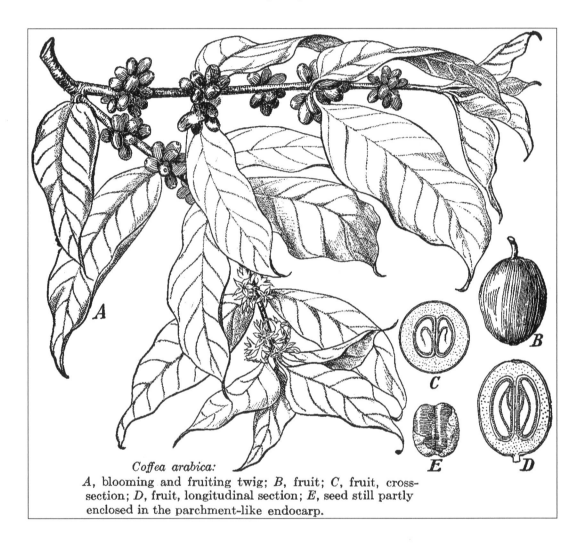

Coffea arabica:
A, blooming and fruiting twig; B, fruit; C, fruit, cross-section; D, fruit, longitudinal section; E, seed still partly enclosed in the parchment-like endocarp.

The coffee plant originated in Ethiopia, which to this day produces some of the best coffee beans in the world. There are as many as 150 coffee species grouped in the family Rubicae. Among botanists, coffee plants are divided into two main groups: *Coffea arabica,* which represents about 80 percent of the world's coffee production, and *Coffea canephora,* with about 20 percent. Today, various species of coffee are grown in more than seventy countries. The best yields are from regions around the tropical belt, such as Latin America, Africa, and Southeast Asia, in climates similar to where it originated. Although many believe coffee is native to Brazil, it was not introduced to that country until 1727. Brazil now leads the world as the largest coffee producer.

Coffee grows as a small tree or vigorous bush, up to 10 to 12 feet high. It likes high elevations, though it is intolerant of freezing weather conditions. New coffee plants take three to five years after planting to produce their first fruit. Once they do, the plants keep producing beans for fifty to sixty years. Certain plants are reported to have lived for more than a hundred years before ceasing bean production. The plant blooms a highly scented white flower, which after fertilization takes nine months for its fruit to ripen. The fruit looks about the size of a cherry and comes in red or purple. In each there are two seeds, or coffee beans.

The spread of coffee did meet some resistance. Muslim countries embraced it, and so it was considered a "Muslim drink" and not for Christians to imbibe. Not until Pope Clement VIII proclaimed it a "Christian beverage" was the prohibition against drinking it revoked. The first coffeehouse opened in Italy in 1645 and many such shops sprang up throughout Europe. They were often sponsored and encouraged by the Dutch East India Company, which began large-scale importation of coffee from Ceylon and Java. The British East India Company made coffee popular in England. They promoted the famous Queen's Lane Coffee House, established in 1654 and still in existence today. France was first introduced to coffee in 1657,

Java or Coffee

The word *coffee* comes from the Italian *caffè,* which is derived from the Ottoman Turks, who called it *kahve.* Just as there is disagreement among coffee lovers as to which beans make the best coffee, linguists are also in dispute. Arab linguists claim *coffee* derives from the word *qaha,* meaning "to have no appetite," as coffee was considered a beverage able to dull hunger. Others call it *java,* from the island where it was harvested, or *kaffa,* from a region in the Middle East noted for producing quality beans.

followed by Austria and Poland in 1683. After the Battle of Vienna, soldiers captured beans from defeated Turks and quickly found the drink appealing. Coffee was introduced to North America during the colonial period but it didn't achieve the same popularity as in Europe. The demand for the drink, however, increased during the Revolutionary War as a result of the reduced import of tea due to the British blockage of that commodity. Teahouses were seen as traitorous and loyal to the Crown, especially after the Boston Tea Party. Coffee then became the best strong beverage suitable for Americans. Now 54 percent of Americans have at least one cup per day, with 68 percent drinking it within the first hour of waking up.

CORN
Zea Mays
Popping Through the Ages

Corn is a cereal grain belonging to the genus *Gramineae* in the *Maydeae* family of grasses and is related to sugarcane and sorghum. Domesticated and cultivated at least eight thousand years ago and modified from its most likely ancestor, a tall wild grass called *Balsas teosinte*, corn still grows naturally in the central Balsas River valley of Mexico. Native Americans carefully chose the best grains or seeds, slowly improving the crop until it became what we know today. The Aztecs, in particular, vastly improved corn's nutritional value through a process called *nixtamalization,* which involved soaking the kernels in wood ash, limestone, and crushed seashells. Nowadays there are numerous hybrids and genetically modified versions of the plant, though corn first became a popular and important food commodity due to its natural resilience and ability to adapt to varying soils, lengths of seasons, and water conditions.

Whence It Came

There's solid archeological proof that corn spread north and south of its axis in Central America, even serving as a form of currency for natives on both American continents, as well as an important trading item. When the Viking explorer Thorwald wintered in Vinland in 1002, he reported seeing "wodden cribs for corn." Soon after Christopher Columbus related to Spain's King Ferdinand and Queen Isabella his brother's encounters with dense agricultural societies and cornfields 18 miles long, the crop was transported to Europe. Natives called it by its Haitian name, *marisi,* or the Arawak *mahizi,* literally meaning "that which sustains life." The word *mahiz* eventually led to *maize. Corn* is an Anglo-Saxon word that was used to describe many grains.

We Don't Need Help

Corn is an annual plant that grows in temperate and tropical climates on dry fertile soil. It needs full sun exposure and must have a sufficient quantity of water (again, dependent on the strain and environmental conditions). In one growing season, most varieties produce a stalk anywhere from 2 to 20 feet in height. The seed heads, or ears, grow for the purpose of becoming seedpods, and sprout from the middle of the stalk above its leaves. The female ears are called husks and have elongated stigmata called silks. The male tassels bloom at the top of the stalk and release pollen that falls in the wind, to be captured by the female silks. Each tassel produces 25 million pollen grains and is a sure way to beat the statistical odds of pollination, thus achieving total self-sufficiency.

Once fertilized, the ears grow into cobs, which are filled with kernels, or seeds. Technically, the kernels are the plants' fruit, even if we consider them a vegetable grain. The corn harvest begins when the silks turn brown and cobs are full with grain.

A Long List of Uses

It's nearly impossible not to come into contact with some form of corn on a daily basis. There are more than four thousand different uses of the plant, which is instrumental to the production of cereal, cooking oil, syrup, ethanol fuel, fireworks, soap, detergents, chewing gum, potato chips, peanut butter, baby food, paint, whiskey (including bourbon), tortillas, popcorn, and so on. In medicine, corn is used in antibiotics, vitamins, and in acid preparations. Corn oil is rich with vitamin E and linoleic acid, and a starch that makes it an ideal ingredient for baking and adding to meat products, pudding, creams, and sauces. Once a waving stalk on the prehistoric shore of a river, corn is now a cornerstone of many multibillion-dollar industries.

CORPSE FLOWER
Amorphophallus titanum
The Giant and His Odor

Sometimes the experience of merely reading about a plant is nothing compared to seeing it in person. A corpse flower is one such specimen—glimpsing it is a wonder, but just don't get too close when you look at it, as its odor is equally spectacular. As its name indicates, the corpse flower stinks like a dead mammal! Its native Sumatran name is *bunga bangkai; bunga* means flower and *bangkai* is translated as "corpse," "carrion," or "cadaver." The first part of its scientific name is a combination of two Greek words: *amorphous* means "shapeless" and *phallus* means—you know what—and *titanum* means "giant." This is one scientific name that describes its organism perfectly.

The corpse flower is a species endemic to equatorial rain forests in Sumatra, part of the *Rafflesia* genus from the same region. However, botanical gardens and private collectors worldwide keep them for their hugeness and for their shocking and renowned stench. The inflorescence of this giant flower can reach up to 9 feet and possesses a gentle spadix of flowers surrounded by a spathe, similar to a big petal. On the outside, the spathe is green, and inside it is a dark burgundy color. The amazing spadix is hollow, shaped more like a big loaf of French bread than a phallus, but it doesn't take much imagination to see the comparison. On the lower part of the plant, the spadix bears two circles of tiny flowers, of which the upper ones are male flowers, while the lower ones are intense red-orange carpels.

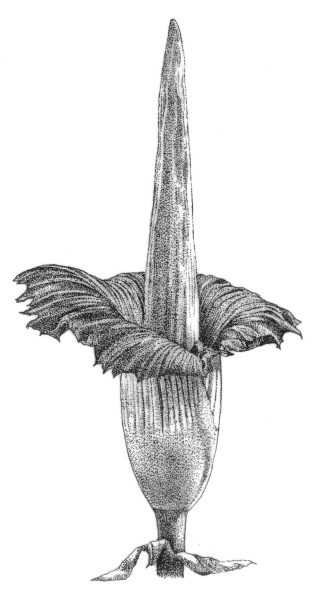

Serve the Pollinators What They Want

Though the old saying "You can catch more flies with a spoonful of honey than a gallon of vinegar" is good advice, this plant knows an even better way to attract insects. The awful rotten-meat odor it produces attracts beetles and flesh flies from the family *Sarcophagidae,* who are the chief pollinators of the corpse flower.

What Makes It Smell

It takes this plant all year to store up enough energy to make itself stink during its short blooming period. The smell seems to combine spoiled eggs, a dead animal, and sweaty, week-old dirty laundry. Corpse flowers produce a compound of sulfurous chemicals, cadaverine and putrescin, which break down carrion. The odor is strongest at night, an attempt to attract nocturnal insects laying their eggs in carcasses, such as flies and certain beetles. These insects relish the odor and fly to it, walking up and down the plant, thus serving as efficient pollinators. Though they do not lay their eggs on the plant, each year these insects are fooled by the corpse flower's unique adaptation.

During the blooming period, which lasts less than a week, the top of the spadix/phallus/French bread part of the plant warms up to enhance its odor, becoming the same temperature as the human body. Both male and female flowers grow inside the same inflorescence; the females are first to open, then, after one to two days, the males follow. This clever cycle prevents the plant from self-pollinating, instead allowing flies and bugs to facilitate cross-pollination. The leaves surrounding the flower can be up to 18 feet tall and 15 feet across. Though they fall off each year, new ones grow annually, despite the energy-consuming bloom, after which the plant becomes dormant for four months, until the cycle begins again. It takes the plant about seven to ten years before it has its first bloom. After the first time, it can bloom every second year.

Corpse Flower in Botanical Gardens

Many botanical gardens have corpse flowers, which in odorous bloom attract many visitors—because who doesn't like a good stink? The first one to bloom away from its natural habitat was in the Royal Botanic Gardens in London in 1889. In the United States, a corpse flower shocked the noses of New Yorkers in 1937 when one bloomed at the New York Botanical Garden. According to Guinness World Records, the tallest corpse flower bloomed in 2010. It was displayed at Winnipesaukee Orchids in Gilford, New Hampshire, and measured 10 feet, 2¼ inches tall. Sadly, there is presently no way to gauge or record which specimen of this plant won for foulest smell in the plant kingdom.

CUCUMBER
Cucumis sarivus
Cylindrical Blessing

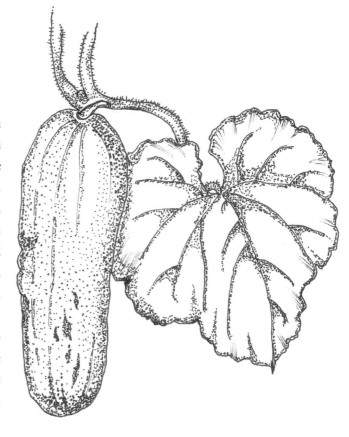

Cucumbers are the fourth most-cultivated vegetable in the world and one of the healthiest foods in existence. Cucumbers are best when they are organic, though today you'd be hard-pressed to find one that hasn't been sprayed with pesticides, which penetrate its skin. The cucumber is native to India and was known to be cultivated for at least three thousand years in western Asia, whence it spread from India to China, Italy, and Greece. The Romans cultivated cucumbers with great success and introduced them to the whole of Europe. They were cultivated in France in the ninth century, England in the fourteenth century, and America in the sixteenth century.

The cucumber is an annual, herbaceous prickly vine of the gourd family Cucurbitaceae and of the genus *Cucumis*. The fruits are green and cylindrical, and can grow up to 24 inches long and about 4 inches in diameter. The cucumber likes to grow in fertile soil and requires ample water, as its root grows very shallowly and spreads only along the superficial layer of soil. The cucumber has two differential flowers, male and female, on the same plant, making it a monoecious plant. There are approximately an equal number of blossoms of both male and female flowers. Many varieties are now grown in greenhouses and require manual pollination, but if outdoors, the plants rely primarily on honeybees and some other insects from the bee family as their chief reproductive aids. Commercial cucumber growers border their fields with beehive boxes.

Green Cylinder of Health

The cucumber is an extraordinarily healthy food, rich in vitamins, minerals, and important ingredients. It has almost every B vitamin, although it consists of 95 percent water. The cucumber also contains vitamin C at 11 milligrams per 100 grams, and is a strong antioxidant. In addition, the green gourd is rich with iron, magnesium, potassium, phosphorus, zinc, calcium, sodium, manganese, and iodine. Even cucumber skin is healthy, containing large amounts of vitamin C—eating only one cucumber provides about 10 percent of the recommended daily requirement. The skin is also useful in treating sunburns and skin irritations when rubbed directly on the wound or burn. It also contains lignans, such as secoisolariciresinol, pinoresinol, and lariciresinol, all known to help prevent breast, ovarian, prostate, and uterine cancers. Because the cucumber's fruit is low in calories and high in water content, it is a great filling food for people wishing to lose weight. Doctors recommend it for patients with diabetes as well, since one of its hormones can help pancreas cells produce natural insulin. Cucumbers are also good for treating arthritis, low and high blood pressure, heart conditions, and digestive diseases, and can help lower cholesterol in all who include this impressive plant in their diet.

CYANIDE GRASS

Sorghum halepense
The Colonel's Mistake

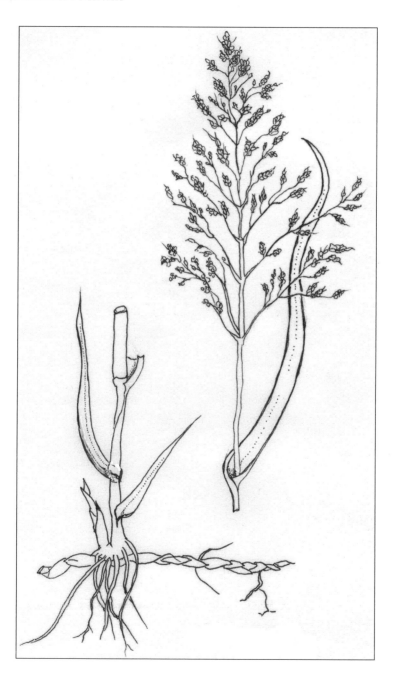

Johnsongrass, also called cyanide grass due to its unique chemical makeup, belongs to the family Poeceae. The common name stems from one Colonel William Johnson, who grew this plant on his Alabama plantation in 1840. Johnson had heard the grass was fast growing and could stop erosion and make hay, but he couldn't have imagined how thoroughly it would eventually overrun the whole of the southern United States. It took us a while to learn that if grown in certain soils, or as soon as it is wilted by frost, the plant turns deadly, such that a mouthful of it can kill a full-grown cow in an hour. The plant is native to the Mediterranean area, coming to the United States by way of the Caribbean, where this rapid-growing "weed" was named in honor of the unsuspecting colonel who cultivated it.

Officially *Sorghum halepense,* this annual plant can grow from 3 to 9 feet in height, ultimately forming a wide shrub. Its stalk is smooth and vertical, and its branches contain narrow leaves. On the top of the stalk, a tassel forms that has a dark violet color. The grass prefers fertile and sandy soil and warm and dry climates, though it can adapt to almost any terrain and grows at great speed, often outcompeting other nearby plants. Cyanide grass reproduces via seeds and rhizomes, which are underground networks of stems and offshoots. As a result, Johnsongrass usually spreads faster than herbicides can prevent.

Cyanide grass blooms from July to September and ripens from September to November. It produces much pollen, which is primarily dispersed by the wind. Each plant can produce 8,000 to 25,000 seeds per year.

In some climates, the grass does make for an edible food for livestock, though there is no way to know just by looking if the deadly toxins are present. If the cow starts swelling at the stomach, you'll know the batch of grass is bad. This deadly chemistry, the manufacturing of hydrogen cyanide, sometimes called prussic acid, is yet another effective defense mechanism. In the United States the plant is on a botanical version of the "Most Wanted List," the "Federal and State Noxious Weeds" directory, which classifies the grass as an invasive species.

However, the plant is not entirely without redeeming qualities. One man's weed is another man's treasure. In many parts of the world, people use the plant's grains in natural medicines to treat respiratory problems, kidney aliments, and urinary tract infections. In Nigeria, certain tribes use sorghum extracts to make poison arrows.

CYPRESS
Cupressacaeae
Solemn and Stoic

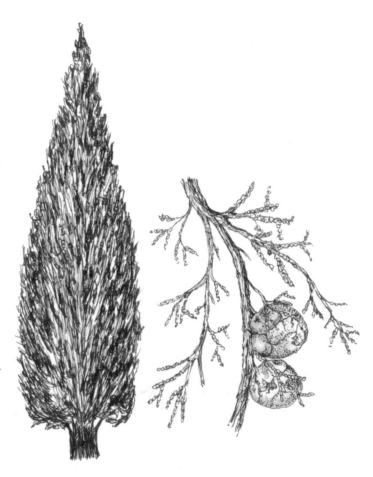

The cypress is a magnificent plant of the genus *Cupresus* and family Cupressacaeae, and has about 12 varieties. The tree gets its name from a tale in Greek mythology: A boy named Cyparissus was out hunting one day when he accidentally killed one of Apollo's sacred stags. Though Apollo was outraged and about to seek revenge, the boy pleaded for forgiveness. In the end, Apollo reluctantly showed mercy, turning his dead stag into a tree and proclaiming it a monument to grief.

The Italian cypress (the tree is indigenous to the Mediterranean) grows tall and straight, like a green column. Ancient Romans called it the "mourning tree" and planted it in graveyards and placed its branches on the dead; even to this day when a pope dies, members of the Vatican rest cypress branches beside him. The tree does have a solemn essence, towering grandly and seeming almost sorrowful, if we permit ourselves a moment of anthropomorphic reflection.

Records indicate that the Egyptians, Phoenicians, and Greeks used cypress in shipbuilding, and many unearthed relics of sarcophagi and temple doors, in addition to religious statues, were found to be made of the wood. The Persians believed the tree was a sample of the flora that grew in heaven. The Bible indicates that Noah's Ark was made from cypress wood, the same material Christians believe made up the cross on which Christ was crucified. Indeed, many attribute religious significance to the tree, particularly since many species of cypress have an incredibly long life span of thousands of years.

Present Throughout History

A tree called the **Zoroastrian Sarv,** a Mediterranean cypress growing in Iran, is 4,000 years old. **The Senator,** a name given to a pond cypress in Longwood, Florida, is 3,500 years old, and the **Alishan Sacred Tree,** a Formosan cypress in Taiwan, is 3,000 years old.

The cypress species is predominantly an evergreen perennial, and it can grow either like a bush or a tree. A few species are deciduous. But in general, cypress grows very fast (especially when young), almost 2 feet in a single year, and very tall, from 65 to 130 feet. It flourishes in all types of soil, in temperate and subtropical climates, and appears on every continent except Antarctica. Cypress grows at high altitudes in rocky soil, or even submerged in water, as does the bald cypress of the Everglades. In general, cypress bark is dark brown or red-brown, but as it ages the older bark frequently turns gray and looks as if it is peeling with scaly plaques. A cypress's treetop can form various shapes, but almost all have narrow foliage and short branches. This foliage can take different colors as well, ranging from bluish to light green or dark green. Some leaves are thin needles or like smooth, long hair. Cypress bears male and female flowers. Pollen is dispersed by the wind, and cypress's fruit is a cone that looks like a nut with scales. A fertilized cone takes 18 to 24 months after pollination to mature, going from green to brown.

In 2006, an entire ancient forest of bald cypress was discovered buried off the coast of Alabama in the Gulf of Mexico. The 50,000-year-old forest was so well preserved by silt and the oxygen-free environment that when one of the trees was cut, it still released the fresh resin smell found in a living cypress.

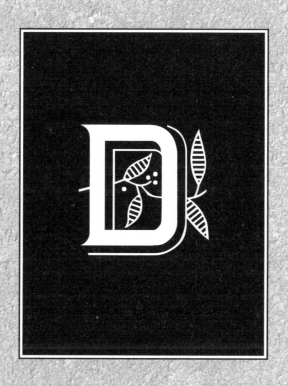

DAHLIA
Dahlia hortensis
Hybrids Galore

The dahlia is a native of Mexico and Central and South America, from which Swedish botanist Andrew Dahl carried a specimen back to Europe by ship in 1784. The man was quite a gatherer and cataloger, having been a student of Carl Linnaeus, the famous scientist who invented the scientific nomenclature of kingdoms, families, genera, and species we use today. After Dahl's death, another scientist gave this tubular-rooted, perennial flower, which has since been cultivated into more than 1,000 varieties, Dahl's name in honor of his "discovery" of the plant. Within years of its introduction to Europe, the flower became a favorite of European gardeners, though the Aztecs had grown it centuries before, appreciating it less for its beauty than for its effectiveness in treating convulsions. They also made the flowers' stiff, straight stems, which become hollow soon after picking, into a straw for drinking all kinds of beverages. Aztecs even ate the roots, which make a sweet potato kind of dish still found in the regional cuisine.

Not only can the dahlia's seeds produce next year's flower patch, but its cluster of tubular roots, which resemble a bunched-up group of skinny potatoes, all have an "eye," which, if kept moist during winter, will sprout a new plant in the spring. The flower's ability to transform into so many variations or hybrids lies in its chromosomes. There were originally 36 wild species in its group, but there are thousands today. It has eight sets and contains what are called transposons, or "jumping genes." A successful survival technique, this ability has been a way to attract any number of pollinators throughout the eons, despite environmental shifts and the dense foliage in which it has competed.

Is There a Black Dahlia?
Although the dahlia produces a colorful, concentric flower with many petals (again, depending on type of hybrid), it lacks scent. Therefore it

had to adapt to bloom in a wide range of colors to attract pollinators. In other words, no matter how the surrounding flora changed, the plant always found a way to makes its brilliant burst of a flower stand out, like a billboard or advertisement for pollinators.

Although the flower comes in an array of colors, no actual "black dahlia" exists. "Black Dahlia" refers to a case about the murder of a young woman in Los Angeles in 1947—the longest unsolved crime in the city's history, spawning numerous books and movies. Much like the plant, the story retains the ability to transform into seemingly endless variations.

DEATH CAP
Amanita phalloides
The Killer Beneath the Tree

Although not a plant and in their own fungi kingdom, mushrooms have been used throughout history as a food staple in many regions. Mushrooms from the wild are a tricky food to harvest. Some can be deadly, delicious, or both. If you aren't 100 percent sure of your ability to properly identify mushrooms, don't even think of collecting any you find in the wild. More people die from wild mushrooms than from bear attacks. The death cap is one such fatally toxic shroom, and a sly one, too, taking until long after a person has left the "scene of the crime" to knock them mysteriously dead.

People who eat death caps will feel fine for the first ten to fourteen hours, after which diarrhea, vomiting, and cramps take hold. Bizarrely, a reprieve of normalcy follows this distressing period, lasting a few days— just long enough to make one think his or her recovery is complete. This is not so—the mushroom's sneaky toxins are now doing their deadliest work! After three or four days, the liver or kidneys will fail, and the person will die. *Finito, ende, kaput*—mortality by way of mushroom. The *Amanita phalloides* is the number one cause of mushroom poisonings worldwide.

Accurately identifying toxic mushrooms is difficult since most look similar to the classically edible variety. The death cap even has an almost visually identical match, the paddy straw mushroom (*Volvariela volvacea*), and so precisely identifying this villainous plant is a real trick. Actually, the death cap isn't the only lethal member of the *Amanita* genus; others include *Amanita bisporigera*, *Amanita virosa*, *Amanita verna*, and *Amanita ocreata*. The collection goes by the name "destroying angels" (why angels? who knows), and all are equally toxic, differing only in their drier caps and white color.

Poison of Choice

The known history of poisons goes back to 4500 B.C. Many different plants and mushrooms have been used to kill people (often kings) in silence and mystery. Rome was a real minefield of poisonings; emperors often used toxic plants to quietly kill enemies and rivals. Nero's predecessor Claudius, for example, was said to be poisoned by his wife, Agrippina. The question is not whether she committed the crime, but rather what plant she used. Some think the aconite plant (believed to be able to kill even if only touched) was responsible, though still others implicate a mushroom like the death cap. Nero, unsurprisingly, possessed much knowledge of poisons, using many deadly herbs and mushrooms to kill unwanted family members. Historical rumors say Romanos II, the Byzantium emperor, was poisoned by his wife, Theophanos, who supposedly used a poisonous plant of unknown variety. The Umayyad caliph Umar II died after one of his serfs put a mushroom extract in his food.

Where They Grow

The death cap grows internationally, both in late summer and the fall when in temperate latitudes. In Europe and North America it appears from late August to late November; in South America and Australia from late February to May. Like most fungi, death caps favor the darker and loamier soil around tree roots. They have what's called a mycorrhizal relationship with some trees, where a fungi wraps its mycelia—or thread-thin branching—around the tree's roots, feeding it specific nutrients only the mushroom can absorb from the soil. This ultimately makes the tree strong and healthy. This clever adaptation ensures the mushroom and its subsequent generations will have a "rent-free" environment in which to flourish.

Death caps have a cap (or mushroom head) about 6 inches wide, and a stalk that can grow up to 5 inches. Depending on the environment, the cap can be whitish, yellowish, brownish, or greenish, and is sticky to the touch. The underside of the cap contains feathery gills, while at the base of the stalk there is a smaller, white cup. *Amanita phalloides* uses spores for reproduction that are similar to the seeds of herbs. The death cap has a specific intense smell that attracts different insects to its gills that are not affected by its poison. The spores stick to the insects, which then fly away and spread them, allowing the birth of new mushrooms—the life cycle of death.

Chemical Warfare

Scientists have studied the death cap's murderous biochemistry for decades. This species' toxic mix evolved primarily to ward off "enemies" that might want to eat it. The main toxic element is the alpha-amanitin in combination with *beta-amanitin.* These are called *anatoxins,* and if they aren't enough to kill you, the death cap will use its reserve weapons, named *phallotoxins,* to finish you off. Thirty grams, contained in half a cap of the mushroom, is a sufficient dosage to kill an adult, and drying, freezing, or cooking won't even reduce the toxicity. In a cruel irony of nature, the death cap is alleged to be very tasty—according to an ill-fated mushroom lover just before he died.

DIVINER'S SAGE
Salvia divinorum
Mystery of the Deep Forest

The diviner's sage is another mysterious herb containing psychoactive chemicals. It is a popular plant for those who wish to experience "visions," because of its hallucinatory and dissociative effects. It is also known as Ska Maria Pastora, or seer's sage, and belongs to the genus *Salvia,* which includes nearly 900 species. Botanists, however, do not know whether it is a hybrid or a cultigen, adding to the mystery of this plant. The natural (endemic) habitat of diviner's sage is the isolated cloud forest in Sierra Mazateca, Mexico, where it grows in hidden, shady places with high moisture. Mazatec shamans traditionally use it for religious practices (*divinorum* means "diviner"), but also as support for their healing séances.

Self-Replicating

Salvia divinorum is a type of semitropical sage. It grows from 3 to 9 feet tall with hollow stems and oval leaves (up to 9 inches long). It is emerald green with rare white flowers that have purplish calyxes. This plant prefers high altitudes (1,000 to 6,000 feet) and thrives amid evergreen forests with black soil, low light, and high humidity. The minty aroma of this herb is one of its key characterizations, since *Salvia* belongs to the mint family of Lamiaceae. Diviner's sage is a semitropical perennial and can grow year after year if not exposed to frost. Once full-grown and nearing old age, it searches for a second chance at life by extending its branches to the soil, in hopes that it will break away and reroot. If only we could use this trick when our last days loomed near.

Perhaps because of its self-replicating abilities, the plant rarely produces seeds. Even when humans assist its pollination, the fertility quality of the pollen is weak. Observations show that plants grown from seeds usually lack vigor, so this plant primarily reproduces through self-replication. However, growing *Salvia divinorum* indoors is often easier, as it is not climate-specific. Harvesting this plant is legal in most countries, but as with other psychoactive plants, overuse can be dangerous.

Westerner's Discovery

Jean Basset Johnson first described the diviner's sage in 1939 during his study of Mazatec shamanism. In the name of science, he consumed ample amounts of the herb and documented his personal testimonials under the plant's influence. However, the psychoactive mechanism of *Salvia divinorum* was not identified until the 1990s, by Daniel Siebert and his team. They identified the strongest active hallucinogen of *Salvia* as salvinorin A, present in a dried plant at 0.18 percent. It is not toxic and does not cause organ damage, but it is a potent, natural hallucinogen. According to many who have tried this herb, common hallucinations include haunting demons, or even a person transforming into a demon to haunt someone else. Most agree that each trip is a unique experience.

Many Names

The Mazatec people of Mexico have no indigenous name for *Salvia divinorum,* but they strongly believe that the plant is an incarnation of the Virgin Mary. Names such as *Ska Maria Pastora* and *Ska Pastora* refer to "the leaf of herb of Mary, the Shepherdess." Several Spanish names have similar references, such as *Hierba Maria, La Maria,* and *Hojas de la Pastora.* Mazatecs also call it *hoja de la advinacion,* or "leaf of prophecy." Contemporary researchers, such as Gordon Wasson, claim that *Salvia* is probably the mythological *pipiltzintzintli* mentioned in Aztec writings as the "Noble Prince" of the plant world.

DRAGONWORT

Artemisia dracunculus

Do Dragons Practice Aromatherapy?

Dragonwort, or tarragon, is a polymorphic, perennial herb from the family Asteraceae. Some of the species in this family are used as culinary aromatizers, meant to add a scent to vegetables that have little odor.

Others include French tarragon, Russian tarragon (which doesn't lend itself as well to culinary use), and wild tarragon, which grows in many countries worldwide. Some sources trace the etymology of the term to the Persian word *tarkhun*. Dragonwort grows in organically rich, well-drained, dry to medium-moist soils with full sun exposure. It cannot survive in wet soil, and therefore thrives best in sheltered locations. This plant should be cut in early spring and declumped every third year to keep it robust.

Artemisia dracunculus is native to temperate Asia, Europe, and western North America. It grows 4 to 6 inches in height, with branched stems and lanceolate leaves. These leaves have an intense, glossy, green color covering their perimeter. Flowers bloom in the summer, appearing in small *capitulae,* less than 1/8 inch in size, bunched in groups of about forty greenish yellow florets. Some species of dragonwort produce seeds that frequently turn out to be sterile. To compensate, it reproduces via its rhizomatous roots, which shoot stems underground, sprouting new plants along the way.

The Aromatic Medicine

Tarragon's aroma is reminiscent of anise, and like this herb, it also contains estragole. In addition to its culinary usefulness, tarragon also has a few esoteric medical benefits, like its supposed ability to cure hiccups. In aromatherapy, three or four drops of dragonwort's essential oil, combined with a heated lump of sugar, produce a soothing aroma. Dragonwort appears mostly in herb gardens but can also grow successfully in window boxes or containers. Many find it suitable for ornamental planting.

Two other species that are similar to *Artemisia dracunculus* are *Dracunculus vulgaris* (or dragon arum), a flowering plant from the Araceae family, and *Arisaema dracontium* (or green dragon), an herbaceous perennial originating from North America. The dragon part of its name is derived from the Latin *dracunculum*. However, it is uncertain why dragons are meant to symbolize this plant, given that it does not resemble common dragon imagery whatsoever. However, a clue lies in ancient folklore, which tells of the herb's use in recipes concocted to repel dragons. Apparently dragons don't like aromatherapy.

Traditional Culinary Use

Artemisia dracunculus is considered one of the four most important herbs in French cuisine. It is used in preparing fish, chicken, and eggs and is the main flavoring element of the famous Béarnaise sauce. In Armenia, Georgia, and Azerbaijan, it is used to flavor the traditional soft drink, *tarhun*. Russians, Ukrainians, and Kazakhs also enjoy this soft drink and believe it to be healthful. In Slovenia, the recipe for a traditional cake, *potica,* calls for dragonwort as its main spice, and Hungarians use the leaves to flavor their most popular chicken soup.

EGGPLANT
Solanum melongena
Teaching Patience

Found by the earliest inhabitants of India, the first eggplants were smaller than the globe-shaped fruit we know today. Belonging to the often-deadly nightshade family, it's the eggplant's flower that is poisonous. These toxins occur in the fleshy seedpod as well, but they dissipate with maturity. The size of the first eggplants (also known as *guinea squash, aubergine,* or *mad apple*) is lost to botanical antiquity, though we know it was still a palatable food prepared by earlier people using numerous means. It was among the first wild plants to be actively cultivated into different varieties. The plant grows to about 2 feet in height, blooms a purplish flower (depending on the strain), and can produce a half dozen or more of its 8-inch-long, bottom-heavy vegetables from its somewhat woody stem.

Fruit or Vegetable?

To the botanist, nothing is a vegetable. Even the eggplant, something nearly every chef and home cook would decidedly call a vegetable, is in scientific terms the seed (really the ovary) of a flowering plant. You say "tomato" or "tomahto," or "potato" or "potahto" (which, incidentally, are both related to the eggplant), but to the plantanical purist, an eggplant is literally the plant's fruit. In technically precise terms, the eggplant is a berry-bearing herbaceous plant, meaning that its stem and leaves die and wither at the end of a season, once its seeds are given a good send-off. The eggplant was serious about making its ovary desirable. A toxin in its flower ensures the plant won't be eaten during growth, making potential consumers wait until its tasty seedpod is big and fat—a real strategic achievement in the competitive world of seed dispersal.

ELDERFLOWER

Sambucus

For the Body and Soul

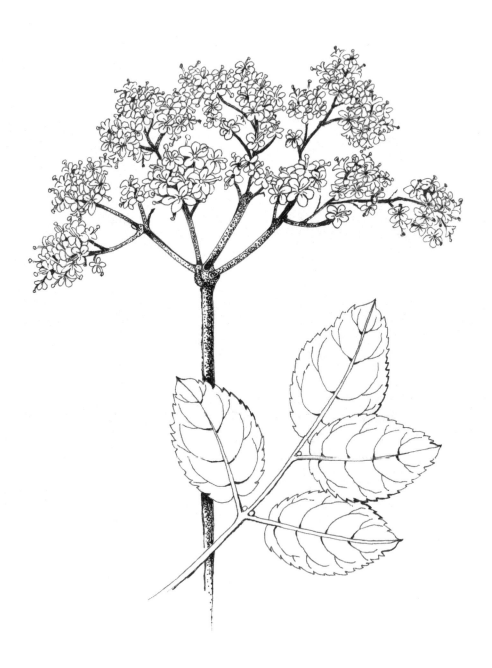

Elderflower is part of the honeysuckle family, with 20 different species growing in temperate and subtropical zones. They are usually small shrubs, but when nurtured some have grown 20 feet in height. Their white flowers rise in ornamental clusters, like a ready-made bouquet. Though a delicacy of sweetness, an elderflower doesn't bother dissuading predators from destroying its flowers, as it blooms so quickly and produces seeds at such a rapid pace.

Humans prize the elder's berries, which give a potent dose of tasty sugars. The blackish blue (occasionally red) berries are well suited for use in jams, juices, and pastries. Both the flowers and berries are edible, but the berries have to be cooked. They are poisonous raw. The flowers, when distilled, make a sugary drink, which can be imbibed straight, made as a tea, or turned into wines and cordials. Sambuca, a favorite Italian liqueur, is made from the plant's flowers. Even yogurts and certain brands of marshmallows use the flower's nectar as an ingredient, which is so versatile that certain mouthwashes have it in their formula. Who knows, maybe the first cavemen took a swig of it before courting! Fossilized remnants of the plant have been discovered in numerous Stone Age excavation sites, showing elderflowers were apparently used for multiple purposes. Ancient medical books cite it as a cure for numerous ailments, like excessive sweating or coughing fits, and it is still used in liquid drops for red eyes. Its bark and stems are not often sold raw, as these can be dangerous if misused.

The plant's scientific name is taken from the writings of Pliny, a first-century Roman naturalist and cataloger. Before the discovery of its many food and medicinal uses, its hollow stems were used to make natural flutes, called sackbuts, which many a lonely shepherd learned to play. Like the peaceful melodies of a flute, many hail the elderflower as good for both body and soul.

People have long loved the elder for its beauty and host of benefits. Naturally, superstitions grew

The elder *part of the plant's English name has nothing to do with the plant's age, but meant that it was good to use to start fires.* Elder *is a derivative of an Anglo-Saxon word for kindling.*

around the plant; for example, if someone dared to kill one of the stouter varieties to make furniture, the chair or table fashioned from its timber would seek revenge. A chair might fling itself across the room or move about on its own and haunt the home's residents for abetting the plant's destruction. In Christian mythology, Judas chooses to hang himself from the branches of an elder tree—perhaps as a last symbolic plea for mercy or kindness.

ELM
Ulmus
The Liberty Tree

The elm is probably one of the most painted trees in the world. You will find this graceful tree with sensitive foliage within the landscapes of master painters such as Ferdinand Georg Waldmüller, George Innes, John Constable, Childe Hassam, and Karel Klinkenberg, and of countless practicing artists, all inspired by the elm's appearance. It wasn't only aesthetics that attracted artists to elms, though. The tree has a rich mythology in literature and art, though it is also simply planted for its beauty and great economical value. Elm has long been the preferred timber for fine furniture, wagon wheels, chairs, coffins, keels for old wooden ships, and strong longbows.

Multi-Useful

Other uses of the elm tree include medicinal ones. The tree's inner bark, especially, is used for a skin salve and as a nutritional supplement. Its leaves are cultivated and harvested and used as livestock fodder. The tree's seeds are also nutritious, containing 45 percent crude protein and about 7 percent fiber. Europeans have long acknowledged the tree's nutritional value. In 1812, the bark of the elm saved the Norwegian people from a famine and starvation.

Belonging to the genus *Ulmus*, family Ulmaceae, elms are decidu-

ous and lose their leaves each year. The tree's genus first appeared about twenty million years ago, in the Miocene period. Its origins were in today's Central Asia, but it spread and flourished in the temperate climates of the Northern Hemisphere, Eurasia, and Indonesia. Elms are found in many types of natural forests. In the late 1900s they became a favorite ornamental tree for streets, parks, and gardens, both in Europe and North America.

The tree can grow to heights of 70 to 90 feet, with branches spreading to widths of 40 to 70 feet. Some elms live a long time, more than two hundred years. Elm leaves have alternating shapes, with either single or double jagged or serrated edges. It is a hermaphroditic genus with perfect petalous flowers, pollinated mostly by wind and bees. Elm fruits are round, rich with chlorophyll, and spread primarily by wind. The tree is tolerant to a wide range of soils and pH levels, though it demands good drainage. In 1997, the European Union started the Elm Project, aiming to conserve all of the elm's genetic resources and to strengthen its resistance to Dutch elm disease, which has devastated the species for many decades.

The elm became a symbol of freedom and victory. For example, after the final victory of the parliamentarians over the monarchists during England's Glorious Revolution in 1688, planting elms was considered a fashion among the supporters of the new order. In the United States the tree also became a powerful political symbol. The famous "Liberty Tree" of the American Revolution was a white elm from Boston, in front of which the first resistance meetings were held in 1765. The British tried to cut it down in 1775 but were prevented from doing so. Later, it became an established tradition for all American presidents to plant an elm. The French Revolution also used *Les arbres de la liberté* (Liberty Trees), most often elms, as symbols of their revolutionary battles and hopes, inspired by the Boston elm. The famous Elm of La Madeleine, planted in France in 1790, survives to this day. It was this revolutionary moment that probably inspired so many painters to use elms as symbols of freedom. Such trees shouldn't be cut down or killed by anyone.

Elm Mythology

When the hero Orpheus from Greek mythology rescued his beloved Eurydice from the underworld, he paused to play a love song for her. As a result, the first elm grove grew instantly on the spot. In Homer's *Iliad*, mountain nymphs planted an elm over the tomb of the father of Andromache. Elms were often mentioned in pastoral poetry as symbols of idyllic life. The Celtic people believed elms were protectors from the underworld and planted the trees to guard burial mounds and aid the dead during their passage into the other world.

ERGOT

Claviceps purpurea
St. Anthony's Fire

St. Anthony's fire is a name once given to a fungus, known today as ergot, that grows on rye and other grain-producing plants. In human beings and other mammals this can cause St. Anthony's fire disease, also known as ergotism. The fungus generally affects oats, rye, wheat, and barley, which can quickly spread the disease among human populations.

St. Anthony's fire disease has killed millions throughout agricultural history. In A.D. 1000, an order of monks called the Order of St. Anthony was formed and trained to treat the disease. In the Middle Ages, these monks built and operated the world's first hospital system, the Hospital Brothers of St. Anthony. They eventually opened more than 350 facilities throughout Europe, specifically created to combat the terrible blight. The monks used balms that tranquilized and improved the circulation to aid the immune system in detoxification. Patients suffering from the infection experienced severe skin rashes, including deep burning sensations in the limbs. Sometimes patients even lost their limbs because of restricted circulation of the blood.

The alkaloids that the fungus produces can cause hallucinations, irrational and unconventional behavior, convulsions, and an untimely demise. Other symptoms after consumption of ergot-contaminated grains include strong uterine contractions, sudden unconsciousness, nausea, and seizures.

The medicine ergometrine is used to induce uterine contractions. Similarly, when ergot is taken as a medicine after skillful preparation it can induce abortion without killing the mother. It helps control maternal bleeding that can occur after childbirth as well as other hemorrhages. In products like "Cafergot" (a proprietary medicine with the ingredients ergotamine, tartrate, and caffeine), ergot is added to the mix to help with cluster headaches.

Ergot could be considered a catalyst for modern medicine, since it affected so many and spurred scientific inquiry about what caused the disease. St. Anthony's fire disease was very common in Europe in the medieval period, but some intentionally used ergot as a poison to wipe out enemy populations by adding it to grain stores.

Ergotamine found in the plant affects muscle fibers. When taken in large doses, it can paralyze nerve endings. If a person consumes too much ergot, he or she will likely suffer from St. Anthony's fire disease. To prevent infection, make sure baked foods are made from inspected flour supplies.

Ergot can affect humans and animals equally. Cattle and other herbivores that consume contaminated rye and wheat will also succumb to the disease. There are several ways for farmers and production companies to identify and disinfect flour of St. Anthony's fire before selling it to consumers. Farmers cut the heads of the cereals affected by the fungi before milling. Sometimes, harvested crops are "cleaned" through a visual check; farmers will examine and remove dark purple and black ergot fungi, thereby neutralizing any suspected blights. The ergots collected from this process are buried more than 2 feet deep in the ground to prevent germination. Today, most commercially prepared foods for humans, birds, and animals are generally free from ergot infections. St. Anthony's fire disease typically crops up today only in people and animals who consume directly and care-lessly from the fields. Therefore, it is best to consume commercially cleaned or organically prepared and sold products, since the flour normally goes through a heating processing that kills the fungi.

EUCALYPTUS
Eucalyptus globulus
Take a Deep Breath

This unusual-looking tree is part of the myrtle family, which contains as many as 400 different species. It originates from Australia, although varieties are also grow in the Malayan islands. It has since been exported around the world to warmer climates, since it's very fast growing and a ready source of timber, not to mention beautification. The largest of the species, the king gum, reaches heights of over 300 feet, with trunk girths of 25 feet—a whole lot of wood. However, those who imported the trees in hopes of reaping quick timber profits found that the best timber from the Australian varieties took hundreds of years to reach similar magnitude. What was touted as a "eucalyptus gold rush" of timber wealth that occurred in California during the early twentieth century quickly faded, since in American soil the trees failed to produce plank-size boards as rapidly as had

been hoped. However, that timber rush left vast forests of these stunning trees that remain to this day.

Many types of eucalyptus go by the common name of *gum tree*. Their sap, known as kino, is sticky and feels like superglue. The leaves are oblong and rigid, and look and feel like green leather. The leaves stand vertically, stiff off their stalks, angling their edge (and not their face) upward to the light.

Why the Long Face?

Rigid and upstanding in youth, the leaves of eucalyptus trees begin to droop with age, seeming to hang in melancholy and turn sideways. Though puzzling at first, this strategy is now understood to allow older trees to conserve water and not dry out as quickly, since most species grow in regions with excessive sunshine. This leaf switching is yet another novel adaptation by plants to meet the challenges of a stationary existence.

A Difficult Food

The tough, leathery leaves of the eucalyptus provide food for only one animal, the koala. But in order for this marsupial to digest the leaves it had to acquire a special bacterium in its digestive tract. This bacterium, which, incredibly, is transferred from mother koala to its infant by spitting into the newborn's mouth, ferments the leaves and makes them digestable. Although eucalyptus oil has a pleasing menthol aroma, it gives the koalas a repugnant body odor.

Another by-product of the eucalyptus is its aromatic resin. Aborigines of Australia used the plants' sap to treat burns, blisters, wounds, and insect bites. When the first British colonists encountered eucalyptus forests, they referred to the plant as a "fever tree." They found that when they were infected with what they called "tropical fever," the refreshing and uplifting scent from the plant cleared the sinuses and seemed to restore health. Now the oil from the leaves is distilled and used in aromatherapy. The well-known Vicks VapoRub, which generations of parents have daubed on the chests and under the noses of children, contains eucalyptus oil. The famous little blue jar of salve was invented by a North Carolina pharmacist named Lunsford Richardson. He first called it Magic Croup Salve in 1905, and marketed it as a treatment for croup, among other respiratory ailments. When he went to print the label for his new product, his last name, Richardson, was too long, so instead he chose that of his brother-in-law, Dr. Joshua W. Vick.

FENNEL
Foeniculum vulgare
Aromatic Creativity

Fennel is a perennial, highly aromatized, and highly favored plant
from the family of Apiaceae, genus *Foeniculum,* of which it is the sole
species. It is an umbelliferous plant, with feathery leaves and yellow
flowers, considered native to the Mediterranean, though naturalized

worldwide, and thrives particularly in dry coastal soil and on riverbanks. Apart from its famed culinary use, fennel is also food for some species in the Lepidoptera order, such as the mouse moth and the anise swallowtail butterfly.

Etymologically, the word comes from *fenol* or *finol,* which is from the Latin *fenum* or *faenum,* meaning "hay." In Hindi, fenol is known as *sonp* or *saunf. Foeniculum vulgare* is a straight plant with hollow stems, fresh green in color, and can grow up to 2½ feet tall. Its finely dissected thin leaves are long for the plant's size and can reach over 1 foot. The fennel's flowers come in terminal umbels, like little umbrellas, only a few inches wide. These, however, are packed with thirty to fifty flowers with short pedicels. The herb's fruit is a dry, grooved seed about 2 inches long.

Hail Fennel

Fennel has been cultivated for a considerable part of history. It appears in Greek mythology; Prometheus used dry fennel stalks to perform his legendary act of stealing fire from the gods. A giant fennel seed from the species *Ferula communis* formed the sacramental wand used by the Romans to summon Dionysius, the god of drinking, at the start of their many lush festivals. The original Greek name for fennel was *marathon,* or *marathos.* It comes from the Battle of Marathon, literally "a plain with fennels," the supposed site of the epic bloodshed. Old English *finule* is one of nine plants mentioned in the pagan *Nine Herbs Charm,* an Anglo-Saxon book of recipes for magic potions and remedies dating back to the tenth century.

Fennel is cultivated all over the world, mostly for its edible, intensely flavored leaves and fruits, which contain the strong aromatic compound anethole. This herb is highly adaptive and can take root in many open sites, including roadsides and pastures in northern Europe, the United States, Canada, Australia, and Asia. One cultivar of fennel, *Florence fenne,* has a more mild flavor, and is sweeter and more aromatic; smaller than the original, this type of fennel, besides being a decorative plant, is also used as a vegetable, both cooked and raw, as *purpureum* and *nigra.*

Fennel seeds have traditionally been used to alleviate bloating, heartburn, loss of appetite, intestinal gas, and colic, but the plant is also useful for fighting respiratory infections, backache, coughs, bronchitis, visual problems, and bedwetting; it is even used against cholera. Native Americans used fennel poultices against snakebites. In some regions, women use this herb to increase the quantity of their breast milk, to bring about menstruation, and even to increase their sex drive. Its oil has also been used to flavor laxatives and is a component in some cosmetic products. It's also a main ingredient, with the absinthium plant, in the emerald-green liquor absinthe.

FERN
Pteridophyta
A Plant from the Beginning of Time

Ferns belong to the botanical group Pteridophyta, which contains more than 12,000 species. They are one of the oldest plants on this planet. According to fossil evidence dating back 360 million years, the land before the fern's arrival was merely a reddish soil devoid of nutrients.

Algal mats and bacteria were the only organisms that could survive the harsh conditions. Land plants prior to ferns were algae-like. Ferns were among the first plants to have leaves, stems, and roots. Mosses may have preceded their arrival, but ferns were the first to develop true pinnate leaves and an internal transport sieve system (known as xylem and phloem) to distribute nutrients, thus paving the evolutionary way for the vast array of flora we know today. Early ferns grew as tall as trees and came in numerous variations. Most of the earliest species from this period are extinct, but there are a number of prehistoric specimens still

🌳   The Big, Bad Book of Botany

in our midst—surviving continental shifts and countless epic climatic changes.

Most of the existing fern species appeared about 145 million years ago, during the early Cretaceous epoch, which makes them contemporaries of the dinosaurs. Ferns have no seeds or flowers and reproduce by spores, similar to mushrooms. There are five groups of ferns, including horsetails, marattioid ferns, ophioglossoid ferns, whisk ferns, and the largest group, leptosporangiate ferns, also called monilophytes.

Nevertheless, the ferns we see are remnants of ancient flora, and though they have no economic significance—most have little food value—their simple beauty still astounds. To most humans, ferns seem mainly ornamental, but ecologically they are able to cleanse contaminated soil by adding nutrients. In addition, recent studies show they can even clean chemical pollutants from the air. Ferns play a role in homeopathic medicine and hold significance in both mythology and art.

Unlike the stereotype of ferns hiding in shady, moist woodland nooks, many fern species grow in a diverse variety of conditions, from dry, desertlike rock areas and mountain elevations, to open fields and bodies of water. However, they frequently seem to favor marginal habitats, often growing where no other plant can survive. Generally, ferns fare best in four specific environmental types: shady and moist forests; acidic wetlands, such as swamps and bogs; crevices in rock faces without full sun exposure; and, of course, the tropics. You'll see them everywhere from the Scottish Highlands to the depths of the Amazon Basin. Many tropical trees, called epiphytes, are actually of the fern species—as many as 25 to 30 percent.

Many of the species have very particular requirements and can only exist within specific pH ranges found in soil. For example, the climbing fern in eastern North America grows best in moist, intensely acidic soils. The "bulbet bladder" fern can grow only on limestone. In addition, some ferns strictly depend on their association with various species of fungi that add nutrients to soil. With their wide flexibility, it's not so astonishing that ferns have prevailed for millions of years. They are highly adaptive survivors.

Because ferns reproduce by spores, their life cycle is similar to those of other vascular plants. Here is a typical life cycle of a fern: The plant produces a small, flat, delicate structure, sometimes looking like a thread, called a prothallus. Here it enters into the "diploid phase," where it produces haploid spores, or eggs cells with a single set of chromosomes. These cells divide in a process called meiosis, which reduces the chromosomes by half. In the next phase, the spores undergo cell division, or mitosis, growing into haploid gametophytes, which then go through mitosis once more, producing both eggs and sperm on the same prothallus. The sperm portion of the plant then fertilizes the egg, which stays connected to the prothallus. Once fertilized, the spore is ready to produce another fern.

Simple! But not really. The process of sporogenesis is yet another example of nature's amazing ability to foster species under virtually any conditions. This reproductive system, in constant repetition for 150 million years, allows for the birth of new ferns all over the planet, and may continue to do so until the end of time.

FIG
Ficus carica
Mediterranean Sweetness

Part of the Moraceae family, *Ficus carica* is unique in a genus with more than 1,000 species, most of which are giant tropical rubber trees. Almost universally known as *fig*—other names are *common fig* and *edible fig*—its name is very similar in Italian and Portuguese (*figo*), French (*figue*), and German (*feige*). The Spanish call it *higo* or *brevo,* while Haitians named it *figue* to differentiate it from their smaller, dried bananas, which they call figs. The fig is indigenous to western Asia, and spread over time across the whole of the Mediterranean region. Its cultivation goes back thousands of years; evidence found in Neolithic sites suggests fig gathering or cultivation dates back to at least 5000 B.C. Over time, fig growing

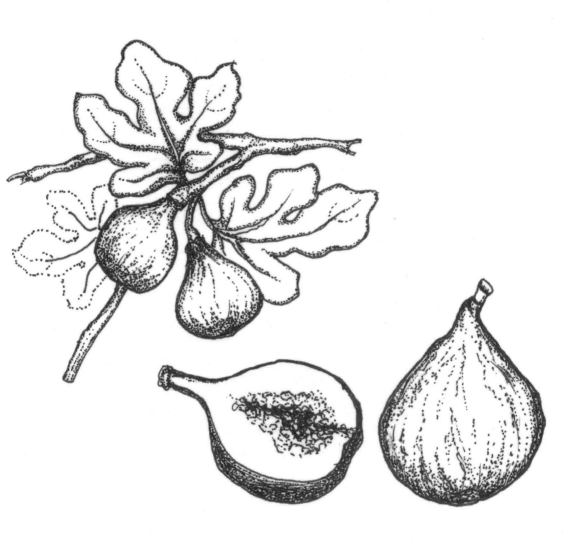

extended to Afghanistan, the Canary Islands, and even to Germany. Today the plant is still mostly cultivated in the Mediterranean and in mild-temperate climates, though it will grow in tropical and subtropical areas as well.

Ficus carica is a small tree, 9 to 18 feet tall, consisting of lots of spreading branches and a relatively lean trunk—about 6 inches in diameter. Roots are shallow and wide, covering 30 feet close to the surface or on top of the ground around the tree. In harder soil it will bore downward 8 feet or so with a stronger root. Leaves are palmate, divided into three to seven main lobes. The blade grows up to almost an inch long and as wide, and is rough and fairly thick on the surface, with a soft, hairy underside. The fig plant produces a copious milky latex for sap. Its fruit is known as a syconium—a fleshy, hollow receptacle with a tiny opening at the apex, partially closed by small scales. The fruit is pear-shaped, from ¼ inch to 1 inch long. It ranges in color from yellowish green to dark purple, bronze, or copper.

The common fig has all female flowers, which need no pollination. However, three less prevalent varieties have male and female flowers. The *caprifig* achieves pollination by a small wasp, *Blastophaga grossorum*. The *Smyrna* is cross-pollinated by caprifigs. The *San Pedro*, an intermediate fig, has its first crop reproductively independent, like the *common fig*, while the second crop depends on pollination. The fig's skin is tender and thin, and its wall is whitish, amber, pale yellow, rose, pink, red, or purple. People consume figs fresh (juicy and sweet when ripe) or dried, and use them as a baking ingredient or in extraordinary jams. The fig's seeds differ in size but are generally small, so there can be 30 to 1,600 seeds per fruit.

We cultivate figs in a few different ways. The vegetative method is the most common. After gathering seeds from dried figs and storing them in plastic bags or wrappings, farmers need only to add small amounts of moisture, and germination will begin in a few weeks. Once the sprouts bud and the leaves open, the plant grows to just an inch (which can take one year), before it is ready for transplantation to its final home in a field. For summer propagation, it is best to plant the seedlings in a sandy soil mix or moist perlite; when new growth starts, move the little plants into full sun exposure. Spring crops need their shoots cut before the tree starts vegetating; it should then be set into a shady place with a sandy soil mix or moist compost.

Cultural Aspects

Fig cultivation has accompanied much of human history, and the plant is iconic in many different cultures. The book of Genesis tells of Adam and Eve covering their nakedness with fig leaves after tasting the forbidden fruit from the tree of knowledge of good and evil.

There has never been a consensus on what exactly the forbidden fruit was in the Garden of Eden. For centuries, most thought it was a fig. Later, during medieval times, Christian scholars claimed it was an apple. Figs, not apples, were likely to be more abundant in the area of modern Iraq, thought to be the site of the Garden of Eden. But, then again, it was the garden where anything could grow.

Because of the story in the Bible, artists have often favored fig leaves for covering up parts of nude bodies in paintings and sculptures. Also, there are numerous passages in the Bible that feature the fig. For example, one section describes Jesus being hungry and finding a fig tree that has only leaves and no fruit. Jesus curses it (which is very astonishing!), and the tree then withers. The Bible also famously says, "each man under his own vine and fig tree," to indicate peace and prosperity. The Koran also depicts the fig many times. However, the plant's most significant role in history may be in its relation to the Buddha, who, according to legend, first gained enlightenment under an old, sacred fig tree.

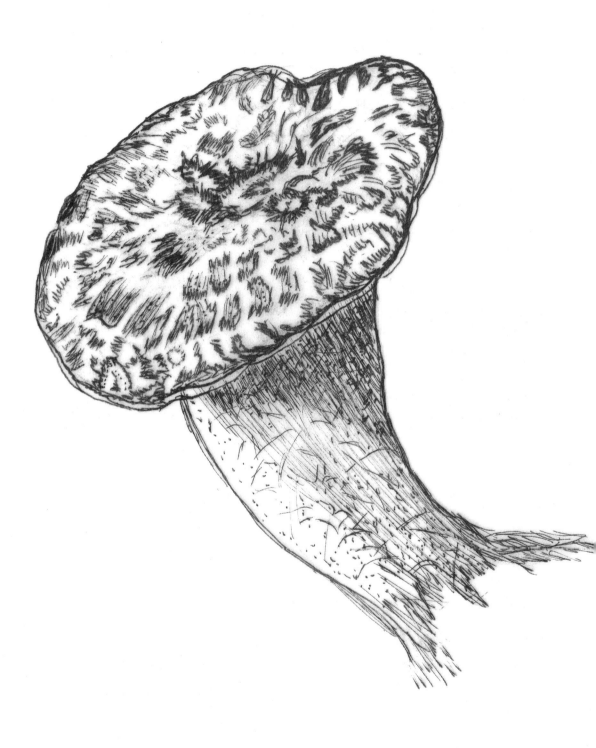

FUNGI
Fungal Lineage
The Strange Kingdom

Fungi, like animals, plants, and bacteria, are placed in their own taxonomic kingdom. They are distinct from the rest of the plant world. Though many naturalists had long considered various fungi to be plants, in the 1950s the American ecologist Robert Whittaker argued that fungi needed their own classification.

This large group of *eukaryotic* organisms (their cells contain a nucleus) includes molds, yeasts, rusts, puffballs, smuts, morels, truffles, and, of course, the most famous—mushrooms. So far, about 100,000 species have been discovered, but many believe there are as many as 1.5 million. The main characteristic that distinguishes fungi from plants is on the cellular level. Fungi have cell walls containing chitin, while the cell walls of plants contain cellulose. The part of the fungus that we see is only the "fruit." Fungi cannot make their own food like plants do, and they have no chlorophyll. Fungi are mostly parasitic. Nevertheless, fungi are of great importance and function as the chief decomposers (or recyclers) in nature.

Fungi grow all around the world, though usually in hidden places, and play a profound role in nutrient cycling and exchange. Even though they subsist on dead matter, many of them are *symbionts* of animals, plants, or even other fungi, meaning they give back as much as they take. Some fungi are a prized food source, like mushrooms and truffles; another, yeast, is important as a leavening agent for bread, as well as for fermentation of beer, wine, and soy sauce. Others form useful antibiotics, and recently some detergents have begun including certain fungi enzymes. They are even added to biological pesticides—some species produce the bioactive element *mycotoxin,* which is extremely toxic to animals and humans. A few controversial species of fungi contain some psychotropic compounds and are traditionally used in some spiritual rituals.

Like certain infamous mushrooms, some fungi also contain pathogens deadly to people, animals, and even plants.

With their vast numbers and characteristics, fungi can grow in a range of habitats, from extreme desert areas to deep-sea sediment. Some can survive strong ultraviolet rays and even cosmic radiation during space travel, which has led some speculative theorists to believe the first fungi on earth may have arrived on asteroids or from another world. In addition, fungi reproduce through many complex phenomena. Depending on the environment, most species of fungi can practice either sexual or asexual reproduction. Asexual reproduction occurs through spores or by mycelial fragmentation, where the mycelium divides into pieces, each of which grows into a separate new organism. Asexual fungi spread much more rapidly than the sexual variety. A third reproduction method, practiced by fungi such as *Penicillium* and *Aspergillus,* is *parasexual.* The process, called plasmogamy, involves a fusion of two parent fungal cells. Although parasexualism is considered important in hybridization and in the evolution of fungi, exactly how and why fungi adapted as they have remains unexplained. Fungi form a strange and secret kingdom, perhaps with many biological and chemical treasures yet to be revealed.

GARLIC
Allium sativum
Vampire Killer

A small vegetable with many meanings, uses, benefits, and myths, garlic is highly regarded worldwide. In some regions it not only is considered a precious food but retains a folkloric symbolism as a protector against evil and illness. Garlic is guaranteed to make every meal more flavorful and healthy, and provides great benefits to our cardiovascular system. Its seven thousand years of use on this planet speaks for itself; even ancient Egyptians found uses for the plant, both medical and culinary.

Garlic belongs to the *Allium* genus of the Amaryllidacae family, and is a close cousin to onions, chives, leeks, rakkyo, and shallots. Its flowers are hermaphrodites that are pollinated by bees and other insects. Humans cultivate the plant for its bulb, which is usually 2 inches long and wide, consisting of numerous small cloves. Both the bulb and cloves are "packed" in paperlike tiny sheaths of white, pinkish, or purplish color. Garlic can grow up to 4 feet tall, with two long green leaves; its cloves have a firm texture but are still easily crushed. Describing its unique and intense taste is no simple task—a hot pungency hits the palate, but not without a subtle background of sweetness to it.

During the era of bubonic plague in the Middle Ages, people wore crosses and a veritable grocery store of vegetables, including onions, leeks, and garlic, around their necks, in the hope of warding off the evil disease. Although there is no science to prove that wearing garlic did any good, it perhaps helped people to keep their distance from one another and reduce the chances of catching this communicable disease.

Where It's From

Allium sativum is thought to have originated in southwestern Asia, though today the plant is cultivated throughout the world, and China is the leading producer. Garlic needs soil rich with highly organic material, although it will grow in a wide spectrum of terrain and acidity. Two of the most popular species are elephant garlic, actually a wild leek, and single-clove garlic, which originated in Yunnan, China. Garlic prefers mild climates and doesn't bloom year-round. Although it can undergo sexual reproduction, garlic nearly always propagates asexually by depositing its cloves in the soil.

Growing

In colder regions, garlic grows from autumn until spring, when it is ready for harvest. To prevent frost, which causes white rot or mold, from endangering the plant's growth, cloves need to be planted quite deep within the soil and close to one another, with enough space for bulbs to grow and mature. It grows well in dry, loose, well-drained, sunny fields. Farmers select only large cloves for planting, as they yield bigger bulbs. The scape, a leafless flower stalk, will grow above the ground, but farmers remove this prior to harvest so the plant can concentrate all its energy into the bulb. Scapes can, however, be eaten, either cooked or raw.

Health Benefits

Garlic, both raw and cooked, has many widely praised health benefits. It improves the whole cardiovascular system, unblocking blood vessels and lowering the body's level of triglycerides and cholesterol; it also has anti-inflammatory and antioxidative effects. Garlic is also recommended for cancer prevention and improving the metabolism of iron, as well as for antiviral and antibacterial protection. It can even function as an antiseptic agent. Consuming garlic regulates the sugar level in the blood and boosts testosterone levels. Most famously, garlic is known as the best vegetable for warding off vampires, a legend that even predates Bram Stoker's iconic *Dracula*.

GIANT HOGWEED
Heracleum mantegazzianum
Turn and Run!

Right off the bat: do not touch this plant! While it won't kill you, giant hogweed can easily land a person in the hospital. It contains sap that in combination with sunlight and moisture can cause painful blistering, severe skin and eye irritation, and even permanent blindness and scarring. So it's worth the effort to learn what giant hogweed looks like. A noxious herb belonging to the carrot family of Apiaceae, hogweed can grow perennially or biennially; it can reach up to 14 feet high, with a hollow, stout stem 2 to 4 inches in diameter and dark purple-reddish pigmentation. The big, incised, and compound leaves can be up to 5 feet wide; on the flat, formed top of foliage grow white flowers, or heads, around 2 feet in diameter.

Giant hogweed, *Heracleum mantegazzianum,* goes by many other names, such as *cartwheel flower, giant cow parsley, giant cow parsnip, wild rhubarb,* and *wild parsnip.* It is a phototoxic weed, considered noxious in most cases. The phototoxic effect comes from compounds called furocoumarin derivatives, which are designed to ward off predators and are active in all parts of the plant, including the roots, stem, flowers, and seeds. The plant is native to Central Asia, more precisely to the Caucasus region, but has now spread to Britain, the United States, Canada, Ireland, Sweden, Finland, France, Germany, the Czech Republic, Belgium, and Latvia.

One Final Gift

Giant hogweed lives no more than seven years. Its roots are tuberous, and each year they produce perennial buds, though the flowers appear only in the last year of its life cycle, blooming in its final days, from spring to midsummer. During this finale, the plant produces numerous white flowers inside umbrella-like heads, growing up to 3 feet in diameter. The hogweed then bears 1,500 to 100,000 oval, dry, speck-size flattened seeds, which it entrusts to the wind for dispersal. After the mature seeds are released, the plant dies, usually in autumn. Despite the toxicity, giant hogweeds are highly appreciated among beekeepers; many believe that bees are able to make the sweetest possible honey from its nectar—another example of nature's strange sensibility. It's as if this final gift of sweetness is its redemption for its years of poisoning. Even more bizarrely, cows and pigs are able to consume giant hogweed without any harm.

Antidotes

If you touch *Heracleum mantegazzianum,* quickly and thoroughly wash the affected area with water and soap, and keep yourself away from sunlight for forty-eight hours. Contact your doctor and report the plant's location to the appropriate agency. Don't even think of rubbing your eyes with your hands after touching giant hogweed—you could become permanently blind, or develop some nasty purplish or black scars that can last for years.

A 1971 song by the band Genesis, "The Return of the Giant Hogweed" (off the *Nursery Cryme* album), relates the history of giant hogweed's introduction to Great Britain in the nineteenth century, where it was once touted as an ornamental plant: "Turn and run! Nothing can stop them. Around every river and canal their power is growing."

Whatever else Genesis might have meant with the song, this is the best possible advice when dealing with hogweed. If you ever encounter the plant, abandon curiosity and courage—just turn and run!

GINKGO
Ginkgo biloba
Leaves like Duck Feet

In traditional Chinese herbalism, the ginkgo is a champion specimen. Ginkgo tastes similar to almonds and smells like rancid butter; some claim it can cure Alzheimer's disease, increase blood circulation, act as an antioxidant, and alleviate lung ailments. The ancestral origins of this plant go back an amazing 270 million years. Gingko extracts have played a crucial role in Chinese medicine for centuries, while Western medicine has only recently started to study their benefits. The German government has already approved the plant for use in the treatment of poor concentra-

tion and memory loss. Most interesting is that ginkgo would likely not exist today if not for ancient Buddhist monks in China and Japan, who cultivated it as a sacred tree. Scientists believe ginkgo evolved from seed ferns, of the order Peltaspermales. Ginkgo plants have an incredible longevity of one thousand years or more.

Ginkgo biloba is basically a living fossil—it is the only surviving species of ginkgo today. To survive so long as the sole remaining member of its family should earn the plant a deep bow from botanists everywhere, though perhaps we owe some (one-handed!) applause to the monks for keeping it alive. *Ginkgo* are classified as gymnosperms and first appeared in the Permian period of prehistory, an era before flowering plants. Some argue ginkgos may now be evolutionarily closer to conifers than to other gymnosperms. Ginkgos flourished during the Jurassic and Cretaceous epochs, converging in later periods into a single polymorphic species, named *Ginkgo adiantoides,* which is practically indistinguishable from the *Ginkgo biloba* trees we see today.

Pinch the Nose

Present-day ginkgo differs from its predecessors in its fan-shaped, light green leaves. The Japanese call it *I-cho,* meaning "tree with leaves like a duck's foot." Ginkgo leaf edges are wavy with parallel veins, and lack a central vein. Its bark is smooth and gray. This flowerless plant can grow from 30 to 100 feet high and produces a massive amount of seeds, which have been a staple of Chinese cuisine for centuries. When gathered in a sort of compost heap manner, the seeds give off an overpowering smell, often described in horticultural literature as "repulsive," "disgusting," or "offensive," even earning comparison to the odor of vomit. The smell comes from a malodorous chemical known as butyric acid, which is found in every ginkgo seed.

Built-in Adaptation

Ginkgoes grow wild only in China, but people cultivate the crop worldwide. Its long evolutionary history has made it a highly adaptable plant that can succeed in practically any temperate climate. Ginkgo is extremely resistant to pests and pollution, which has allowed it to thrive in urban locales. Given its slow rate of evolution, it is very possible that ginkgo has developed unique strategies for surviving that have allowed it to exist for as long as it has through countless changing environments. One advantage is the plant's large seed production, which statistically favors propagation. Another helpful characteristic is the plant's habit of "bolting"—a rapid growth spurt whereby the 30-foot trunk forms before any elongate branches appear. This periscope-like method of shooting its trunk to the sky may have given the plant a preliminary sample of the environmental conditions in which it has found itself.

GYMNOSPERMS
Protective Parents

Gymnosperms are flowerless seed-bearing plants, such as cycads, conifers, gnetophytes, and ginkgos. The name comes from the Greek *gymnospermos,* meaning "naked seeds," which describes the plants' seeds, also known as ovules, which appear unenclosed in an unfertilized state. Fossils indicate gymnosperm evolution probably began about three hundred million years ago; most became extinct, except for ferns. Gymnosperms comprise about 1,000 living species in 88 genera, divided into 14 plant families; they are remarkably diverse in their leaf types and reproductive structures.

Self-Sufficient

Gymnosperms also differ from other seedless plants in that they do not rely on pollinators to transport the male gamete to the female gamete; they accomplish this feat with nothing more than the wind. As such, gymnosperms must produce a large amount of pollen, which many of us can't help but notice every spring. Next, the pollen is located in conelike structures named strobili (from the Latin word for pinecone, *strobilus*). The pines and a few other plants in this family have seeds with "wings" that help in dispersal. Each male can produce 1 to 2 million pollen grains a year—success in statistical abundance! They also have an inventive pollination strategy: they use sticky surfaces of the seed-bearing part of the plant to catch pollen grains. After pollination has been achieved, the droplets contract and evaporate, closing the grains inside the pollen chambers to make contact with ovules. This is what's happening inside a pinecone.

Gymnosperms have significant economic uses. Species such as pine, spruce, fir, and cedar (all of them beautiful trees) are used for lumber. Other uses include production of soaps, nail polish, varnish, gum, food, and perfume.

HEMLOCK
Conium maculatum
Socrates's Choice

Hemlock is yet another highly toxic plant that can cause serious health problems, even death. *Conium* is a genus of two species of herbaceous, perennial, poisonous flowering herbs in the Apiaceae family. The hemlock species, *Conium maculatum,* is native to the Mediterranean region, and the other, *Conium chaerophylloides,* comes from southern Africa. According to Merriam-Webster, the word *hemlock* comes from the Old English *hemlic,* which was the name of the tree. The plant has other names, such as *woomlicks, beaver poison, poison parsley, bunk, hever, caise, devil's flower,* and *gypsy flower.* It even has more regional nicknames: *break-your-mother's-heart* (wow!), *lady's lace, scabby hands,* and others. A very inspiring plant, obviously. *Conium* derives from the Greek *konas,* meaning "vertigo" or "whirl"—both symptoms of the plant's intoxicating poison.

Hemlock is a biennial, herbaceous plant that can grow from 3 to 5 feet tall. It has a smooth green stem, often streaked or spotted on the lower half with purple or red—a warning from nature of the plant's toxicity. Its leaves have an overall triangular shape, divided and lacy, and grow about 1½ feet long and nearly as wide. Its small white flowers, clustered in umbels, are ½ inch in diameter. When crushed, a hemlock leaf or root emits an unpleasant, rank odor, similar to that of parsnips.

Hemlock is native to the temperate regions of West Asia, Europe, and North Africa but has since spread to North America, Australia, and New Zealand. It often grows near surface waters, such as streams and ditches, as well as on waste areas, roadsides, and the edges of cultivated fields. In some countries, it is treated as an invasive plant. *Conium maculatum* prefers damp areas with poorly drained soils; it flourishes in early spring, before other foliage appears. All parts of the

Hemlock is not actually related to the hemlock tree, which is in the pine family and not at all poisonous. The tree gets its name from its needles, which, when crushed, give off a similar smell to the toxic hemlock shrub.

plant are poisonous, though once dried the toxicity drops significantly. But don't hold any illusions of attempting to use dried hemlock—it is still dangerous. Though never safe for humans, hemlock is nice food for some larvae of the Lepidoptera order (these guys are nearly indestructible!), such as the silver-ground carpet moth.

In Socrates's last moment of lucidity he mentioned the god Asclepius, a mythological deity noted for healing. Scholars surmise that Socrates conceived of his death as the freeing of his soul from the unreasonableness of humanity and the confines of his body. However, Plato's dignified description of Socrates's death might be a bit romanticized, since hemlock poisoning would be a lot more painful and accompanied by convulsive gasping for breath.

The Mix

Hemlock contains conhydrine and N-methylconine, but its most poisonous alkaloid is coniine, which has a chemical structure similar to nicotine. This poison disrupts the central nervous system—a small dose can cause respiratory collapse. Coniine causes death by blocking the neuromuscular junction, which eventually stops your ability to breathe, causing you to suffocate. This won't happen right away—drinking hemlock tea only makes you feel drunk at first. It may take from forty-eight to seventy-two hours for the full toxic effects to manifest. If you find yourself so poisoned, only artificial or mechanical ventilation can save you.

The Gentleman's Choice

According to Christian mythology, the hemlock plant became poisonous after growing on the hillside of Jesus's crucifixion. When his blood touched the plant, it turned forever toxic. However, the most infamous poisoning by hemlock is attributed to the Greek philosopher Socrates, who chose a hemlock drink as his preferred means of death—most sources say that he drank it mixed with water or as a tea. In the *Phaedo,* Plato claims that Socrates first felt a numbing in his limbs, after which the sensation overtook his entire body. Socrates maintained full awareness throughout his poisoning, and even continued to speak to those around him who witnessed his death. His last words reportedly were:

"Crito, we owe a cock to Asclepius. Please, don't forget to pay the debt." Socrates willingly drank the poison after being sentenced to death for his speeches and for his belief in humanistic and democratic principles. When he was ordered to either publicly deny his ideas or die, he chose death. However, because he was a respected gentleman, the court gave him the right to pick the manner in which he wished to have his death sentence carried out. Hemlock tea was his first choice.

HORSERADISH
Armoracia rusticana
The Great White Root

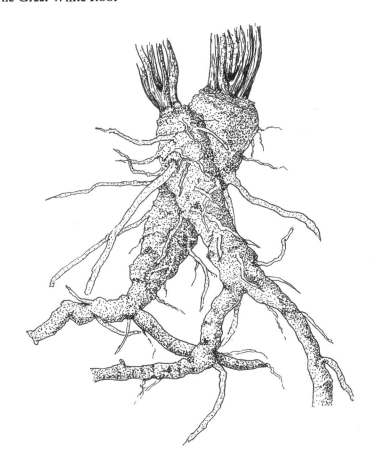

Horseradish has enjoyed hearty cultivation and appreciation throughout the three millennia of its known history. Prized for its gastronomic and medicinal qualities, horseradish is useful as a treatment for rheumatism; as an aphrodisiac (perhaps its most beloved quality); as a flavorful additive for chicken, beef, and seafood; for making the fabulous horseradish sauce; and so on. Also known as *Armoracia rusticana*, horseradish is a perennial plant belonging to the family Brassicaceae, which also includes wasabi, broccoli, mustard, and cabbage. The herb has roots in southeastern Europe and western Asia, and today grows worldwide, cultivated primarily for its tapered white roots, which have a strong aroma. Horseradish grows up to 3½ feet tall, and its leaves are large and intensely green, growing directly from the roots, since the plant lacks a stem.

Horseradish is a perennial, but in colder zones it might live only for a year, since the plant fares poorly in long winters. Without a long growing season, it will go dormant, and it will not resprout on its own. The best time to harvest it is right after the first frost destroys the plant's leaves; at this point, farmers dig up and divide the roots, collecting the main section as their crop and replanting the smaller offshoots the following year. Sometimes horseradish left undisturbed in gardens can spread underground shoots and become invasive.

Horseradish's biomedical properties offer a plethora of health benefits. The volatile oil, known also as mustard oil, has strong antibacterial properties, while 100 grams of fresh horseradish contain about 80 milligrams of vitamin C—a huge dose by natural standards. The horseradish's peroxidate enzyme proves immensely useful in both biochemistry and molecular biology.

Though known mostly by its English moniker, horseradish has various regional names in Central and Eastern Europe, where it originated. In Germany and Austria the plant is known as *kren*, in Ukraine as *khrin*, in Romania as *hrean*, in Slovakia as *chren*, in Bulgaria as *khryan*, in Croatia as *hren*, and in Macedonia as *ren*. The English name dates as far back as 1590, as a combination of the words *horse* (also meaning "large," "strong," and "coarse" in those times) and *radish*, derived from the Latin *radix*, meaning "root." Ironically, despite the name, the horseradish plant is poisonous to horses.

Myths and Facts

Ancient Egyptians were aware of the plant as early as 1500 B.C., and the ancient Greeks used it for low back pain and as an aphrodisiac. Jews still use it during Passover seders as a bitter herb. Its most spectacular, though mythological, appearance is in the legend about the Delphic oracle's words to Apollo: "The radish is worth its weight in lead, the beet its weight in silver, the horseradish its weight in gold." During the Renaissance, horseradish consumption spread from southeastern and central Europe to Scandinavia and England. By the late 1600s, the plant had become a standard accompaniment for oysters and beef in England. It arrived in America in 1806, and commercial cultivation began there in the 1850s, when the first horseradish farms were planted in the Midwest. Today, U.S. farms produce nearly 6 million gallons of prepared horseradish every year.

HOT LIPS PLANT
Psychotria elata
Mother Nature's Psychedelic Kiss

What a name, what a plant! When you see a picture of *Psychotria elata* for the first time, you might think Mick Jagger's lips were Photoshopped onto some plant, while he sang, "I can't get no satisfaction." Though these spectacular red lips are usually called flowers, they are actually leaflike bracts, a part that is at the base of the flower. Some of the plant's other nicknames are even more provocative, such as *hooker's lips* or *hooker's kiss*. Nevertheless, just as a heavy red lipstick might help human beings attract more suitors, so too do these luscious bracts lure pollinators, mostly hummingbirds, bees, and butterflies. For these suitors, the Hot Lips plant produces an abundance of oval berries, first in a passionate purple and then deep black when ripened.

Psychotria elata grows in South America, but only in the tropical regions of Panama, Ecuador, Costa Rica, and Colombia, as well as in Africa and the Pacific area, particularly in rain forests. *Psychotria* is a genus with more than 1,900 species, from the family Rubiaceae. Plants from this genus are small, understory trees, meaning they grow below larger trees, preferring strictly tropical forests.

Don't Be Tempted

Don't hurry to kiss these sensual lips, as many species from this genus produce a kind of psychedelic chemical, named dimethyltryptamine, or DMT. While you might be familiar with the explosion of pleasurable hormones that come from kissing another person, these lips will send you on a trip of a different kind. But not all are dissuaded from taking this risk; shamans and recreationists consume the plant hoping to initiate an out-of-body experience. It is for this reason the plant gets another of its nicknames: *A kiss from the Motherland,* or *A kiss of Mother Nature.*

Even more interesting is the limited duration of these most seductive colors; the Hot Lips plant will show its red petals or lips for only a very short period of time, attracting a flock of hummingbirds and a horde of bees. Within hours, however, the red yields its real flowers of white, which appear between the lips of its leaflike bracts. Among plants, it is one of the pure exotics. Unfortunately, we may soon have to kiss these lips good-bye forever, as deforestation of tropical regions threatens to drive it into extinction.

HYDNORA AFRICANA
Plant of the Living Dead

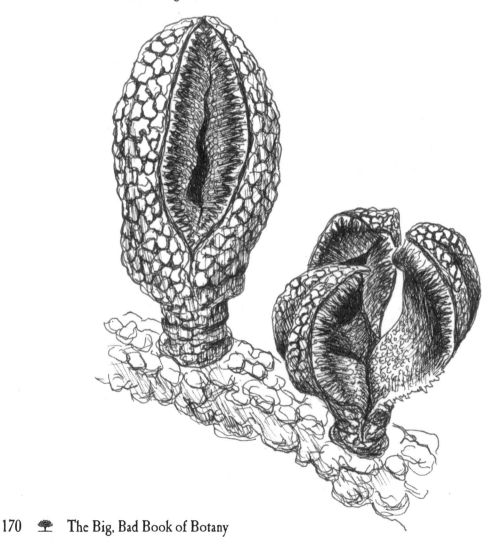

Hydnora africana is a bizarre-looking plant that smells like feces and lives in southern Africa. It is has a fleshy flower, which, some note, resembles female genitalia. It takes one year for its bud to develop into a mature flower and form into this shape. The *africana* species is parasitic and grows entirely underground, apart from its bloom. The plant looks like a fungus in its closed condition; its stem is shaped like a worm, it has numerous seeds and edible fleshy pulp, its pulp is rich in starch, and its fruit appears as a half-rounded berry with thick skin. None of this plant's leaves are visible, which gives it the appearance of something actually growing that looks dead. As the plant ages, it turns from gray to black.

Its fruit is a traditional food of the Khoi people of southwestern Africa and reportedly very delicious, with a sweetish taste. It is extremely astringent and is also used by natives of the regions for tanning hides and preserving fishing nets. In local homeopathic medicine, it is used to treat diarrhea, dysentery, and bladder and kidney complaints. When made into a liquid, its infusion is used as a face wash, which helps in acne treatment.

What's with the Shape?

Hydnora africana's flowers are bright red in color, hollow inside, fleshy, tall, and strong like wood. The flowers are borne on the surface of roots, since it has no stems. Succulent in texture, its underground structure consists of tubular roots with three openings, called perianth segments. It actually resembles an elongated truffle. Not only is it edible by birds and mammals, it is also nontoxic to humans. Its pollen and its flowers are also edible. Its wide-open and inviting shape makes it a welcoming meal for birds and animals. Many foragers seem to relish the plant's berries, and when they defecate they spread the seeds far from the parent plant. Although *Hydnora* is derived from the Greek word for "fungus," it is also known as *jakkalskos* and *bobbejaankos,* since it's a favorite food of jackals and baboons.

The roots are completely white, and so they are very easily differentiated from the plant. Its flower is a kind of intricate trap, which has a cavity with white ovules at the bottom. These ovules will mature into seeds. When the flower opens, it resembles a white, threadlike structure with gaps between the sepals. The openings are large enough for a beetle to enter, though it will then face difficulty in leaving the flower; the shape creates a maze, ensuring the wandering insect will pollinate the bloom. The flower also emits unpleasant, dunglike odors, to which mostly dung beetles are attracted. The flower's perianth segments are bright orange with downwardly pointing hairs. These hairs effectively direct the beetles to go down into the lower portions of flowers, ensuring that they will spend more time there than they intended, thus collecting pollen before they finally escape. Whatever we might think of *Hydnora africana's* evocative shape, anatomy, in nature, is rarely incidental.

HYDRILLA
Hydrilla verticillata
Vitamin Bovine

Hydrilla verticillata, or *hydrilla,* as it is commonly known, is an aquatic plant with a long stem and pointed leaves. The stems grow to an amazing 25 feet, while its leaves are only ½ inch long. It is a fast-growing plant, adding 1 inch to its mass per day. A perennial plant, hydrilla can grow in any body of freshwater. During unfavorable conditions, the plant dies, but the roots, buried below the lake, stream, or pond bottom, remain alive, and once the climatic conditions become suitable, it regenerates, no matter how long it has had to wait. There are two types of hydrilla: one with both male and female flowers, and the other with separate, single-sex varieties. The former type is monoecious, and the latter is dioecious.

The Good with the Bad

A species of Asian hydrilla was introduced as an exotic decorative plant for aquariums in North America in 1960. It soon became a problem when it started growing as a wild plant, covering entire waterways with thick, densely proliferating leaves, making it difficult for humans to swim, and also disturbing recreational boating. The roots of the plants prefer to be anchored at the bottom, but even if uprooted, the plant can survive by letting its roots float on the surface, forming a thick mat. This adaptation, good as it is for hydrilla, can prevent sunlight from reaching underwater, which in turn can hinder or kill other plants. On the flip side, it forms a protective cover for fish, frogs, and insects, and even provides a food source for crabs and turtles.

The Danger of Imports

Managing the spread of hydrilla is not easy, and removing it by hand requires considerable time and expense. Various methods exist, all developed by aquatic plant managers to control it from clogging waters. Unfortunately, bombarding an exotic species of this nature with herbicides can cause side effects not yet fully revealed, and can increase human exposure to carcinogens. Fluridone and endothall are among the few known herbicides that are effective against hydrilla. Fluridone, however, is very costly and acts very slowly. Endothall is a contact herbicide, and while it often shows quicker results, combating hydrilla is still a risky, uphill battle that does more collateral damage to the environment with each passing season.

What Is It Good For?

Apart from treating abscesses and debris in wounds, there are no significant medical uses for *Hydrilla verticillata*. Even still, health stores sell the plant as a supplement, as it contains calcium, vitaminB_{12}, protein, and minerals, and is claimed to be good for the immune system, weight loss, and healthy skin. In its native regions, people have collected it as fodder for animals. Recent studies indicate that cows fed hydrilla gave 20 percent more milk; chickens laid 14 percent more eggs when it was added to their diet. This may be due to the high presence of calcium in the plant. Some researches say that it ranks among plants with the most calcium content; it is measured in hydrilla at 13 percent.

If hydrilla establishes an economic value as cow feed, it could shake its classification as a weed, which could stem the spread of herbicides intended to get rid of it into waterways.

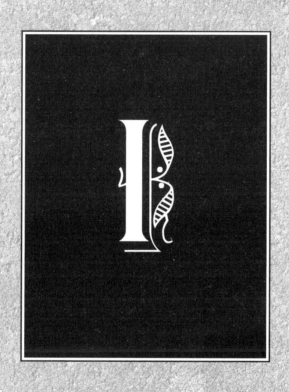

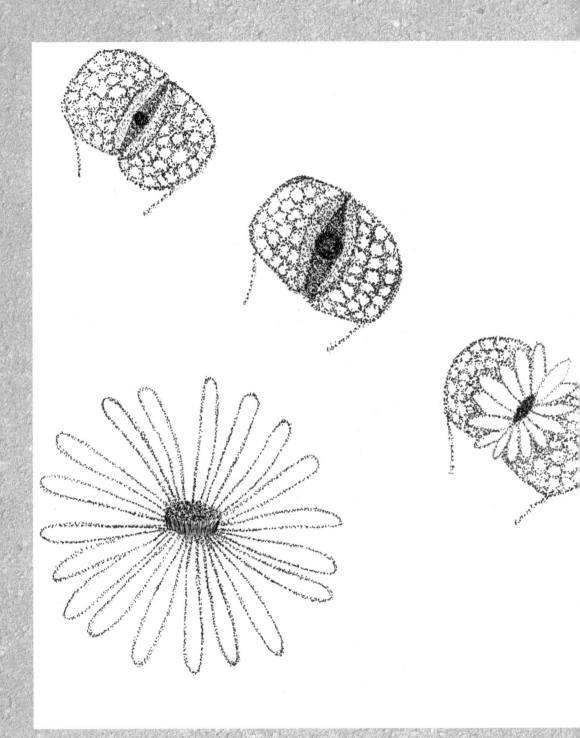

ICE PLANT
Carpobrotus edulis
The "Me First!" Plant

The ice plant belongs to the stone plant family. There are more than 150 species of ice plants, the best known of which is the purple ice plant, also known as the hardy ice plant, or *Delosperma cooperi*. The name *ice plant* comes from the leaves, which have glistering surface hairs that reflect and refract sunrays like tiny ice crystals. It has pale pink, purple, white, yellow, and orange daisy-like flowers, and fleshy leaves. A few ice plant species are bushy shrubs, while others are low-growing spreaders. It is a native of South Africa, where ice plants are evergreen; in other locales, the plants grow as perennials.

Ice plant shoots can grow more than 3 feet in a year, and each shrub or bush can spread wide, covering a tremendously large area of 165 feet in diameter, or more. The plant produces fruits that look like either a type of raspberry or a fig, depending on the species. But all ice plant fruits consist of hundreds of tiny seeds, which make the plant's chances of propagation great. The fruits are edible and are made into jams and tarts in South Africa. The gelatinous juice of the leaves is used in medicines. Ice plants have green leaves that are triangular in shape and change into flowers in the blooming season. Despite the "ice" in their name, these plants don't like cold weather, which causes root rot and death. They can, however, thrive in poor soil conditions and don't need very much water. New plants can arise either from a planted seed or cuttings from a mature specimen. Using a cutting is the fastest way to grow ice plants, particularly for people who wish to plant them for their flowers, which bloom year-round. Ice plants are drought- and insect-resistant, and a choice for landscaping that requires little maintenance—they can provide fast-growing green ground cover even in dry, hot areas, and can also help control erosion.

IVY

Hedera
From Decorative to Poison

Ivy plants are evergreen creeping or climbing plants of the family Araliaceae and especially the genus *Hedera*. Native to central, western, and southern Europe, ivy comprises around 15 species, with more than 100 subvarieties: the most common are wall ivy, ground ivy, grape ivy, Boston ivy, and English ivy. These plants have been held in high esteem since

Some Popular Varieties

Boston ivy: Boston ivy is a perennial vine covered with small green flowers and dark green leaves. It can grow to a height of 2 feet.

English ivy: English ivy climbs walls and covers the sides of buildings, and is also known as true ivy. The leaves are gray and yellow and are ruffed or pointed.

Devil's ivy: Also known as the money plant, it can grow up to 65 feet in length, and the leaves are yellow and green, shaped like hearts.

Poison ivy: A woody vine whose leaves produce urushiol oil, which can cause severe rashes, blistering, or inflammation of the skin.

Swedish ivy: The one ivy that does not cling to walls. Actually native to Australia, this variety is very popular in Sweden as a houseplant.

Roman times. They were considered symbols of love and fidelity because of their habit of clinging to whatever surfaces surround them.

Most ivy plants bear flowers and nectar fruits that are eaten by insects and a few birds. Some species of ivy can keep on growing upward to heights of 90 feet from the root. As evergreen plants, they need less maintenance in terms of water and sunlight. Ivy can also be planted indoors in pots for ornamental purposes. The creeping varieties are even useful in the prevention of soil erosion. Many find ivy adds texture and color to a property and a quality of old-time elegance to houses up which it crawls; thicker varieties have even been used to create sound barriers between adjacent buildings.

In Indian mythology, ivy plants are treated as a symbol of wealth and prosperity, while in Roman culture they symbolized love and fidelity.

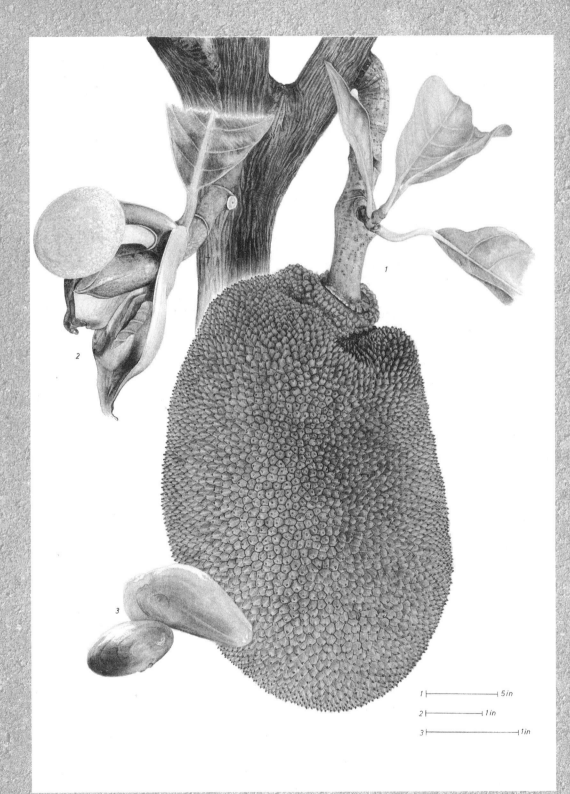

JACKFRUIT
Artocarpus heterophyllus
A Wealth of Fruit

If you've never eaten jackfruit, then simply imagine biting into a large, 30- to 100-pound oblong or egg-shaped greenish yellow seedpod with a whole fruit stand of combined tastes. Although its flavor is unique, some report tasting a blend of apple, banana, pineapple, and mango all in one. It has an earthy smell that may put some off, but to most people the fruit is a tasty delicacy. Considering the fruit's wide spectrum of vitamins and other nutrients, the jackfruit is certainly one of nature's most splendid gifts.

Artocarpus heterophyllus belongs to the family Moraceae and is also known as *jack (jak)* or *jaca,* derived from the Malayan term *chakka.* In the Philippines it is called *nangka;* in Cambodia, *khnor;* in Thailand, *khanun;* and in Vietnam, *mit.* Jackfruit is considered native to Southeast Asia and is widely cultivated in India, Nepal, Bangladesh, Vietnam, Sri Lanka, Malaysia, Thailand, the Philippines, and Indonesia, as well as in Africa, Mauritius, Brazil, and Jamaica.

Jackfruit is a handsome tree, growing 18 to 66 feet tall, with evergreen, glossy, 8-inch-long leaves. The leaves, stems, branches, and trunk all contain a white, sticky latex sap. Its flowering blooms come from large branches, or directly from the trunk, or sometimes even around the base of the tree. It is a monoecious species, growing tiny male flowers in clusters 5 inches wide and rounded, as well as ellipsoid, female flowers on the same tree. Fruits come in different sizes and weights, and some huge ones grow to over 36 inches long and are 2 feet wide. Inside the fruits, there are large bulbs (perianths) with yellow, banana-like flesh, and a pithy core. Each bulb has an oval, brownish seed (called an endocarp) measuring only ½ inch long, but they are numerous, with as many as 100 to 500 seeds inside a single fruit.

However, not all are big supporters of this tree. In Tijuca National Park in Brazil, the jackfruit is considered an invasive species: from 2002 to 2007, the park's manager organized a cutting of more than 55,000 trees. Its aggressive nature notwithstanding, many have found uses for these trees beyond their coveted fruits: the jackfruit's wood is a good material for many musical instruments.

Health Benefits

Jackfruit is noted for its extraordinary wealth of vitamins and health benefits: it

- protects the body against viruses.
- regulates blood sugar.
- protects the thyroid gland.
- protects bones.
- stabilizes blood pressure.
- supports regular bowels.
- acts against night blindness.
- supports blood clotting.
- prevents anemia and blood disorders, and strengthens blood cells.

JASMINE
Jasminum
Lady Flower

Jasmine is one of the most popular flowers worldwide, prized especially for its soothing fragrance. Since ancient times, the plant has represented pure beauty, in both music and poetry. *Jasminum* is a genus of vines and shrubs within Oleaceae, a family of about 200 species originating from tropical regions of Africa and Asia. Europe has only 1 native species of jasmine. People cultivate jasmine all over the world as an ornamental flower, but as an agricultural crop it produces high-quality essential oils and syrup for flavoring and for teas, and it is an ingredient in perfumes. Jasmine blooms with an air of mystery, as its flowers open only during the night—due, of course, to temperature oscillations—but the act only adds to its romantic mystique.

There is a great tradition in South and Southeast Asia of women wearing a flower of jasmine in their hair for symbolic reasons. In southern India, married women don the flower as a sort of wedding ring. Nowadays single women in the region may also wear it, though there remains a strong tradition against widows adorning themselves with the plant.

Depending on the climate and species, jasmine can be either evergreen or deciduous; the latter variety loses its leaves in autumn. It grows as a shrub and has leaves of different sizes. On some types the leaves are either pinnate or trifoliate. Jasmine's famous flowers are usually white and yellow, though in some cases they can be lightly reddish, and grow to about an inch in diameter. They bloom in clusters containing at least three flowers, but single flowers can also occur on the branches' ends. Its calyx—the cuplike part of the flower—is bell shaped and produces a very gentle and fragrant aroma. After the flowering ends, the plant gives berries, which turn black when ripe.

A Stalwart Specimen

Jasmine is very suitable for gardens. All species of the plant prefer fertile, well-drained soil with full or partial sun exposure. Summer species need sheltered spots, full sun, and southern or southwestern exposure, while winter ones are more tolerant of partial shade and prefer southeast to northwest exposure. Most tender species require a minimum night temperature no lower than 55 degrees Fahrenheit. Though the plant can procreate with its seeds, gardeners would do best to use hardwood winter cuttings for growing outdoor varieties of jasmine, and internodal softwood, or semiripe cuttings taken during the spring and summer, for those more delicate specimens that need greenhouse environments to survive. In fact, many of the more heavily cultivated varieties are bred purposefully not to produce seeds.

Jasmine Culture

Indian culture prizes jasmine for use in rituals, religious ceremonies, marriages, and more. Other countries use jasmine as a national symbol: In Pakistan, *Jasminum officinale,* known as *chambeli,* is the official national flower; in Indonesia, *Jasminum sambac* was adopted as the national symbol in 1990 and is the primary flower for weddings, especially on Java. Jasmine is also beloved in the Philippines, which adopted it as the country's national flower in 1935. Hawaiian culture has dedicated countless songs to the flower, Thailand considers it a symbol of motherhood, and in Syria jasmine is the symbol of Damascus, also known as "City of Jasmine." Jasmine is even now a common name for girls. In many Indonesian and Asian countries it is beautiful to see the white-reddish flower worn by a woman with black hair, traditionally above the left ear.

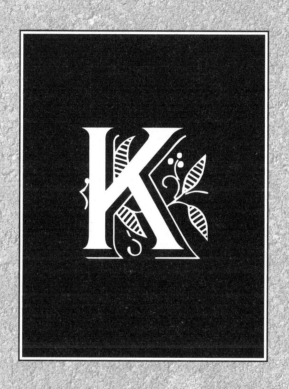

KHAT

Catha edulis

Chewing Euphoria

A "chewing" plant popular among recreational drug users, khat contains a psychoactive alkaloid that causes effects similar to those of amphetamine (a stimulant), including euphoria, increased excitement, alertness, friendliness, confidence, ability to concentrate, intense flow of ideas, and so on. Some sources claim that the experiences one encounters after ingesting khat, which can vary wildly, depend on the social environment in which it's used. Much like coca, the plant has a long tradition of use, dating back to the fourteenth century. It seems to have originated in or around Ethiopia, but explorers or traders transported it to the Arabian Peninsula, and beyond, where its use has spread rapidly. Khat leaves contain the stimulant, which is best extracted by chewing. Overuse can be addictive, similarly to nicotine and alcohol, which explains why khat is now illegal in many countries.

Catha edulis is a slow-growing plant, reaching 3 to 15 feet in height, usually preferring arid conditions with temperatures of 40 to 95 degrees Fahrenheit; in equatorial areas some khat trees can grow up to 30 feet tall. Its leaves are evergreen, 2 to 4 inches long, and nearly as broad. It bears small flowers with five white petals that grow on short auxiliary cymes, or branches, which rise above the flower and are 4 inches long. The fruit of khat is an oblong three-valve capsule with one to three seeds inside. The plant reaches its full height after seven to eight years. Except for water and sun, it requires practically no maintenance. A month before the harvest, growers water the plant heavily to moisten and soften the stems and leaves, making the leaves all the more suitable for chewing. A healthy, mature khat plant will produce harvestable leaves four times per year.

Khat is known by many other names, depending on the region. Here are the most common: *African salad, Abyssinian tea, African tea, bushman's tea, chafta, iubulu, kafta, mandoma, marongi,* and in the West, *Arabian tea.*

When chewing khat leaves, one experiences an immediate increase in heart rate and blood pressure. Within thirty minutes, euphoria as well as hyperactivity will set in, after which appetite will decrease radically.

Long-term and continued use is dangerous and can cause serious depression and sporadic hallucinations. Risk of myocardial infarction, or heart attack, increases with use, though that can afflict even first-time users. In a number of cases, usage has induced permanent psychosis. Khat can cause oral cancer, liver damage, acute coronary syndrome stroke, and, of course, death.

Firsthand Encounter

The initial experience of chewing khat is often one of euphoria. The reporter John Vidal described his experience with khat with friends during his travels through Ethiopia, which appeared in the British newspaper the *Guardian* on February 5, 2004. Here's an interesting excerpt: "After ten minutes there was a slight numbing of the gums. After fifteen minutes, [my friend] started jabbering loudly. At twenty-five minutes, we were laughing uproariously. After forty-five minutes, Ethiopia's trouble had slipped away, and a sense of well-being, alertness, euphoria, and lucidity took over."

KIWI
Actinidia deliciosa
The Good Girl from China

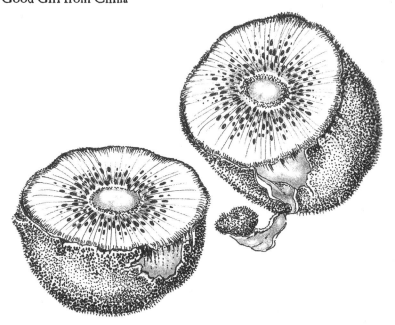

The kiwi, or kiwifruit, has an interesting history. Even today, it has only recently gained global popularity. The fruit has a bittersweet flavor and looks a bit odd—greenish yellow in color, a hairy, overgrown Ping-Pong ball shape—all of which belies its significant nutritional value. Kiwi is native to China, where it is known as *yang tao* and was declared a national fruit. In 1960 the Chinese officially changed its name to "Chinese gooseberry." Today, kiwi is cultivated worldwide; Italy, France, New Zealand, Chile, Japan, and the United States are leading commercial producers.

Botanically, kiwi is a berry of a wood vine belonging to the genus *Actinidia*. The most famous cultivar group is Hayward, with oval, egg-size fruits 3 inches long and 4 inches in diameter. The kiwi's skin is fibrous, and its greenish brown, bright green, or golden flesh contains rows of tiny, black, edible seeds. The fruit's body is soft and has a unique sweet flavor.

The kiwi grows best in temperate climates that have full summers of a few months or more. Commercial cultivation requires the aid of sturdy support structures, since the plant's weak vines can't support all of the fruit; kiwi farms can give several tons per hectare. Commercial crops usually employ a watering system for irrigation and frost protection during the spring. The vines of the kiwi require vigorous pruning, similar to grapevines; its first fruits are borne one year after planting, though yield decreases as the vines get older. They are usually replaced with new ones after the third year.

Kiwi has male and female flowers on the same plant, allowing for dioecious pollination. Male flowers pollinate the females via wind or by brushing together as the vines entwine. In many cases, one male vine will grow next to three to eight female vines coming from the same root. Some cultivars are able to self-pollinate, but plants directly pollinated by male flowers always give a greater yield, and of higher quality. This is no easy feat, though; kiwi flowers are not so attractive to bees and other insects. Some producers resort to mechanically blowing collected pollen onto the female flowers.

Kiwi is a great source of vitamins C, K, and E, as well as dietary fiber. A medium-size kiwi fruit provides about 46 calories. Since the fruit and skin also contain actinidain and flavonoids, however, some people have allergic reactions that result in mouth and throat irritation. New studies suggest that people allergic to bananas, pineapples, papayas, and latex are probably allergic to kiwi as well. Nevertheless, the health benefits of kiwi are worth exploring. Kiwi phytonutrients give us great antioxidant protection, control blood sugar, strengthen the cardiovascular system's well-being, and protect against asthma and macular degeneration. With kiwi's increasing renown and popularity, different varieties have become more available, including the so-called *hardy kiwi* and the *silvervine kiwi,* both of which have smooth skin and a size similar to a cherry.

KUDZU
Pueraria lobata
A Plant of All Trades

There is an old saying: nature has an answer for every problem and a remedy for every disease. Whatever you believe, kudzu—vilified as a weed in the southeastern United States—has some amazing properties. For example, although most experts claim there is no real cure for alcoholism, *Pueraria lobata* taken as an herbal remedy has a great record in helping people reduce their drinking. And that's not all: kudzu is used in East Asia in treatments for many other health problems, such as deafness, diabetes, diabetic retinopathy, menopausal syndromes, gastroenteritis, and cardiovascular diseases, particularly angina.

Kudzu also goes by the name *Japanese arrowroot;* some botanists believe its origins lie in Japan, where it is called *kuzu.* The plant belongs to the pea family of Fabaceae, in a subfamily called Faboideae. It is a climbing, trailing, and coiling vinelike edible plant, considered a noxious weed where it exists as an invasive species. Kudzu can climb trees and usually kills them by covering the tree's leaves with its own. Sometimes kudzu causes serious ecological consequences, especially in the southern United States. Since it grows so rapidly, it "wins," or destroys nearby plants,

According to a study by Harvard Medical School researcher David M. Penetar conducted in 2012, kudzu's extract, called puerarin, did show some positive results for alcoholics. Penetar concluded: "People still drank, but they drank less."

by what's called *interference competition.* By climbing over native flora, it can effectively "steal" their light supply, thus preventing their ability to thrive—even killing them. Still, some use the plant for erosion control and for enhancing soil, since it can increase nitrogen content and transport minerals to the topsoil from deep below.

Kudzu is also useful as animal food; in the United States, many goat farmers use a kudzu-based feed (containing about 18 percent crude protein and 60 percent digestible nutrient value). The plant also makes a good material for basketry and fiber arts; it has long runners and large vine material that is great for weaving. Kudzu fiber, originally called *ko-hemp,* was once important to the production of paper and clothing. The plant is also useful for making cellulosic ethanol, and in the United States kudzu is an ingredient in lotions, soaps, and compost.

Kudzu Food

The plant's roots contain a wealth of starch, a traditional food ingredient in East Asia. People from Vietnam usually flavor this starch with pomelo oil and use it as a refreshing drink. In Japan, the starch is called *kuzoko* and is traditionally used for dishes such as *mizu, kuzumochi,* and *kuzuyu.* Some have even made jellies from kudzu flowers. In East Asia, the plant has been used for making tinctures and tisanes for centuries. Practically the whole plant, including flowers, leaves, and roots, contains strong antioxidant elements.

LAVENDER
Lavandula
The First Deodorant

A splash of color and beauty, an intangible sweet aroma, an aura of calm and balance—these are the inherent qualities of one of nature's most exquisite handiworks, the lavender plant. Lavender holds a special place for many, even for non–plant lovers, due to its pleasant, calming fragrance. From gardens to kitchens, healing to craftmaking, lavender is extremely versatile, and ranked among the top 40 ornamental and medicinal flowering plant species. The genus belongs to a family of aromatic mint herbs, Lamiaceae, well-known for flavor, fragrance, and medicinal use, and therefore holds great economic value. The familiar name *lavender* comes from the Old French word *lavandre* and Latin *lavare* ("to wash"), from its use as a soap and additive to baths since early antiquity. It was likely the first deodorant—some Stone Age "cavemen" might occasionally have smelled okay!

The history of lavender stretches across thousands of years of human history. Egyptians, Phoenicians, and Arabs used the plant as a perfume and in mummification (by enfolding the dead bodies in a lavender-dipped covering). Early Greek societies regarded lavender as a holy herb, naming it *nardus* or *nard* in reference to a Syrian city, Naarda, where it grew abundantly. The Greeks used the plant in temples to prepare the holy essence *nard,* as well as to cure diseases varying from insomnia and backache to mental illness. During the Roman era,

---

What's in a Name?

Lavender's scientific name, *Lavandula*, was coined by the famous botanist Carl Linnaeus. *English lavender* or *Old English lavender* (*L. angustifolia*), *French lavender* (*L. stoechas* or *L. dentata*), and *Spanish lavender* (*L. stoechas, L. lanata,* or *L. dentata*) are some of the widely used names for different lavender species. *Lavandula angustifolia* is one of the most widely cultivated varieties and most commonly referred to as simply lavender.

the popularity of lavender was at its peak and it became an esteemed commodity. Soon it became associated with soaps, baths, perfumes, insect repellent, sachets, and potpourris, and was used as a flavoring agent. Today it is most commonly known for its beauty and floral fragrance and has multiple uses, such as in aromatherapy, the perfume industry, food dishes, traditional medicine, and as an ornamental plant. Lavender is quite the sustainable crop, since it has the ability to grow under poor irrigation conditions and without the need of pesticide and fertilizers—what smells sweet to us, leaf-munching bugs don't like!

Lavender is native to the Old World and originates mainly from the Canary Islands, northern and eastern Africa, the Middle East, the Mediterranean, Southwest Asia, and southeast India. The plant is an extremely drought-tolerant shrub and grows well in dry, sandy, well-drained soils; it favors full sunlight. Although many members of the genus are cultivated extensively in temperate climates, it does bloom in other areas as well. In ideal conditions, lavender needs good drainage, since waterlogged soils and climates with high humidity make it susceptible to root rot or fungus contamination.

The genus mainly comprises small, herbaceous, short-lived perennials with shallow roots. The perennials are slightly woody or shrubby at the base and belong to the category of small, woody shrubs. The plants are generally 1 to 3 feet tall and adorned with gray-green feathery leaves. The shape and size of the leaf differ greatly across the genus. In some species leaves are simple, while in others they are pinnately toothed or have multiple pinnates that are dissected. Lavender leaves are generally rooted with a silvery gray covering of fine hairs or trichomes, botanically known as indumenta (a major source of essential oils). The flowers are borne in five to ten whorls (rings), which together form long, slender floral spikes, rising above the foliage. The spikes are usually unbranched and indeterminate, though in some species they are branched. The flowers in the wild species are highly scented, and blue, violet, or lilac in color. Different lavender species boast even more flower colors: white, pink, purple, blue, violet, yellow-green, and red.

The flowers depend on insects, especially bees and butterflies, for pollination.

Lavender has a long history in traditional and modern herbalism. The plant is grown commercially for large-scale production of its sweet essential oil, obtained through distillation from the flower spikes and comprising a complex mixture of phytochemicals, including terpenes (camphor), linalool, and linalyl acetate. Lavender oil serves as a base ingredient in many cosmetic items, such as perfumes, cleaning supplies, soaps, shaving creams, bath salts, lotions, and lip balms. The soothing and relaxing qualities of lavender oil are highly effective, primarily against headaches—it has proved very popular in aromatherapy to help reduce anxiety and stress. In addition, many use it as an antiseptic, anti-inflammatory, or pain reliever, as well as an ointment on insect bites and stings. Lavender is also effective for treating acne, sunburn, sunstroke, burns, and coughs and respiratory infections (asthmatic and bronchitic spasms).

Herbalists prescribe lavender to treat head lice, hyperactivity, microbial activity on gums, airborne molds, and insomnia. Recent laboratory studies suggest lavender extract may have promise in fighting cancer; certain components in the oil have been shown to reduce the size of breast cancer in mice. The buds, flower spikes, and flowering tips of lavender are widely popular as condiments in salads and flavoring agents for baked goods and desserts—it's even used to flavor sugar, creating what's commonly known as lavender sugar. Lavender is a favorite for potpourris, and many now use it in lieu of rice (which can kill birds after expanding in the stomachs of those that eat it) as an ideal wedding confetti.

LEAF OF GOD
Tabernanthe iboga
Passport to the Past

Leaf of God, bitter grass, tree of knowledge: these are some of the common names of the sacred iboga tree of West Central Africa. The plant has a long history as part of traditional rituals and religious practices in the Bwiti religion and other secret religious societies in the Gabon province of Central Africa—particularly among the Mitsogo, Babongo, and Fang peoples. For hundreds of years, *iboga* has served as a keystone in the development and expansion of religious systems, and is used in a variety of festivals and rites.

The key to its religious popularity is the alkaloid contained in the root of the plant, which allowed ancient people to access religious "psychedelic" experiences. Historically, many early religions throughout the world used vegetable hallucinogens for healing, magic, religious ceremonies, and spiritual teaching. A drink made from this plant can seriously alter one's perception of the world, and affects cognition and motor skills.

Invisible Suit

The Leaf of God has served as an important spiritual pillar for the establishment and expansion of numerous religious systems. Ancient peoples believed the plant could offer a glimpse of who you really are or help you gain an understanding of your true, unique individuality. Africans even once believed consumption of the plant could make one invisible to Western civilization, particularly slave traders.

Among traditional African religions, *iboga* helped transport one to the "land of the dead," where one's ancestors discussed the truth about the person's past lives and the future evils he or she could expect to encounter. Frequently, ingestion was an important initiation rite into these religions; boys of around thirteen took massive doses, often for extended periods. The community at large would often ingest the plant on special religious holidays, though in smaller amounts. Similar doses also proved useful as a stimulant to aid in hunting, maintain alertness, and to heal sick people or drive out evil spirits.

Tabernanthe iboga is noted for its psychedelic or hallucinogenic properties. The *iboga* belongs to the family Apocynaceae (dogbane) and is indigenous to Gabon, the Republic of Congo, and the Democratic Republic of the Congo (former Zaire) in west-central Africa. The plant grows well in humid tropical forest understories, in well-drained soil, and loves moderately shady conditions.

The Leaf of God is actually an evergreen herbaceous perennial shrub and usually attains a height of 5 to 7 feet. However, under certain ideal conditions it may reach the height of a small tree, 30 feet or more. The stem is long, erect, and extends branches out in pairs. Its leaves are narrow and dark green. The white-pink tubular flower cluster grows on long, slender, pedunculated inflorescences just above the point of branching. The shape of *iboga*'s fruit varies from elongated ovals to spheres and the fruit is yellowish orange in color. The yellowish root of the plant is the most concentrated source of the plant's hallucinogenic chemicals, which might make it more appropriate to call *iboga* the "Root of God" instead.

LEPIDODENDRON
The Gasoline Plant

The geological history of earth is replete with once-dominant species that have gone extinct, leaving behind nothing but fossilized clues of their existence. The Carboniferous period (359 to 299 million years ago) is one such epoch, characterized by both tropical and warm temperate climates. These climate conditions were ideal for life, and thus the period was a showcase for many of the earliest and greatest biological events, including the establishment of terrestrial life. Amphibians and reptiles appeared, and vast swaths of swamp forests took shape. Through a process called permineralization these swamp forests eventually formed into coal beds, and they are the source of our gasoline today. The name of the epoch, Carboniferous, actually means "carbon-bearing." Morphologically, carboniferous plants resembled many present-day tropical floras. It was also at this point in history that small shrubs made the leap to large, tree-size plants, and the plant world began to develop the complex vascular system we see today.

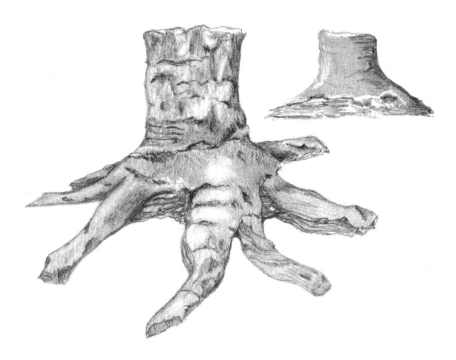

Lepidodendron was among these first vascular plants of the Carboniferous period, and is distinguished as one of the first giant land plants. Today's *lepidodendron* is called a *giant club moss* or *scale tree,* but it was once part of a now-extinct genus of ancient arborescent (treelike) plants. These plants grew as dense forests in wetlands and contributed significantly to the formation of the tropical coal forest flora of the Carboniferous period. The next time you fill your car up with gas, know that it probably contains the remnants of *lepidodendron* trees, which once harvested the energy of an ancient sun.

Lepidodendron and other plants in its genus are evolutionarily linked to the moss, or lycopsids, of today. These early treelike plants were large, exceeding a height of 100 feet and with diameters as wide as 3 to 5 feet. These fantastic plants were preserved as specimen fossils in coal ball deposits of carboniferous shales, and left impressions of their leaf pattern, which resembles alligator skin or tire treads.

The name *Lepidodendron* originates from the Greek words *lepido,* meaning "scale," and *dendron,* "tree." The plants had soaring, long, thick trunks and did not branch until fully grown. At maturity, each plant was topped with a coronet of bifurcating branches and tinted with cushions of long, thin, spirally arranged leaves. The leaves were shed from older parts of the stem, which left densely packed, diamond-shaped leaf scars, principally composed of green photosynthetic tissues and marked with minute apertures or pores known as stomata. The trunk, or stem, was green with thick bark. The roots of *Lepidodendron* were not really true roots, and scientists instead identify them as *stigmaria.* Stigmaria bear round, nodelike structures on the surface, themselves the remnants of ribbonlike rootlets arranged radially from the stigmaria—much like the spikes of a bottlebrush. *Lepidodendron* replicated through sophisticated, encapsulated spores, called megaspores and microspores. Upon germination, each megaspore developed into the female gametophyte—the egg-producing part of the plant. The microspores, for their part, contained the sperm-producing male gametophytes.

Lepidodendron generally lived for twelve to fifteen years and were monocarpic, meaning they reproduced only once before dying. The plant's fruit, or cone, is called a *strobilus,* or *lepidostrobus*—essentially an enfolded megasporangium (a structure that bears one or more megaspores) similar to that of seed plants. However, the existence of a true fruit cone is still a topic of scientific debate, as a fossil has never been found demonstrating its existence. Whatever their fruiting might have looked like, by the Mesozoic era drastic changes in climate conditions had taken place, and these giant plants became extinct.

LICORICE
Glycyrrhiza glabra
Sweet Root

Over the millennia of our existence, human beings have depended on plants for the protection and restoration of health. The biological importance of their capabilities, made possible by their chemical (or phytochemical) makeup, cannot be overstated—put simply, we would not exist without them. Even with advances in scientific research, we are not always able to completely behold all that plants have to offer. Nevertheless, plants lie at the foundation of human medicine. In the past few decades, we have witnessed a trend to duplicate the biologically active molecules found in plants and transform them into pharmaceuticals. Particular attention has been paid to one such plant, *Glycyrrhiza glabra,* for its potential in the fight against eczema, dyspepsia (indigestion, gastroesophageal reflux disease), upper respiratory infections (cold, cough), chronic hepatitis, peptic ulcer disease, and liver cancer, specifically hepatocellular carcinoma.

Glycyrrhiza glabra has an exceptionally sugary flavor, leading to its more popular nickname: *licorice* (which means "sweet root" in Greek). The plant is indigenous to the Mediterranean and certain parts of Asia, including Greece, Turkey, Spain, Caucasian and trans-Caspian Russia, Italy, Iraq, and northern China. It grows best in well-drained soils. The plant has an admirable history in human medicine, stretching over thousands of years. Both Eastern and Western civilizations have made extensive use of licorice roots in treating a variety of illnesses, varying from the common cold (as an expectorant and carminative) to liver disease, and as a flavoring agent in candies and tobacco. The plant was introduced to England by Dominican friars around the fifteenth century. History records cultivation of the plant beginning in England in 1562. In all probability, it was English settlers who introduced the plant to the New World, after which its popularity and usage flourished even more.

The licorice plant belongs to the legume family (peas, beans) of flowering plants. The plant is a subtropical herbaceous perennial and usually grows in rich soil to a height of 4 to 5 feet. Its woody stalks are 3 to 6 inches long, with featherlike leaves and leaflets that grow from both sides of a common axis (pinnate leaves). The leaflets are generally eight to sixteen in number, and somewhere between oval and lanceolate in shape. The licorice plant has an extensive branching root system, which principally comprises a main taproot, root branches, and numerous long-runners, or thinner roots that spread out. The long, cylindrical taproots are soft and fibrous and are the part that most frequently finds medicinal use among humans. The main taproot grows horizontally, brown on the exterior and yellowish on the interior. The flowers are small, and purple, blue-violet, or white-pink; they grow in loose clusters from the leaf axils. Licorice seeds come in long, oblong protective cases known as seedpods; due to the low germination rate of the seeds, vegetative methods of propagation (by means of harvested roots) allow for the spread of the plant without sexual reproduction.

William Thomas Fernie, an occultist/scientist, wrote Herbal Simples Approved for Modern Uses of Cure *(1897), which boosted this plant's forgotten benefits. He presented a detailed description of the active constituents of the licorice root, identifying glycyrrhizine (a demulcent starch), simple sugars, amino acids, and mineral salts, and finally explained why the plant was so beneficial.*

The flavor and delightful aroma of licorice come from its water-soluble, biologically active mixture of different substances such as anethole, flavonoids, pectins, triterpene, saponin, amino acids, mineral salts, polysaccharides, and simple sugars. Licorice root is 30 to 50 times sweeter than sugar and more than 150 times more so than sucrose. The plant owes its extreme sweetness to a mixture of potassium, calcium, and magnesium salts of glycyrrhizic acid, also known as glycyrrhizin, a triterpenoid compound. Accordingly, practitioners of traditional medicine prescribed licorice to treat diseases caused by high sugar levels and to keep a patient's blood sugar down. The interior yellowish color of the licorice root is mainly due to the presence of flavonoid liquiritin, isoliquiritin, and other substances. Among the natural isoflavones, glabridin and hispaglabridin and vitamins A and B are present in licorice and have noteworthy antioxidant activity. The isoflavones glabridin and glabrene possess estrogen-like properties and thus act like xenoestrogens—naturally occurring compounds that imitate estrogen.

Licorice root is one of the oldest and most frequently employed botanicals in all pharmacopoeias, nearly always mentioned in Egyptian, Greek, Roman, Hindu, Assyrian, Babylonian, Chinese, and even Sumerian texts. Many early peoples discovered the plant's abilities as a demulcent (soothes and coats irritated membranes) and as an expectorant (lessens phlegm and congestion). In modern medicine, licorice extracts are a popular flavoring agent to mask bitter tastes and are added to syrup preparations. In addition, licorice has therapeutic benefits against numerous viruses, such as hepatitis A and C, human immunodeficiency virus, cytomegalovirus, and herpes simplex. This antiviral property of licorice is mainly attributed to glycyrrhizin and glycyrrhizic acid. After oral consumption of licorice root, intestinal bacteria hydrolyze glycyrrhizic acid (the main ingredient of licorice) into glycyrrhetic acid—one thousand times more potent an inhibitor of 11-beta-hydroxysteroid dehydrogenase than glycyrrhizic acid. Both of these components retard hepatic metabolism of aldosterone and suppress 5-beta-reductase activity; in moderate doses they can help the liver tremendously.

Hardly a One-Hit Wonder

In addition to this slew of health benefits, more recent research has revealed that licorice's glycyrrhizic acid also inhibits various other aspects of organ inflammations. Yet another well-documented effect of licorice extract is from its antioxidant properties, which, studies suggest, can lower serum liver enzyme concentrations and improve hepatic tissues significantly. In addition, deglycyrrhizinated licorice (licorice without glycyrrhizin) inhibits the growth of *Helicobacter pylori,* and doctors prescribe it for healing stomach ailments and ulcers. Some studies have shown licorice to be effective against autoimmune conditions such as lupus, scleroderma, and rheumatoid arthritis, and others have indicated that it possesses anticancer and anti-allergic properties. Since licorice supplementation has some side effects, including elevated blood pressure, hypokalemia (potassium loss), and edema, people should use caution to avoid overconsumption or misuse. Licorice components also exhibit significant anti-inflammatory effects, partly due to inhibition of phospholipase A2 enzyme, an enzyme central to various inflammatory processes.

Licorice ropes (and that black cube variety) have been around for some time. Many believe the first licorice candies were produced in Holland during the 1770s.

LIE DETECTOR BEAN
Physostigma venenosum
Calabar Justice

Prehistoric judicial systems would often determine guilt or innocence by subjecting the accused to a dangerous experience traditionally known as "trial by ordeal." Whether one survived such an ordeal was left to divine control, and escape or survival was taken to indicate innocence. The roots of this custom lie in the Code of Hammurabi and the Code of Ur-Nammu, the oldest known systems of law. Numerous West African tribes depended on the *calabar bean,* also known as *ordeal bean* or *lie detector bean,* for rulings in their early courts. These tribes used the power of the beans (really highly poisonous seeds) to detect witches and people possessed by evil spirits. Courts would feed numerous seeds, what they called "ordeal poison," to the accused; if he or she was innocent, God would perform a miracle and allow the accused to live—and the court would have its ruling. If the reverse was true, of course, guilt would be "proven" the moment its sentence was successfully carried out.

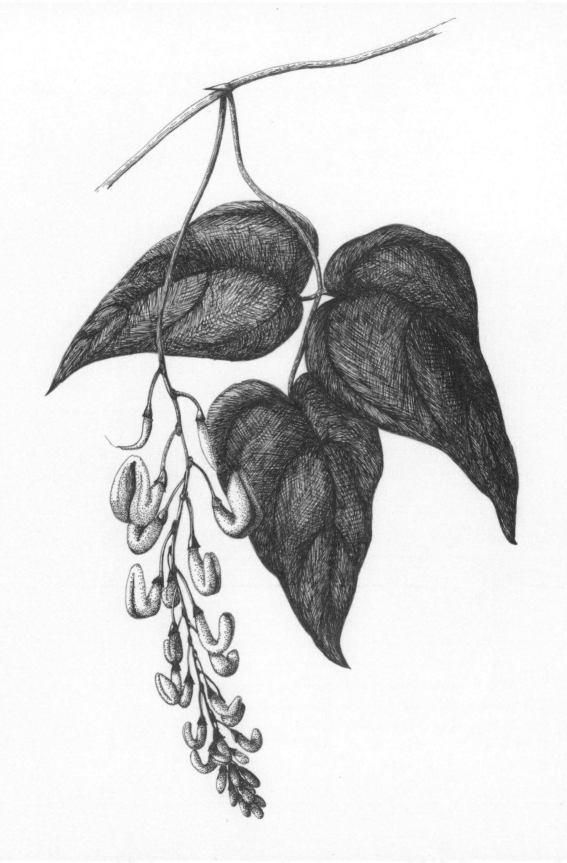

Calabar bean is the seed of a climbing leguminous plant scientifically known as *Physostigma venenosum* and is poisonous to humans when chewed. However, if one swallowed the whole bean intact, it might prevent the release of its toxins. The plant is indigenous to the coastal area of southeastern Nigeria known as Calabar and was first noticed in 1846, though it took until 1861 for botanists to describe it. Its scientific name, *Physostigma venenosum,* came from the appearance of "a snooping beak-like solid appendage at the end of the stigma."

The plant is a large, herbaceous perennial vine, with a woody stem at the base. It produces a large, purplish flower with intricate visible veins. Once pollinated, the flowers yield a thick brown pod of a fruit, which contains two or three large kidney-shaped seeds. The seeds ripen throughout the year; however, it's not until the rainy season (June through September) that the plant is able to produce its best, most toxic beans.

How It Kills

The alkaloid content in a calabar bean is only slightly above 1 percent, and the most potent of the alkaloids are calabarine (with atropine-like effects) and physostigmine, of which the latter is mainly responsible for the bean's poisonous properties, which act on the nervous system. This compound disrupts communication between the nerves and organs. In this regard, it acts similarly to nerve gas, which results in contraction of the pupils, profuse salivation, convulsions, seizures, spontaneous urination and defecation, loss of control over the respiratory system, and ultimately death by asphyxiation.

Some Benefits

Since physostigmine affects neurotransmitters in the brain, scientists have begun conducting studies to see if the alkaloid might aid in reversing Alzheimer's disease or perhaps anticholinergic syndrome, a process by which neurotransmitters dangerously "freeze up" during or after anesthesia. Though itself toxic, this alkaloid proves an effective antidote for poisoning from another deadly plant, *Atropa belladonna.*

MAGNOLIA
Magnoliaceae
An Ancient Beauty

Magnolia, named after French botanist Pierre Magnol, belongs to a genus of flowering plants that includes a number of different magnolia species. Plants in the group have gone by many names, including *beaver tree, Indian bark, Chinese magnolia,* and *swamp laurel.* Depending on the type, magnolia plants can grow as shrubs or full trees. The genus has an ancient lineage, with some fossils indicating the plant dates as far back as far as ninety-five million years.

Magnolias owe their wide popularity to their beautiful flowers. The official state flower of Mississippi and Louisiana, magnolias are also the former state's official tree. Indeed, there are so many of these trees in Mississippi, its nickname is "the Magnolia State." The much-heralded flowers can be white, red, pink, purple, or yellow, and most bloom in early spring before the plants' leaves open. These leaves come in diverse shapes and are evergreen or deciduous, depending on the species. All magnolia species, however, produce large flowers of striking beauty, which also fill the air with a delicate fragrance.

The Bee or the Flower?

The magnolia might answer the question of which came first, the flower or the bee. Since the plant most certainly arose long before the evolution of bees—as well as any blooming flower—the dispute can be put to rest. Botanists believe flowers developed at first to attract beetles to do the pollination work.

Magnolias prefer open areas and don't fare well in crowded forests. This has less to do with resource competition and more to do with free-flowing air; without enough wind circulation (which thickets of other plants can certainly hinder), the plant is much more liable to succumb to diseases. One of the magnolia's worst enemies is a powdery mildew that forms on its branches and can be a huge detriment to the plant if not dried out by the wind. Moist soil is important to magnolias, which explains why one so often sees mulch spread at the base of landscaped trees.

Although people value it most for its flowers, the magnolia also has other uses. The Chinese and Japanese have found uses for the plant in the treatment of asthma, cough, headache, stress, anxiety, weight loss, abdominal pain, and stomach problems. In Japan, the leaves of magnolia plants are used for wrapping food and in cooking numerous types of entrees. As a lumber, the magnolias provide a soft, cream-colored wood that is used for intricate carvings, furnishings, and moldings. Most trees of this species grow naturally in East and Southeast Asia, which is why the mentioned remedies, as well as the magnolia lumber trade, are so localized in the region. North America, Central America, and West India are also all hotbeds of magnolia growth, and even South America boasts an abundance of certain species. Although these plants are everywhere, only a few species are grown as foliage or decorative plants.

Plant an Ancient Tree Today

When planting a magnolia, you must pick the site carefully. All magnolias prove difficult to move once established, since digging around their roots can severely injure or even kill them. Many grow huge, very tall, and heavily branched. Thus you should pick an area that has plenty of open space. Magnolias will never look their best if crowded together, so keep this in mind when planting. The soil should be fairly rich, well drained, and with a pH between neutral and slightly acidic. Most magnolia trees and shrubs will require full or at least partial shade, and they will need regular waterings in order to thrive.

MANGO
Mangifera indica
The Ancient Smoothie Plant

Mangifera indica 'Jean Ellen'

The mango tree is an African evergreen, cultivated primarily in tropical climates and known best for its edible fruit, the succulent mango. There are at least 27 species of mango tree that bear edible fruits, and countless hybrids and cultivated varieties. In ideal conditions, the tree has a long life span, with some bearing baskets and bushels of bulbous fruit for three hundred years. The common mango tree grows large, reaching heights of 115 to 130 feet. Its branches and foliage can spread to a diameter of around 65 feet. It stands out among other trees due to its towering size and dark leaves.

Mangifera indica "Angie"

The leaves of *Magnifera indica* are evergreen and fairly hefty, with lengths of 6 to 14 inches and widths of 3 to 7 inches. Brand-new leaves are orange or pink, although they rapidly change to a glossy red when they begin to mature. When completely mature, the leaves turn a deep green.

The flowers of the mango tree are moderately sized, all white, and can range from 4 to 6 inches long. Each flower, comprising five small white petals, has a mild, sweet odor. The fruit of the mango tree, also known as a mango, is green when young and takes somewhere between three to six months to completely ripen. When completely ripe, the fruit turns from an orange to a deep red-yellow and gives a pleasantly sweet smell when peeled. Mangoes have a pit in the center, which contains one somewhat large seed. The mango seed, like a bean seed, has an embryo and will germinate after a few months.

People have cultivated mango trees for their precious fruit for thousands of years, and today they are cited as the largest commercially produced crop in tropical regions (regions with frost are inhospitable to the plant). In early colonial times, the fruit was often exchanged like money, especially in the Caribbean. During the 1700s in the Dominican Republic, for example, one cup of goat's milk was worth two mangoes.

The fruit of the mango tree can either be eaten raw, pickled, dried, or cooked. Ripe mangoes are generally sweet to the taste, but unripe mangoes are usually sour. One can encourage an unripe fruit to ripen faster by leaving it at room temperature for three to five days, which naturally brings out its sugars as it begins to decay. Most mangoes have a soft, pulpy texture, similar to that of a common orange. Certain varieties of mango, though, have a hard texture like that of a cantaloupe. Although they may look and feel like oranges, mangoes have a unique citrusy taste all their own.

Don't Live in Paradise?

There are many people who would like to grow mangoes but they live where frost hits throughout the fall, winter, or spring, making such cultivation (at least outdoors) impossible. Several dwarf mango trees, however, have been bred and produced by hybrid plants, and can be kept indoors and grown in containers. These plants will still flower and bear a fruit that will taste like a mango. Still, nothing beats the flavor of tropically grown fruit that falls loose from its tree with only a touch. When peeled and eaten, as messy and juicy as it is, right on the spot, mango has a unique effect on the taste buds. It is great in smoothies, or *batidos,* if you find yourself in the Spanish Caribbean.

MAPLE
Acer cappadocicum
A Botanical Icon

Acer is a common type of tree, though most know it by the name *maple*; the family has 128 species of flowering shrubs and trees. Although these species are widespread, about 42 percent of maples now face the threat of extinction. Most maple trees are native to Asia, although many are native to Europe, North Africa, and North America. They prefer moist climates and can grow in either full sun or the shade. Maples are generally small, understory trees rather than trees that tower over other ones.

Most maple trees are deciduous and grow bright green leaves during the spring and summer. In the fall, the foliage of maple trees is quite a display. The leaves turn to different colors including red, yellow, brown, and orange—all of which goes a long way to explaining why maple trees are so popular as ornamental plants. Their autumn foliage is famous and amazes thousands of tourists ever year. Maple leaves have an abundance of carotenoids, the pigments found in carrots, as well as chlorophyll, which gives them their healthy green color. When the leaves begin to die, the chlorophyll becomes less prominent, allowing the carotenoids to shine, thus producing a spectacular burst of color in autumn.

Maples flowers are usually quite small. Most maples begin budding in late winter to early spring, just after the appearance of new leaves, and the resulting flowers can be green, yellow, orange, or red. This early blooming strategy is effective in attracting bees early on, as they are often the only source of pollen and nectar until other plants begin to produce flowers, too.

Maple fruits are made up of two sections, each containing a wing and a seedpod. The seedpods are attached to the whirlybirds (see "Nature's Helicopters" on this page). After spinning through the air and landing on soil, the pods dry and then split open. Each seedpod usually contains one seed, black and flat, which will require a period of cold-moist stratification before it can germinate. One can achieve this naturally by allowing the seed to be set in soil during the winter, though wrapping it in a moistened paper towel, putting the damp paper towel in a plastic bag, and putting the bag in the refrigerator for about a month is an effective alternative. If attempting this artificial germination, be sure to change the paper towel regularly to prevent the seed from developing rot.

Nature's Helicopters

The fruit of a maple tree is very distinctive. Scientifically termed *samaras,* the common names for these fruits are *whirlybirds* and *helicopters*. These fruits have evolved to spin with the wind when they fall from their tree, thus spreading the seeds over a vast area.

Maple seeds usually mature within a few weeks, somewhere up to six months after the plant originally bore its fruit. The seeds are mature when the fruit is dry and brown, and it will easily fall off the tree in the wind or from other natural causes. One maple tree can produce thousands of seeds, and for this reason, many farmers actually consider the trees pests. Even a single seeding maple tree can lead to the sprouting of many more around it.

Maple leaves are an important food supply for the larvae of many insects. Useful for much more than beautifying landscapes, maples are often tapped for their xylem sap, which is the key ingredient in maple syrup. The maple syrup market is hugely important to the Canadian economy, totaling $140 million in export sales, though most

supermarket brands contain little of the real maple's sap. The syrup might not exist if not for the Algonquin Indians, whom European settlers observed making V-shaped cuts into maples to allow their sweet sap to drip out through a reed. Thus began the tradition of maple syrup, a vital companion of the pancake. The autumn leaf-watching tradition surrounding these trees is strong in many countries and gives real economic benefits from tourism. The maple leaf is so treasured in Canada, perhaps for its symbolic association with strength and endurance, that it appears on the nation's flag.

MARIGOLD
Calendula officinalis
Flowering Guaranteed

Marigolds are flower-bearing plants that are easy to grow, since they adapt to a wide range of soil and climatic conditions. The plant seems determined to unleash its brilliant flowers upon the world, no matter what. Though they will tolerate the shade, most marigolds thrive in full sun, or in places where they get ample hot, sunny exposure; they can even grow in the sunlight reflected from pavement as long as they get sufficient moisture. The flowers will also bloom in poor and average soil, so long as it's not too soggy. Marigolds actually grow a higher quantity of flowers in poor soil; richer soil stimulates the growth of lush foliage, sacrificing the growth of buds and blooms in return. Marigolds are rapid growers whose seeds usually germinate within a few days of planting in a warm, sunny location. Though it is a perennial, its life is nevertheless short, even if it adapted by growing up to nearly 3 feet high, producing flowers and seeds all in less than one month.

Marigold flowers resemble daisies or carnations in their shape. They are available in a wide range of colors, including white, cream, yellow, orange, red, and burgundy, and one plant can often blend two separate hues.

Although they grow easily, marigolds are vulnerable to disease. Powdery mildew can be a threat in damp and humid conditions, but good airflow will alleviate this problem substantially. Soggy soil will induce fungal infections, characterized by dis-

The Aztecs believed marigolds were sacred and employed them in human sacrificial rituals as well as a medicine. To this day in Mexico, marigolds feature prominently in Dia de los Muertos (Day of the Dead) festivals, and many refer to them as the "flower of the dead." The Greeks and Romans used varieties of marigolds native to those regions for dyes and in cosmetics.

colored spots, mildew on the plant, and wilting foliage. Insect pests can also bring about fungal infections. The best way to prevent disease in marigolds is to keep them weeded and provide good drainage for the soil. Marigolds also make good companions to tomato plants, as they prevent the tomato fruit from getting those fat green caterpillars that can so often kill the plant. Marigolds have a strong odor, more pungent than sweet, and many believe the scent exists to repel certain types of threatening insects.

Marigolds make for a fine-looking flower show, whether alive or dead. For a live flower arrangement, cut the flowers off first thing in the morning and put them in a vase of warm water immediately. Later, trim the lower leaves, since otherwise they will foul the water. An indoor flower arrangement may be pretty but will give off a smelly odor that is often quite strong and noticeable.

Marigolds have many notable uses. Some people eat them in a tossed salad. The people of India and Pakistan cultivate the plant for medicinal use, flavoring, dye, and decoration. A staple of flower arrangements even in ancient times, marigolds were the designated markers for pavilions and played a role in sacred fire pits and ceremonies. Today marigolds are a common guest at weddings. Even their essential oils have an ornamental use, providing the ingredient for certain perfumes.

Good Therapy

Marigolds are popular in gardening projects, particularly with the elderly and children, since their hardiness proves very forgiving of would-be gardeners and the inexperienced. Having germinated the plant indoors, one should transplant the young seedling outdoors on a cloudy day so as to prevent the stress of the hot sun killing the plant before it has a chance to take root. Plant the seedlings 8 to 10 inches apart once the danger of frost has passed, and add some organic material to discourage weed growth until the plant gets bigger. Marigolds are quite sturdy when they grow bigger—if you snip off dead blooms, new buddings can grow to take their place. In ideal summer conditions, marigolds will last from midsummer until frost kills them.

MIMOSA
Mimosa pudica
Touch-Me-Not

Here's a plant that defies the rules—if there really are any—of a species's primary motivation to survive and continue its kind. Indeed it raises the question, Is there a limit to what science can tell us about the botanical world? Are these organisms as simple as we imagine them to be, or are there complex causes underlying their behavior we may never understand?

Mimosa pudica, also known as the *sensitive plant, humble plant, shameful plant,* and perhaps its best name, *touch-me-not,* will die immediately after being touched. If you hit its leaves roughly with a hand, the plant's puzzling fragility causes it to die. With one touch, it's over.

The touch-me-not is native to South and Central America but has spread today all over the world, such that scientists have taken to calling it a pantropical weed. This shy lady (*pudica* means "shy" in Latin) prefers shady areas, growing under shrubs or trees. In some regions of South Asia, the Pacific Islands, and Australia, the plant is considered an invasive species.

It grows erect and slender to about 4 feet tall, branching out and creeping over larger areas as the plant matures. The plant has bipinnately compound leaves, meaning the leaves grow opposite each other. The leaf pairs can have ten to twenty-six leaflets on each branch, as well as beautiful, delicate, purple or pink flowers of about ¼ inch in diameter. *Pudica* bears fruit clusters that have two to eight segmented pods, which hold light brown seeds. The herb depends upon pollination from bees and insects, which do manage to touch it without causing its death.

If the plant senses a large animal coming near, its leaves actually try to turn away. If touched, it will die. English botanist Robert Hooke first postulated a theory for this odd behavior in the seventeenth century. His investigation suggested the plant consists of tissues and nerves

Are Plants Telepathic?

In the 1960s, scientist Cleve Backster attached a plant to a polygraph machine. When he threatened to hurt the plant, the polygraph went practically crazy. Another experiment had two plants placed in the same room, with only one connected to a polygraph machine. A group of men entered the room, and one man was tasked to harm the unconnected plant. The polygraphed plant began to display movement on the instrument's readout. The men then left the room and returned sometime later. When the man who had harmed the other plant entered, without touching the plants, the polygraph plant again began to show activity, as if it had a memory. Although these "experiments" are generally debunked as pseudoscience, Backster's instinct might have been heading in the right direction. The Society for Plant Neurobiology recently endorsed a study that examined the extent of plant intelligence. We know plants react to changing environmental factors, such as variations in light, and produce toxins to detract herbivores, and they receive chemical signals from other plants. It was previously believed plants did so via genetically entrenched biochemical mechanisms. New research suggests that the system plants use to respond to stimuli is similar in many ways to animal nervous systems. In any case, George Washington Carver, the famous American horticulturist, always talked to his plants.

similar to those animals use to dissuade predators, like an opossum playing dead. Hooke thought movement of water within the plant allowed the leaves to move; any external stimulus, he suggested, would cause the plant to release chemicals that move the water out of cells and cause the plant's collapse, making it seem dead and thus very unappealing to a herbivore. Such an act would be a novel mechanism for self-defense. In reality, the rapid withering may last only a short time, and once the stimulus disappears, the water may return to the plant's cells, rejuvenating it. Only prolonged touching causes its "suicide."

Despite this plant's fragility, the Global Invasive Species Database has ranked mimosa on a list of invasives that pose a danger to numerous agricultural crops, including coconuts, corn, tomatoes, coffee, cotton, papaya, bananas, soybeans, and sugarcane. Touch-me-not also contains the toxic alkaloid mimosine, which has apoptic and antiproliferative effects (causing cell damage and retarding cellular growth) to these other plants. The touch-me-not name, it turns out, has clearly been well earned in a number of ways.

Even if some scientists are not fully convinced the plant dies as a defense mechanism, it has a long history of providing benefits in some traditional medicines. In India, its pulped leaves are usually used on granular swellings; Indians believe the leaf sap helps fight against sinus infections. The people of the Republic of Congo use the plant's pulp to form a mixture useful as a pain reliever and for kidney aliments. In Senegal, the entire plant is used against uterine cancer and glandular tumors, and mimosa leaves have found use as treatments for nephritis and lumbago.

MISTLETOE
Viscum album
Kissing, Dracula-Style

Mistletoe is a group of semiparasitic plants belonging to the order *Santanales*. While the name *mistletoe* has unknown origins, it possibly derives from the German *mist* or the Old English *mistil,* though this word was used to describe basil. The plant originated in Eurasia, and humans subsequently introduced it in North America and Australia. The plant grows by attaching its viny branches to trees and shrubs. But it doesn't do this just to gain sunlight; it also penetrates the host with its haustorium, a rootlike outgrowth that allows it to absorb and rob the other plant of its nutrients and water, ultimately killing the other plant—Dracula-style.

Mistletoe isn't all bad, though. Many animals use its leaves and young shoots for food. More than 240 species of birds build their nests inside mistletoe plants, whose shape is very suitable for support. Juniper trees entwined with mistletoe have even been known to produce more juniper berries than normal. Areas with a higher density of mistletoe foliage tend to play host to broader animal populations, so it might not be fair to categorically write these plants off as pests. They do contribute to biodiversity.

A Plant with History

Mistletoe is the subject of numerous myths and legends and folklore. The only species native to Europe, *Viscum album,* was honored as the Golden Bough of Aeneas in Greco-Roman mythology. According to some Norse legends, the god Hoor killed his brother Bald with a mistletoe "projectile." In another version, Hoor performed the murder with a sword named Mistilteinn. Some European pre-Christian cultures considered these plants a sign of male vitality, and the plant has come to be associated with romance.

As Christianity continued to influence pagan cultures, it began to rewrite the significance and symbolism of the plant. Some argue Jesus's cross was made from a mistletoe tree (others say cypress), but according to one legend, from the crucifixion on the plant became parasitic. This belief boosted the plant's initial popularity as a hanging ornament in homes; a tradition formed that people should kiss beneath boughs made from mistletoe that were seen as a symbol of the crucifixion. Thus they humbled themselves before the cross and kissed it to receive blessings. Though reports of this practice date back to the sixteenth century in England, it spread as mistletoe grew in popularity as a Christmas decoration in the Victorian era. Since the plant retained its pagan association with fertility, the tradition continued to oblige a woman to kiss a man when standing with him beneath a decorative wreath, bough, or branch. With each kiss, one of the mistletoe's berries was plucked by the female. When all the berries were gone—and the berries are poisonous, by the way—the plant lost its romantic sway, and kissing beneath it was no longer required.

Botanically, mistletoe's evergreen leaves perform photosynthesis, so it can survive without a host. However, its seeds usually germinate on the branches of the host trees or shrubs that the mistletoe entwines with while the plant is young and not yet dependent on its host. After bearing seeds, the older plant, having spent its vital energy on the seeds, only then begins to rob nutrients from the host tree, drawing from it water to keep itself alive. Some mistletoe species give small flowers, which are pollinated by insects, and others have very showy, large flowers, pollinated by birds.

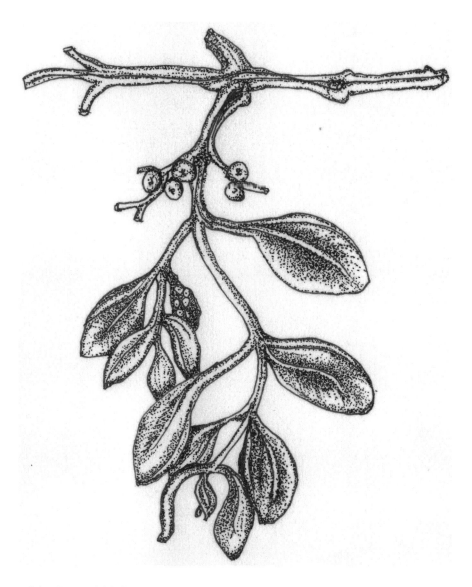

Medicinal Value

Some claim mistletoe extract has cancer-fighting properties, although there have not been any substantive clinical trials to prove this. However, European herbalists use the plant's young twigs to aid respiratory and circulatory problems. You can find mistletoe extract sold as Helixor and Iscador. Although it's been the culprit behind many an unwanted kiss, mistletoe has no known aphrodisiacal effects. Celts used it as a poison antidote.

MONKEY PUZZLE TREE
Araucaria araucana
A Majestic Sight

The monkey puzzle tree, also called the *monkey tail tree* or *Chilean pine,* is an evergreen conifer native to Chile and Argentina. Spanish explorers first discovered the plant in 1780, and Archibald Menzies, a naval surgeon and plant collector during Captain George Vancouver's circumnavigation of the globe (traveling in Captain James Cook's old ship *Discovery*), introduced it to England fifteen years later. Menzies used the seeds as a dessert while dining with the governor of Chile, but he later sewed them in a frame on the quarterdeck, which, by the time he reached back home, had produced five healthy young plants. The "monkey" name dates to 1850, when a proud owner of a tree showed it to his friends, one of whom remarked that a tree with branches so tightly clothed with spiny leaves would "puzzle even a monkey" if climbed.

In addition to its jigsaw-puzzle branch configuration, another distinguishing element of the monkey puzzle tree is its green, glossy leaves, which bear sharp tops and edges; they are thick and triangular, about an inch long and half as wide, but don't fall off for an amazing ten to fifteen years or even more, when the leaves finally lose the ability to photosynthesize. The tree is dioecious, bearing either male or female cones on different trees, and is pollinated usually by the wind. The cones are cucumber-shaped and oblong, about 3 inches in length. After the cones have reached maturity, they simply crumble and disintegrate, releasing 1-inch-long edible seeds that are similar to nuts. The tree can grow up to 150 feet tall, with a trunk circumference of about 6 feet. The whole visual effect of the monkey puzzle tree is quite unusual, even mystical; it certainly looks like a majestic hiding place for an entire troop of monkeys.

The natural habitat of the monkey puzzle tree is primarily the south-central Andes, where it usually flourishes at altitudes above 3,000 feet, and it can withstand temperatures as low as -4 degrees Fahrenheit. The tree has now taken to climates of northern Europe and grows in the Faroe Islands as well. Some specimens can also be found in North America, New Zealand, and Western Australia. The tree prefers slightly acidic, well-drained, volcanic soil, but it is also tolerant of other well-drained types. Its cones drop by themselves, so the harvest is very easy, but as an economical crop, it takes a long wait for a profitable return, thirty to forty years to produce its first seeds. But the tree is patient, and can live to one thousand years. In most European countries the tree is such a rarity, it has enjoyed the protection of law since 1971.

Uses and Benefits

The Latin name *Araucaria araucana* derives from *Araucanos,* a name for the tribes of the Araucana linguistic family, living in Argentina and Chile. They considered the tree to be sacred and harvested its seeds, which taste bitter raw and more palatable if roasted. The natives of the Andes also used the seeds to make flour and for a fermented beverage, *muday.* They even fed the seeds to livestock, especially during the winter. Since its sacredness has dwindled, locals now cut the trees for construction and fuel. The Spaniards considered the monkey puzzle tree one of the Andes' most precious and strong lumbers and often sought it for ship masts, to use as pit props in mines, for railway sleeper cars, and for paper pulp. In the 1940s it was even used to make a few airplanes, since the wood was believed to be good for enduring crashes, but it was ultimately judged too much of a puzzle to shape for stable aerodynamics.

MUSTARD
Brassica
Vigor and Tenacity

Mustard is considered an ancient plant still very suitable for contemporary gardeners. It is easy to grow and can produce seeds in as few as sixty days after planting. Most use the plant as a spice, while a mixture of its seeds, in addition to water, vinegar, and a few other ingredients, create the well-known yellow condiment also named mustard. Some versions of the condiment also utilize the seeds, and even the leaves are edible (known colloquially as "mustard greens"). Mustard plants are several of the known plant species in the genera *Sinapis* and *Brassica*.

Although many believe some varieties of the mustard plant were already established in Roman times, the plant that today forms the key ingredient in the mustard condiment has no wild origins. There is a white mustard that grows wild in Africa and the Mediterranean region, and some theorize it was from this type that the domesticated version evolved. The plant is also related to radishes and turnips, and may derive from cultivated crossbreeding of these plants as well.

It is easy to grow mustard. It thrives in different soils, but does best in well-drained, rich ones. The plant likes constant moisture and cold water, while a light frost even improves its flavor. Farmers sow seeds in the springtime, ⅛ inch deep, 15 inches apart. In the southern regions of the United States, mustard will even grow during September and October, so the harvest occurs in late fall or early winter. Mustard species are practically free of disease or insect problems, and larger critters also don't like their taste. The hotter the weather is, the faster the plants give seeds; they need only thirty to sixty days to mature.

It is astonishing how such an ordinary little plant has such a great reputation. You can find its name everywhere, from the Bible to Shakespeare. So, how does it attract such attention? There can be no other reason but its vigor and tenacity. As proof of its popularity, an excerpt from the Bible praises the plant: "The kingdom of heaven is like a grain of mustard seed, which a man took and sowed in his field, which indeed is the least of all seeds. But when it is grown, it is greatest among herbs, and becometh a tree, so that the birds come and lodge in the branches thereof" (Matthew 13:31–32). Yes, the mustard species known as *Brassica nigra* and *Brassica hirta* can in fact grow as tall as trees in Mediterranean climates.

Health and Nutrition

Some mustard species of the Cruciferae family contain significant doses of vitamin C and beta-carotene, both very strong antioxidants. Despite a current lack of scientific proof verifying such an application, many use mustard plants as a traditional method of cancer prevention. Its greens are also a rich source of calcium, besides supplying a satisfying amount of iron. The nutrients of ½ cup of cooked mustard greens practically speak for themselves:

Protein: 1.6 grams

Carbohydrates: 1.5 grams

Dietary fiber: 1.4 grams

Vitamin C: 18 milligrams

Vitamin A: 2,121 International Units

Folic acid: 130 micrograms

Calcium: 52 milligrams

Potassium: 140 milligrams

Iron: 0.5 milligrams

Calories: 11

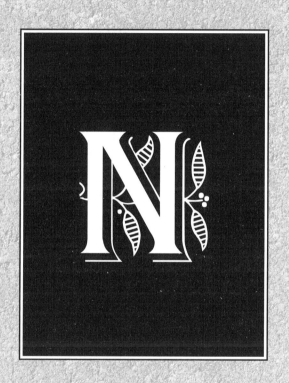

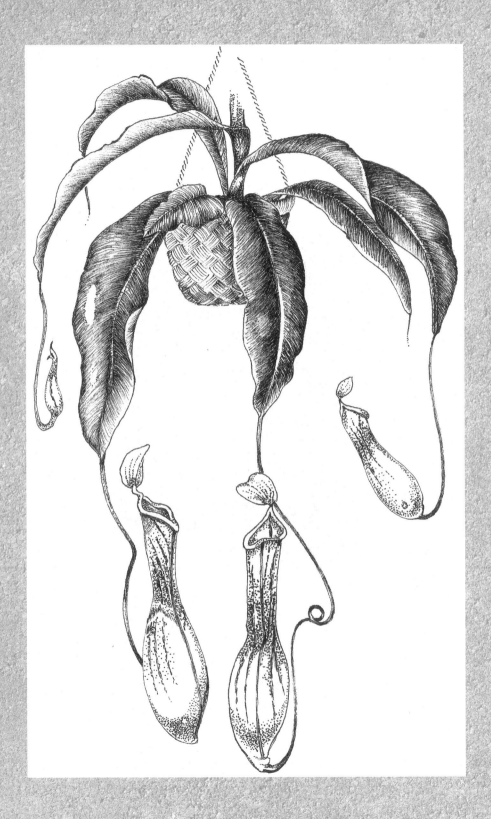

NEPENTHES
Nepenthaceae
Monkey's Luxury

According to Homer's *Odyssey,* the beautiful Helen of Troy ("the face that launched a thousand ships"), responsible for the ten-year war between Mycenae and Troy that resulted in Prince Hector being slain by Achilles, was also a healer. During these years she gave soldiers and their families a drink made of the nepenthes plant, aimed to "relieve their sorrow and grief." Helen supposedly learned the recipe for the potion of "Nepenthes pharmakon" from an Egyptian queen. The Greek word *nepenthe* means "without grief," while *pharmakon* is Egyptian for any "magician's remedy" and, incidentally, is the root word of *pharmacology.*

The plant, which today is used in all sorts of narcotics, goes by the common names *pitcher plant* and *monkey cups.* It grows naturally and mostly thrives in Borneo and Sumatra, but it is also found in India, Sri Lanka, Australia, Seychelles, Madagascar, Malaysia, Indonesia, the Philippines, and China. It belongs to a carnivorous genus of the Nepenthaceae family, consisting of about 140 species and many hybrids. Some species contain a narcotic-like substance in their fluid.

Nepenthes has a climbing stem that stretches more than 50 feet, with a shallow root system. Its leaves are sword shaped, with tips or tendrils that help them to climb such heights. It forms a pitcher shape that starts as a small bud but gradually grows into a mug-size cup that monkeys have been known to drink from. A little water from a puddle, along with fluid produced by the plants (a syrupy or watery liquid containing viscoelastic biopolymers), forms what some primates consider a delicacy. The syrupy fluid actually evolved as an attractant for insects. If not plucked by a monkey, the beautifully colored lime-green pitcher with its ring of red at the top is a very efficient trap for all kinds of insects, which the plant eats. Beauty, like Helen's, is sometimes dangerous.

Both highland and lowland species of nepenthes need plenty of rainfall and some bright light, though less than full sun exposure. The plants need well-drained soil, constant air circulation, and high humidity, and can grow from cuttings, seeds, or tissue culture. Seeds usually take two months to germinate and more than two years to yield mature nepenthes, so it is not a human's ideal method of propagating the plant. Many put root cuttings inside plastic bags or tanks with damp moss, high humidity, and moderate light; these start to root after two months, forming the pitchers after six months. Tissue culture growth is mostly used by commercial farmers. Nepenthes are considered endangered plants—endangered, of course, not by monkeys, but by humans.

The Golden Age of Nepenthes

After the discovery of the nepenthes and their introduction in Europe by Joseph Banks in 1789, interest grew rapidly. Everyone wanted to own one, such that some called the end of nineteenth century the Golden Age of Nepenthes. The craze faded until the 1960s, when the work of the Japanese botanist Shigeo Kurata rekindled interest in this ancient plant and inspired efforts to preserve the graceful, bug-eating beauty.

Coexist or Be Eaten

Some organisms live inside the pitchers of nepenthes, most commonly mosquito larvae, spiders, ants, mites, fly and midge larvae, and even a crab species, *Geosesarma malayanum*. Some of them are attached to one nepenthes species and so are called nepenthebionts. Other species are associated with but not dependent on the plants and are called nepenthophiles. This complex ecological relationship, called an infaunal ecosystem, is not fully understood, but the relationship appears to be mutualistic, meaning that the infauna receives shelter, protection, or food, while the nepenthes benefits from an increasing rate of digestion, expedited breakdown of captured prey, and protection from harmful bacteria.

NETTLE
Urtica dioica
The Little Warrior

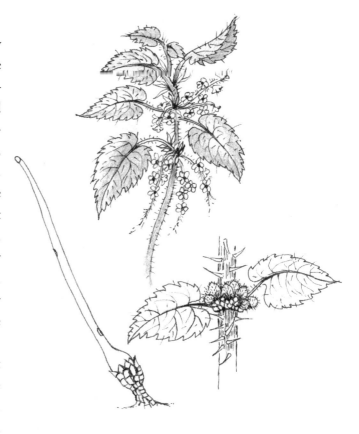

This little warrior with many sharp weapons stands brave and strong across the globe—it's native to practically all parts of the world, including North America, Europe, Asia, and North Africa. Though annoying, nettles are not all bad; they make a great nutritional tea, for example, that's full of iron. Sure, they may first sting you badly, but don't worry—except for a bit of flaming pain, there are no other consequences. Actually, we can even call it a pain-pleasure plant, since in some regions (southern Europe, the Balkans) an old tradition has people intentionally "flare" themselves with the nettles, as they believe doing so can strengthen immunity; this is not so far off, according to some modern medical research. In the Balkans, boys purposely rub themselves with nettle, believing it makes them more attractive to girls.

Nettles' complicated pain-pleasure paradox has inspired a number of idioms and literary references. For example, in Shakespeare's *Henry IV, Part 1*, the character Hotspur urges, "out of this nettle, danger, we pluck this flower, safety." In German there is an idiom translating as "to sit on nettles" that means to get oneself into big trouble. Hungarians say, "No lightning strikes the nettle," meaning that bad things never happen to bad people, while the Dutch phrase *netelige situate* means "predicament." Still, it was the old, wise Aesop who was the source of the most universal nettle metaphor for facing down difficulty. In the fable "The Boy and the Nettle," a boy is stung by the thorn and runs home to tell his mother: "Although it hurts me very much, I only touched it gently." "That was just why it stung you," said his mother. "The next time you touch a nettle, grasp it boldly, and it will be soft as silk to your hand."

However, not all nettles sting; in fact, only five subspecies of the genus *Urtica* do. *Urtica dioica* is most often called *common nettle* or, of course, *stinging nettle,* but is also known as *burn nettle, burn hazel,* or *burn weed.* It grows 3 to 7 feet tall during the summer, dies in winter, and revives in the spring, which is the best time to collect young plant tops for tea and as an ingredient in soups. It is classified as a dioecious perennial, with lots of rhizomes or thinner roots quickly spreading from the main, bright yellow taproot. The plant's beautifully shaped leaves are soft, 1 to 6 inches long, representing the plant's first line of defense, but the most needles are on its wiry stems. Nettle produces small brownish flowers in many colors or inflorescences. Upon contact, the plant will inject you with some histamine, a bit of acetylcholine, then serotonin 5-HT, some leukotrienes, and maybe formic acid. But don't panic; the stinging sensation is temporary and without any serious consequences.

The Nettle Eaters

Balkan boys rubbing their bodies with nettles pales in comparison to the annual World Nettle Eating Championship in Dorset, England, to which thousands of people flock each year to see contestants actually chew and swallow nettles. There's only one rule: each competitor is given a tray with 20-inch-long stalks, after which they strip their leaves and eat them; the winner is the one who strips and eats the most stinging stalks in the shortest amount of time.

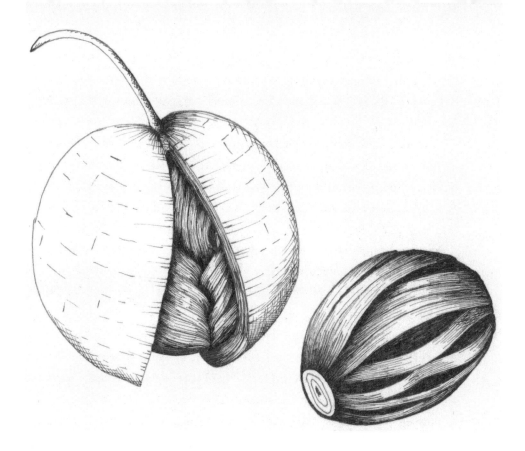

NUTMEG
Myristica fragrans
Sniff or Sprinkle

Myristica fragrans is a tropical evergreen and the primary flavoring ingredient in the nutmeg spice.

The nutmeg tree's fruit is also known as nutmeg. Nutmeg seeds weigh 5 to 10 grams when dried. Nutmeg spice refers to the actual seed within the fruit, while its red, lacy seed coat is used to make mace. Both spices are flavorful and very aromatic. However, nutmeg loses its fragrance shortly after it is ground. This explains why many prefer to buy nutmeg as a whole fruit to grind themselves, rather than buy it

The nutmeg tree reaches about 65 feet in height in temperate climates, but can grow up to 150 feet tall in the tropics.

pre-ground. Both parts of the seed are aromatic when fresh. The smell isn't the only sensory enhancer of nutmeg. The taste of ground nutmeg has a warm flavor, though there are compelling reasons to use the spice sparingly.

Unfortunately, some people abuse nutmeg. Though it's sold in stores, it's less innocuous than it seems—some use nutmeg as a recreational drug; chemicals within the plant have mild hallucinogenic properties. In fact, it has become known as the poor man's LSD, though a lot of nutmeg is required to achieve any effect at all. Ingested in large quantities, nutmeg may cause hallucinations, but uncomfortable side effects will also result, including severe nausea and vomiting. The hallucinogen itself isn't particularly safe, either, since the active ingredient in nutmeg affects the central nervous system.

Nutmeg is a treasured fruit with great economic importance, sold all over the world. However, because it fetches such a good price per pound (for example, $28 per pound in India), there are numerous illegal traders who sell a grade of nutmeg that shouldn't be ground or sold. This grade of nutmeg is known as BWP nutmeg, which means the seed is broken, wormy, and likely infected by pests. BWP nutmegs are only safe for the extraction of essential oils, or for uses other than consumption. Some people do buy these tainted crops and grind them, afterward marketing them as a good, high-quality product—so read the label of origin! These nutmegs usually have certain molds and mildews within them that can cause upset stomach and potentially harm the body—yet another reason to buy nutmeg whole and grind it yourself.

OAK
Quercus
The Nation's Tree

It's a legendary tree, beloved and appreciated, since it has many specific uses and is admired for its sturdy and masterful beauty. The oak is a common symbol of strength and endurance. As such, it is a national tree in many countries. In Germany, it has had many meanings since ancient times. In current times the oak's leaves are displayed on the deutsche mark and the euro. In 2004, the United States Congress made the oak America's national tree. Other countries that display oak in their national symbols include France, England, Cyprus, Estonia, Moldova, Romania, Lithuania, Latvia, Wales, Poland, Serbia, and Bulgaria.

Oak has about 600 different species in the genus *Quercus,* family Fagaceae. It is native to the Northern Hemisphere, including the deciduous and evergreen species. North America has about 250 oak species (90 in the United States, 160 in Mexico). The second-greatest oak diversity is found in China, which has about 100 species. Oak has a very specific spiral arrangement of leaves growing from thick branches. The leaves are lobate or web-shaped. On some species the edges of the leaves are serrated, although most have smooth margins or edges. In spring, oaks produce male flowers, shaped as catkins or flower clusters, as well as smaller female flowers. The fabulous-looking fruits are nuts, known of course as *acorns,* and grow from a cup-shaped structure called a cupule. Each of the nuts contains only one seed. The seed needs 7 to 18 months to mature, dependent upon the species.

Oak wood is highly appreciated because of its density, hardness, and strength. As such, it has many historical and contemporary uses: Vikings used it for their spectacularly resistant longships, as did other European seafaring powers. Since ancient times oak was used for paneling in prestigious buildings and for making fine furniture. In nineteenth-century Europe, oak timber was used to frame houses, since it was considered the most durable. Today, except for furniture, flooring, and veneer production, oak lumber is too expensive to use for framing. It is still the best to make barrels for aging wines, sherry, brandy, Scotch and Irish whiskey, and bourbon.

If a wine has the word barrique *in its name, then you know that it's been aged for at least three years in an oak barrel.*

Other uses include oak wood chips for smoking meat, cheeses, and fish. Japanese oak is used for the best Yamaha drums, as the density of the wood gives a brighter and louder tone. In India it is still used for making traditional agricultural implements. In Korea, oak bark is used for making shingles for traditional roofs. The bark of white oak is also used in medicine since it is rich in tannins, while acorns can be specifically used for flour or roasted for a kind of acorn coffee.

Most Famous Oak Trees

Oak has a rich mythology based on its great strength and age. Even today, many old oak trees are honored. Here are the five most famous ones:

1. The **Emancipation Oak,** at Hampton University in Hampton, Virginia, is considered one of the Ten Great Trees of the world by the National Geographic Society.
2. The **Bowthorpe Oak,** in Bourne, Lincolnshire, England, is 1,000 years old and was the subject of a television documentary.
3. The **Ivenack Oak,** one of Europe's largest trees, is in Germany. It is approximately 800 years old.
4. The **Seven Sisters Oak** is located in Mandeville, Louisiana. It is 1,500 years old and has a trunk 38 feet in circumference.
5. The **Crouch Oak** originates from the eleventh century and is located in Addlestone, Surrey, England. It is the main symbol of the town. Legend says that when she noticed it, Queen Elizabeth I stopped to have a picnic by it.

OLIVE
Olea europaea
Witnessing History

One of the oldest cultivated trees in history, the olive tree has enjoyed many roles and meanings. Even Jesus, before he overturned the tables of usurers and gold traders in front of the Holy Temple, wore an olive branch as crowds welcomed him to Jerusalem. The Latin name for the tree literally means "oil from Europe." It belongs to the family Oleaceae and is native to coastal regions of the eastern Mediterranean, including Iran's coast along the south of the Caspian Sea.

Spanish colonists brought the tree to some regions in present-day Chile, and it soon spread along the Pacific coast of South America where the climate is similar to the Mediterranean. In the eighteenth century, Spanish missionaries introduced the olive tree to California. Japan began cultivating the plant in 1908 on Shodo Island, which today is known as one of the cradles of olive cultivation, as is the Greek island of Crete. According to most estimations, 860 million olive trees grow today worldwide, each springtime giving their spectacularly rich fruits and spreading the unforgettable fragrance that accompanies the blooming of their small white flowers.

The olive tree is an evergreen that grows to about 24 to 45 feet in height. People cultivate it primarily for its fruits, which are used for production of olive oil. Its leaves are silvery green and oblong, while the trunk is twisted and gnarled. Trees vary in their production of either olive fruits or drupes, depending on the species. Most fruits are small, at ¼ inch, with dark flesh, usually harvested when they ripen from green to purple. Some estimate the cultivation of olives began about seven thousand years ago, though the first commercially grown fields are recorded on Crete around 3000 B.C. The olive tree was an essential source of wealth for the Minoan civilization. The oil was used for cooking, as it is now, and as a lotion. Many Greeks made use of the oil on their skin and hair, rubbing it liberally on their bodies on a daily basis.

Olive trees can grow in a number of ways, but planting by cuttings is usually preferable. The trees favor well-drained, clay-rich soil, hot summers, and full sun exposure. The tree has extensive, sturdy root systems that bore down deep and wide, which helps give the trees their extremely long life spans. Today, a few olive trees are known to be the oldest in the world: one in Algarve, Portugal; another in Kastela, Croatia; and one in Bar, Montenegro. All three are more than two thousand years old. In Lebanon, an olive tree cluster dubbed "The Sisters Olive Trees of Noah" is estimated to be six thousand years old—a silent witness to a lot of history.

The Gift of Poseidon

Pliny the Elder reported that an olive tree grew in the center of the Roman Forum, while the great poet Horace mentioned it concerning his diet: "As for me, olives, endives, and smooth mallow provide substance." Homer described how Odysseus crawled under two branches of olive growing from a single stock. The Athenians were especially proud of an olive tree on the Acropolis, claiming that olives grew first in their city, based on the myth that Athens was under special patronship of Attica from Poseidon, who had presented the tree as a gift. Theophrastus, often cited as the "father of botany," records the death of that famous olive tree, which perished in Acropolis when the Persians attacked Athens. Of its resilience, he wrote: "The olive was burnt down, but on the very day it was burnt, it grew again to the height of two cubits."

Olive branches are a nearly universal symbol of peace, glory, and abundance, and have been for much of recorded history. In ancient societies, olive wreaths were used to crown victors both in wars and during competitive games. Archeologists even found remains of olive branches in Tutankhamen's tomb. Both the Old and New Testaments mention olives more than thirty times. Jesus's prayer session before his arrest took place in Gethsemane, an olive garden, and the famous Mount of Olives, where Christ is described to have ascended to heaven, lies just east of Jerusalem. The Koran and the Hebrew Bible also mention the tree, the latter citing it as the source of the seven most significant products of the land of Israel. The people used olive oil extensively in cooking, as well as for sacrificial events, lighting, and anointment of priests and royal officials.

ONION
Allium cepa
A Bulb That Conquered the World

From China and India to Egypt, Iran, the entire Middle East, through-out Asia and across the ocean to South and North America, a plant grows that many consider one of the healthiest foods there are. The onion has figured into thousands of years of human history, and even formed the currency used in ancient Egypt to pay workers who had built the pyramids. Originally, people ate onions raw, as if biting into an apple. Many considered them a source of strength and nutrition, bad breath be damned; onion bulbs were even found inside the tombs of the pharaohs, including Tutankhamen.

However, it was Christopher Columbus who first transported the plant to the West Indies, whence it ultimately spread to both North and South America. Even if Columbus didn't conquer and claim the world for Spain, the onion did. Today, kitchens across the world have onions on hand. People have revered the therapeutic value of onions since antiquity: traditional Indian medicine has made use of them since 2000 B.C., something the ancient Romans and Greeks were able to do as well. Onions were practically an indispensable product in all European cuisines during the Middle Ages. Since onions are fast-growing and inexpensive, many of the world's poor make entire meals from them.

The onion is most cultivated of all species of the *Allium* genus; it is a biennial or perennial plant, but most often it is cultivated as an annual one, harvested in the first season after planting. In addition to the classical bulb of the common onion, the genus has numerous other species cultivated for food, including the *Japanese bunching onion* and the *Egyptian onion,* the latter of which kept the pyramid builders strong and accompanied dead pharaohs into the afterlife. *Wild onion* is a common name for many species from the same genus. The most general division is the one that differentiates between white and red onions.

Onion cultivation takes place in fertile, well-drained soil, but a bit of sand or clay is also good, as this type of planting medium contains sulfur, which the plant needs. Onions can be grown from seeds or from bulbs saved from the last year's crop. The plant does have some special enemies, such as the onion fly (*Delia antiqua*), which lays its eggs on the leaves and stems, after which the larvae make tunnels inside the bulbs, causing them to rot. Another pest is the onion eelworm (*Ditylenchus dipsaci*), a parasitic nematode living in the soil that causes the bulbs to get soft. Soil where this worm is discovered will need to be treated for several years to be onion-fertile once again.

Onion Tears

Slice and dice an onion and there is a good chance this vegetable will bring tears to your eyes. Onions contain a sulfur-like gas produced by an enzyme, called lachrymatory-factor synthase, which is released into the air. The nerves in your eyes believe you are under chemical attack and send a signal to the brain to flush it away, causing you to cry.

Many are aware of the culinary and medicinal uses of onions, especially its benefits for the cardiovascular system, due to its phytochemicals and the flavonoid quercetin, but the plant does have some nonculinary, nonmedicinal uses as well. Since onions have large cells that can be seen by the human eye and are easily viewed under the most inexpensive microscope, they are often used to teach students about plant cell structures. Onions also make a pungent juice or fluid that is used for insect bites and can help hair growth when rubbed on the scalp. Other uses include preventing oxidation or rust on iron, and polishing glasses and copperware. In addition, the water used to boil onions can be put into spray bottles to use as an organic herbicide to help garden plants resist any number of pests. Onion plants also keep moles from burrowing through lawns, because the mole's supersensitive nose apparently finds the odor of the bulbs offensive even underground. Onions are also an ingredient in the production of dyes. And of course, in folklore traditions, onions (along with garlic) are recommended to keep vampires away.

Holy Onion!

Ancient Egyptians actually worshipped the onion, believing that its spherical shape symbolized eternal life. Some findings, however, indicate that people living as early as the Bronze Age, around 5000 B.C., used onions as food. Roman gladiators were traditionally rubbed with onions in order to strengthen their muscles. In ancient Greece athletes ate onions in great quantities, believing they "balanced the blood." Medical practitioners of the Middle Ages often prescribed the plant against coughs, headaches, hair loss, snakebites, and as a cure for impotence. The miraculous onion has even found use as a cure for infertility in women.

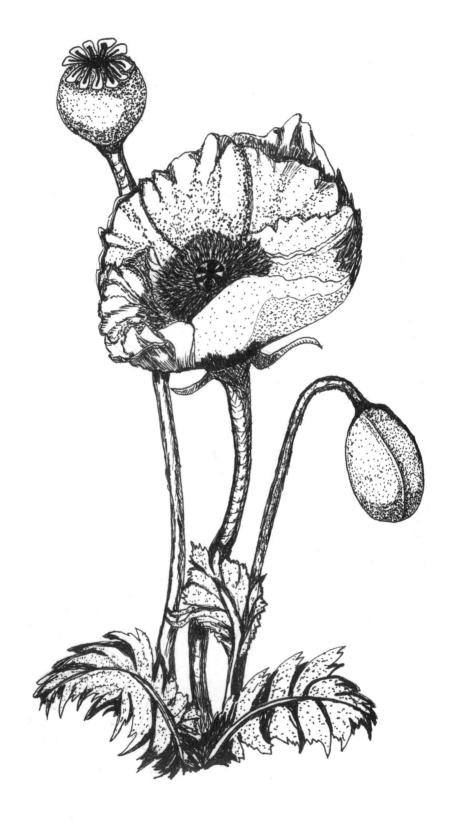

OPIUM POPPY
Papaver somniferum
The Plant of Many Wars

The opium poppy is infamous for its milky, latex sap. Chemically, the plant is rich in isoquinoline alkaloids, which contain a double carbon ring with a nitrogen atom. Commonly found in many species of the family Papaveraceae, these narcotic alkaloids have pain-relieving and sleep-inducing effects, but are also highly addictive; they include codeine, papaverine, noscapine, thebaine, and morphine (named, incidentally, after the god of sleep, Morpheus). In Latin, *somniferum* means "to sleep." Since antiquity, records have indicated that parents in South Asia, the Middle East, and southern Europe gave small doses of raw opium to babies and children to help them get to sleep, although many became addicted.

Commercial opium fields in undisclosed locations cultivate poppies for legal uses. Here an old method known as "poppy straw" governs the harvest; farmers cut dried stalks with pods, or capsules, containing seeds still attached. They later remove the seeds when they release the crop for the culinary market, and any raw opium is extracted from the capsules. Poppy seed bagels owe their seeds to the plant, and although they don't contain any ingredient that gives narcotic effects, consumption of poppy seeds can give a positive result during urine tests for drugs. The seeds have even found use in some cakes, and as a source for making edible and healthy oils.

Archeologists have discovered artifacts from Sumeria, dated to 4000 B.C., that depict opium poppies. The Minoans cultivated the plant, though it was the ancient Greeks who bestowed the name *opium*. In some cultures, people used the plant to fight asthma, improve eyesight, and treat stomach illnesses. A number of writers depict opium (and its effects) in their books, including L. Frank Baum (the poppy field scene in *The Wonderful Wizard of Oz*) and Thomas De Quincey (*Confessions of an English Opium Eater*). The famous French composer Hector

Berlioz was known to use opium and claimed it as his inspiration for *Symphonie Fantastique,* a fable where a young artist uses opium to experience visions of an unrequited love. Historically, people have treated opium as a cure-all for many ailments; the plant has not always suffered the detrimental reputation it has today. In fact, the Royal College of Anaesthetists even displays on its coat of arms the flower and fruit of an opium plant.

Opium Wars

Opium caused two wars between China on one side and allies Britain and France, once in 1839 and again in 1860, as a result of China's efforts to stop the smuggling of opium into China by Western traders. The use of opium in China had reached almost epidemic proportions. The first war ended with China's opening of eleven ports for legal importing of opium, under the Treaty of Tianjin. China later tried to block this agreement, which led to the Second Opium War, itself concluding with the occupation and burning of the Imperial Summer Palace in Beijing by British and French forces. In Afghanistan in 2004, after beating the Taliban forces, NATO commanders, as part of their plan to "win the hearts and minds" of the local Afghans, hatched a plan to destroy opium fields previously financed by the Taliban. Analysis showed, however, that this would wipe out local economies, so orders were changed to destroy only large fields and leave the small crops untouched.

During the U.S. Civil War, stores of morphine were frequently more plentiful to the troops than food rations, such that veterans on both sides, an estimated fifty thousand, became opium addicts. In 1900, morphine addiction was considered such a serious social epidemic that a group called the St. James Society offered free heroin in the mail to anyone wishing to kick morphine.

OREGANO
Origanum vulgare
A Dash of Joy

Oregano, a perennial herb scientifically known as *Origanum vulgare*, is a common species of the genus *Origanum* of the mint family. Oregano is indigenous to warm, temperate regions, mainly in Europe and the Mediterranean. The plant grows from 1 to 2 feet tall with 3-inch-long leaves and longer purple-colored flowers. Some refer to the plant by its nickname, *wild marjoram*.

Origanum vulgare is a perennial, woody-based, aromatic shrub. The ovate, or egg-shaped, olive-green leaves appear opposite each other on the stem. The edges of the leaves are shallowly jagged, and the tips may be pointed or rounded. The purple flowers sit clustered on short, dense terminal or lateral spikes that have colors ranging from white to purple. Oregano favors summer months; a hot, dry climate is better for the

Ancient peoples of Europe used oregano as a food preservative and as an antidote against certain poisons. The father of medicine, Hippocrates, used it to cure stomach problems and respiratory ailments. The word oregano *derives from the Greek* oros granos, *meaning "the joy of the mountains."*

plant, as it's not able to survive in colder temperatures. Most experts advise planting oregano in early spring, in comparatively dry soil and in a region where it can enjoy full sun.

Culinary Herb

Oregano finds an extensive use in kitchens as a culinary herb. The leaves of this plant, both dried and fresh, have a warm, slightly bitter taste and an aromatic smell, and are used for flavoring many dishes. More recently, oregano has gained popularity as the staple herb of Italian-American cuisine; added to pizza sauce, it gives an extraordinary flavor. A wide variety of cuisines, from areas such as Turkey, Palestine, Egypt, and Greece to Latin America, make use of this herb. In Turkey its most common use is to flavor mutton and lamb. Homemade oregano butter is used in soups, salads, and pasta. Oregano also contains therapeutic essential oils.

Medicinal Uses

Since ancient times, oregano has served as a medicinal herb in treating conditions ranging from fever, jaundice, diarrhea, and indigestion to vomiting—all beginning with Hippocrates. The volatile oil extracted from this plant contains carvacrol and thymol, both well known for their antiseptic and antiviral abilities to help control the growth of bacteria, release phlegm, ease burning sensations in the digestive tract, and wipe out most worms or fungi. Its antioxidant properties make oregano helpful in the treatment of high blood pressure, heart disease, and even cancer. When used externally, oregano oils have been successful in relieving muscle and joint pains, swelling, and sores.

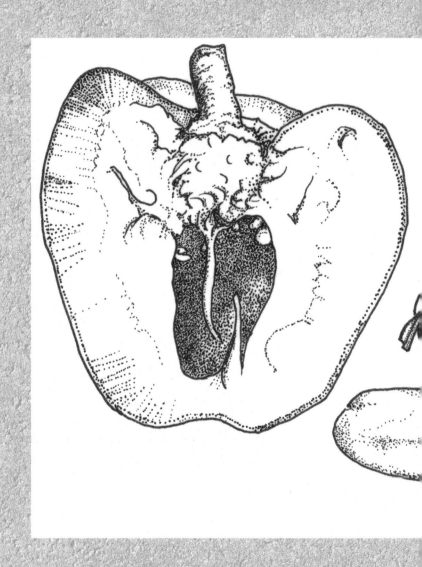

PAPRIKA
Capsicum annuum
The First Spice?

Paprika is a popular spice of the *Capsicum* genus. It is red or deep orange, comes in powdered form, and plays a role in many cuisines around the world, including Chinese, Mexican, Indian, Hungarian, and American.

Paprika, the plant, is native to North America and South America. However, many believe its evolutionary forerunners originated in Hungary. Eventually, it spread far and wide, apparently carried on foot by nomadic races as they traversed the globe. Certain wild varieties

or ancestors of paprika also evolved, perhaps separately, in southern Brazil and Bolivia. Archeological research suggests that paprika was first adapted to domestic use at least six thousand years ago. Aztecs in Mexico knew its numerous varieties before the arrival of the Spanish. Christopher Columbus brought *Capsicum annuum* seeds back to Europe. Cultivation was popularized in Africa, China, India, and other parts of Asia soon after its introduction to Europe, beginning in the 1500s. Now it is grown in almost all countries for domestic as well as commercial uses.

Capsicum annuum grows most productively in dry and warm seasons. Paprika plants occupy little space and are easy to grow, adapting to different soils with little need for fertilizers. It takes at least three months to produce its first fruit, or peppers, after reproduction; the fruit will change in color from green to yellow and to red, mostly commonly referred to as paprika pepper. Farmers then sun-dry the pepper for three or four days— once the pepper can be easily crumbled by hand, it is ready to be changed into paprika powder. After simple grinding or mashing, the peppers become the paprika spice with which we are most familiar. Picked fresh, the pepper remains safe to eat for at least one year. It's no wonder the earliest nomads carried this plant with them; it might well be the first culinary spice used in humans' primitive cuisine.

Uses of Paprika

People generally use paprika to color rice and add flavor to foods, including soups. The spice is also part of ayurvedic medicine (a traditional system of health science in India), meant to relieve pain. Practitioners combine the powder with sesame oil and other herbs to make an external application to alleviate muscular spasm and joint disorders, especially rheumatoid arthritis. In other countries, people use paprika as a home remedy for gout, dyspepsia, and paralysis. Still others use the spice to lower blood pressure and to aid in the killing of cancer cells.

Concerns

Capsicum annuum should not be used in excess in the form of lotions or creams. These can cause burning sensations in the chest or throat, and gastritis. Likewise, one should avoid use before and after surgery, as it can increase bleeding due to its anticoagulant properties. Make sure to cease *Capsicum annuum* use at least two weeks prior to surgery.

PEYOTE
Lophophora williamsii
Sacred Medicine

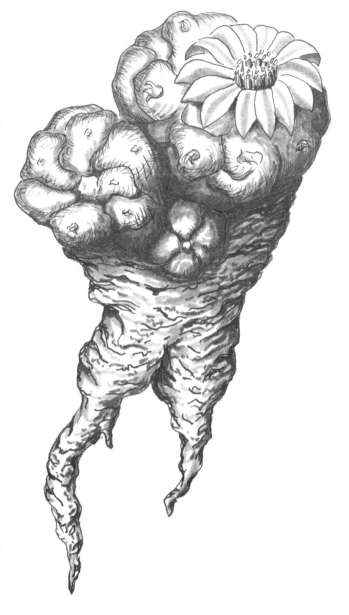

Scientifically termed *Lophophora williamsii,* peyote is a small, spineless cactus plant, indigenous to southwestern Texas and Mexico. The name *peyote* comes from a Spanish word meaning "to glisten," which aptly describes the beauty of this fascinating creature of nature. The word is actually derived from the Nahuatl people, who called the plant *peyotl.* Native North Americans, such as the Huicho of northern Mexico and various local American tribes, have used peyote for at least 5,500 years, according to historians.

Since the early nineteenth century, Native American religious practitioners have used this distinct species of cactus for religious, ceremonial, and healing purposes, considering peyote a sacred medicinal herb, able to combat physical, spiritual, and social ills. The U.S. Bureau of Indian Affairs permitted its use after Native Americans compared its religious significance to that of the Eucharist for Christians. Dr. John Raleigh Briggs, a Texas physician, was first to draw attention to peyote's chemical composition, believing it could have beneficial uses in Western medicine.

Peyote, part of the genus *Lophophora,* grows near the ground and forms groups of numerous, bluish green, reddish green, or yellowish green shoots. These new shoots have sunken tips that form as flattened spheres and can reach only short heights of ½ to 2 inches but are twice as broad. A yellowish or whitish hair, appearing like clustered strands of wool, arises from the cusp areoles. Peyote, a spineless cactus, develops blooms, mostly pinkish in color, which open during the day, reaching a width of maybe ¼ inch.

The plant sporadically bears flowers, which then give rise to edible fruit—small, club shaped, with fleshy outgrowths containing tiny black and pear-shaped seeds. Slow growing, and with strikingly beautiful flowers, peyote can withstand extreme temperatures, and hot and humid climates are actually favorable for its germination. Although the plant can grow at altitudes as high as 4,000 feet, its primary habitat is semiarid regions and deserts, preferably in soil rich in limestone.

Wide Uses of Peyote

Many interpret the effects of ingesting peyote to be spiritual in nature, making it a renowned herb among many, particularly Native Americans. The substantial percentage of phenethylamine alkaloids, mainly mescaline, gives the plant its psychoactive properties. The top of the cactus, referred to as the crown, is composed of buttons, shaped like discs, which harvesters cut from the ground and dry out. These buttons, when chewed or boiled with water to make tea, are a popular delivery method for the plant's psychoactive effects. Since the mixture is exceptionally bitter, many experience nausea before any desired visions occur. Cultivated peyote contains only dashes of the alkaloid, as compared to those harvested in the wild, and are thus less useful for trippers. Apart from this, Native American tribes have used the plant for curative purposes, employing peyote for treating varied ailments like toothache, labor pain, breast pain, skin diseases, colds, and fever.

PHILODENDRON
Philodendron scandens oxycardium
Toxic Decoration

Philodendron is a huge genus of more than 450 species of flowering plants; the number tends to vary, as many of the species are still unknown and unidentified. The second-largest member of the Araceae family is an assortment of fleshy-stemmed, climbing herbs, which commence their lives as vines and gradually transform into epiphytes. Many known species of this genus, such as the heartleaf, often serve as indoor houseplants. The Greek words *philo,* meaning "love," and *dendron,* meaning "tree," come together to give the genus its scientific name. It was Charles Plumier, a seventeenth-century Franciscan monk and a renowned vegetarian and botanist, who first discovered and classified this group of tropical American plants.

Philodendrons are popular worldwide for their decorative foliage. Natural-born climbers, these plants grow everywhere, and are adept at making homes and greenhouses look attractive. The genus contains a highly diverse set of species, coming in many shapes and sizes. They all tend to have long aerial roots with rich green leaves, which may be coppery red underneath or may bear red veins. Some possess heart-shaped leaves, while in some you may find long and narrow or arrow-shaped leaves; still others have ovate or deeply lobed ones. Sizes vary from 3 inches to 3 feet in length. Blossoms come in diverse colors, including shades of pink, red, purple, or greenish white, depending on the different species.

Philodendron is found in many diverse habitats of tropical America and the West Indies. Though most species under this genus prefer humid tropical forests, some may even grow on riverbanks, at roadsides, and in swamps. In many parts of the world, it is common to find a philodendron plant clambering over other plants or trunks of trees, using its aerial roots to gain access to sunlight. Shady spots outside your dwelling with mild climates and moist soil rich in organic matter are sufficient conditions for the growth of philodendrons.

Various species of the genus *Philodendron* have played a role in folk medicine, for a variety of purposes. People in the Amazonian region of Brazil have made medicinal use of different philodendron roots; *Philodendron fragrantissimum* is one such species and is used for both bathing and fumigation.

Philodendron kept as flowering houseplants contain some aroid toxins and calcium oxalate. Toxicosis might occur due to some of the proteins and amino acids not being suitable for human consumption. A philodendron also contains calcium oxalate, which acts as poison in humans and animals. Almost all parts of a philodendron flowering houseplant are toxic, but the leaves and stems are the most dangerous. If someone eats part of a philodendron flowering houseplant, poisoning can occur. Common symptoms of philodendron poisoning are pain or a burning sensation in the eyes, heartburn, loss of motor skills, skin irritation, and nausea. In severe conditions, slurred speech and swelling of the tongue and mouth can occur. The plants are poisonous to cats and dogs as well. There is no antidote, and pets that eat the plant can die from irreversible liver and kidney damage.

POISON IVY
Toxicodendron radicans
The Two-Sided Plant

Actually, *Toxicodendron radicans* isn't even a true ivy species (*Hedera*), but rather is a plant that produces a poisonous sap, urushiol, that can cause irritation, itching, or a painful rash if touched. This "ivy" comes in three forms: as a trailing vine 4 to 9 inches tall, as a climbing vine that grows on trees, and as a shrub that reaches 3 to 11 feet in height. It is native to North America, found primarily east of the Mississippi River. Native Americans used it both as a medicine and as a "chemical" weapon. The first Western colonists quickly discovered its dangerous effects and taught their young from an early age how to identify and avoid it. Eventually, they learned from the American natives that it also held valuable medicinal properties, and used it in herbal medicine to treat arthritis, paralysis, skin disorders, and as a sedative.

Poison ivy has trifoliate, alternate leaves 7 to 10 inches long; the leaf-lets are shiny green on the surface and paler below, ovate, and irregularly toothed. It is a monoecious species, with small, yellowish green flowers that are prevalent in spring and early summer. The fruits are white-greenish, oval, and grow to ¼ inch in diameter. Its slender twigs are gray or red-brownish, and its thick trunk or stalk is densely covered with aerial roots dark gray in color. All parts of the plant are toxic, not just the leaves, which many people don't know.

Still, poison ivy fruits are an important food for many birds, as well as other animals, particularly deer. These animals spread the seeds via defecation and help the plant's regeneration over large areas. Goats also like the plant very much and farmers often set them loose in fields to help control its spread. According to folklore, drinking milk from poison ivy–eating goats could transfer the plants' toxin to people, but there is no evidence to support this.

If you've been exposed to poison ivy's oil, you should wash the affected area within one hour after touching it, using lots of cold running water. Only soap without oils is safe—others can spread the rash. Washing the area with alcohol can be effective, if one rinses with water immediately after (so as not to strip the skin of its natural protective oils, thus making it more vulnerable to the spread of the rash). There is no simple antidote, although some have tried to find ways to build up a natural immunity. Others use the liquid from the jewelweed plant, which often grows near poison ivy, to treat poison ivy rashes.

Toxicodendron radicans *spread to England and Australia, where people today plant it in gardens for its color or as a border plant to dissuade thieves. People in England and Australia also learned that when dried in the sun, the sap turns black and thick like a lacquer. This by-product is used as a dye, a permanent ink, and an ingredient in varnishes.*

The Immunization Technique

As with a number of poisonous plants, many have willingly consumed poison ivy leaves in order to try to build up immunity. Some have been successful, starting with small doses and then increasing gradually until immunity was achieved. However, the side effects of this radical practice include getting internal rashes in the throat and stomach, which surely had to be a wriggling, itching nightmare. Some pharmaceuticals exist for the purpose of helping reduce poison ivy's more serious side effects, but no other immunization is yet available. As the saying goes, don't try this at home!

POTATO

Solanum tuberosum
World's Savior

Officially the world's favorite root vegetable and the fourth-largest food crop (following wheat, rice, and maize), the potato is a lifesaving plant that has provided food to millions of hungry people. In a vote to decide the most important events in human history, the discovery of the potato should rank high. There are more than 4,000 varieties of this plant, classi-fied into smaller groups such as whites, reds, yellows, russets, and so on. In the Andes (Chile, Peru, Bolivia, Ecuador, and Colombia, areas where the potato originated), there are 3,000 varieties, belonging to 9 species; there are also about 200 wild species and subspecies, some of which are crossbred with cultivated ones.

Spanish colonists discovered the plant and introduced it to Europe in the sixteenth century, after which it rapidly spread across the globe. Today annual consumption of potatoes is estimated to be at about sixty pounds per person. Agricultural historians point to the potato as a pri-mary reason for the rapid growth of the world population and urbaniza-tion between 1700 and 1900—this life-sustaining plant has truly altered history.

Southern Peru and northwest Bolivia grew domestic types of potatoes as early as 5000 B.C., and the crop was a main food source for the great Incan civilization. Today, according to United Nations estimates, world-wide production of potatoes is 330 million tons and growing!

The edible part of the plant, its root, actually belongs botanically to the nightshade family, which has a number of highly toxic members. Above its tuberous bulb root, a leafy stalk grows to 24 inches high. It bears white, red, pink, blue, or purple flowers, depending on the variety. Insects are mainly responsible for pollinating potato plants, the most active being the bumblebee, though there is also a significant rate of self-fertilization. Potatoes can grow in vastly diverse soils, which factors as another of their many gifts as an indelible food source.

The potato is an extremely important plant to the world economy. Amid the economic crisis in 2008, and as a preventive measure for possible world food problems, the United Nations declared 2008 as an International Year of the Potato. The agribusiness company Monsanto is a leader in creating genetically modified potatoes and all kinds of agriculture. Now there are many modified potato varieties that have been spliced with compounds from pesticides.

Famine

The Great Famine in Ireland in the nineteenth century is a prime example of how vital the potato is to human civilization. Back then, there was no diversity in potato strains, and farmers merely used one strain over and over again. Nevertheless, Europe, and Ireland in particular, had its entire crop infected with a disease—actually a fungus, *Phytophthora infestans*—named "late blight." Millions starved, and millions more fled to the United States. (In South America, the people plant different varieties within a crop, depending on the soil and altitude.)

Spuds

Etymologically, the word *potato* derives from the Spanish *patata,* which is considered a combination of the Taino word *batata,* meaning "sweet potato," and the Quechua word *papa*. An English botanist from the sixteenth century had used the terms "virginal potatoes" and "bastard potatoes" to distinguish the sweet potato from what he had called the common potato. The name *spud* for a small species of potato derives from the name of a sixteenth-century tool used to dig a hole before planting potatoes.

PSILOCYBIN
Psilocybe cubensis
Magical Mushrooms

Psilocybin, also known as psychedelic or "magic" mushrooms—or even simply as "shrooms"—are at once empowering, mystical, spiritual, recreational, and controversial, indeed dangerous. Some recommend them medicinally, while others have ruled them illegal. Mushrooms in this class all contain the psychoactive alkaloid psilocybin, present in about 40 species in genera such as *Galerina, Copelandia, Mycena, Pluteus,* and *Pholiotina*. There's substantial archeological evidence that humans have used psychedelic mushrooms since prehistoric times, and they frequently appear in cave art in different locations around the world. Since they grow in many regions, it makes sense that many cultures have been using mystical mushrooms for their religious and spiritual ceremonies for ages. Today they are also very popular and many people have taken to using them recreationally for their intense psychedelic effects.

Some of the most common effects of magical mushrooms if about 1 gram of dry mushroom is taken follow. Generally, one enjoys something resembling a spiritual experience, sometimes described as "sensing of God." The experience is also referred to as "ego death." Users claim they felt they were living in the "here and now"—a feeling of having no pain, no past, and no future, and just existing fully in the present. Mushrooms can produce an intense feeling of so-called uncensored perception—as if one is at last "seeing the real world." The experience is surely a radical shift from the usual state of survival-laden consciousness, replete with anxieties and drives to get things done, avoid dangers, and fulfill needs; it induces instead a "let-it-go" sort of mind-set, where one feels nothing is important but being a part of the universe.

But don't have too many illusions that this experience will happen to the user every time, or even once. Many have experienced radical fears and paranoid states of mind after ingesting psilocybin. Which type of effect the user will experience is dependent on his or her psychological background, so one should be extra cautious, as some of these mystical mushrooms are more than dangerous. *Amanita muscaria,* in particular, has the ability to induce permanent psychosis. Some, however, have even claimed that Jesus himself used these mushrooms to enter trancelike states before he began his three-year ministry—though this is a view hardly shared by most Christians.

On the medical front, studies have shown psilocybin mushrooms have the potential to resolve mental health issues such as obsessive-compulsive disorders and clinical depression in a way that is completely impossible for classical medicine to achieve or even understand. Nevertheless, the Imperial College in London claimed that under "proper" use psilocybin can act as an antidepressant. Moreover, some have begun investigations into using synthetic psilocybin not only for treating the most difficult mental health conditions but also for chronic cluster headaches.

Modern Times

Who else but Timothy Leary could have been the first to endorse the use of magical mushrooms in modern Western civilization (it makes some sense; he was also known to praise LSD)? Leary was inspired by an article in *Life* magazine from 1957, written by Valentina and Gordon Wasson, who were the first outsiders to participate in a traditional indigenous mushroom ceremony in Mexico. Leary, of course, traveled to Mexico to experience magical mushrooms firsthand. He returned to Harvard as a lecturer and researcher in 1960, but was dismissed in 1963, so he started propagating his psychedelic experience among the members of the hippie counterculture. The rest is history.

Even in present times, some native groups in central Mexico (and others throughout the world, such as Mazatecs, Nahua, Mixtecs, and Zapotecs) still use psilocybin mushrooms for traditional purposes. One of the greatest insights in the world of mystical mushrooms is given in the literary works of writer Carlos Castaneda, who described his reason for using the plants: "The aim is to balance the terror of being alive with the wonder of being alive."

How to Make a Zombie

Some plants are truly scary. They can turn people into real zombies. The name of such one plant says everything—*Devil's breath*. It grows in Colombia and contains the extremely mentally unpleasant drug scopolamine. There are reported cases of people who used this plant being turned into beings completely lacking free will. Similar effects are produced by *burundanga* plant, another South American "devil," able to wipe out the complete cognition of victims and make them unable to retain any information.

QUININE
Cinchona officinalis
Medicine Cabinet in a Tree

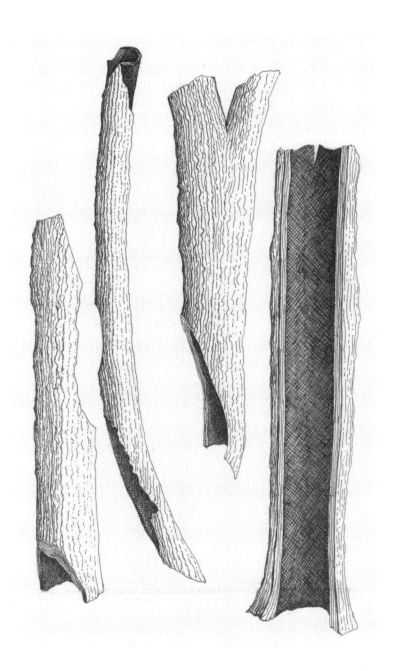

In the case of the cinchona tree—its quinine-producing bark in particular—nature once again confirms the old adage that cures for many diseases grow right before our eyes, if only we'd look. Cinchona is one of the few species of the family Rubiaceae that produces the famous antifever agent quinine, which also cures malaria, saving the lives of millions. Nowadays, it is the *Cinchona calisaya* variation of this tree that is most cultivated for quinine; the quinidine alkaloid found in its bark also contains other medically beneficial compounds, including cinchonine and cinchonidine alkaloids.

Carl Linnaeus named the genus in 1742, inspired by the Countess of Chinchón, the wife of Peru's viceroy, in 1638. Apparently considered open-minded for the times, the countess learned of the tree's medical benefits from native Quechua shamans and recommended it to her fellow colonists. However, even prior to that, records from the 1560s mention the miraculous healing properties of this tree. Jesuit missionaries introduced it as a "fever tree" in England in 1632. A Jesuit and naturalist, Bernabé Cobo, "discovered" it while exploring Mexico and Peru and then brought it to Spain and Italy. By the early nineteenth century, the tree bark's popularity had become so well-known that Peru outlawed cinchona seed exports, hoping to retain a monopoly. Nevertheless, British and Dutch traders smuggled out seeds and cuttings of the cinchona tree, leading to its cultivation in many parts of tropical Asia.

Botanically, *Cinchona officinalis* is an evergreen that grows as a small shrub or a tree, and can reach 16 to 49 feet tall, depending on the conditions. It has rounded to lanceolate leaves, ranging in length from 4 to 15 inches long. Its flowers grow in terminal panicles and come in white, pink, and red. The fruits actually look like oblong nuts and contain lots of seeds.

Other medical uses of the cinchona tree include increasing the appetite, treating bloating, promoting the release of digestive juices, and treating different stomach problems. Many have found it useful for treating various blood vessel problems such as hemorrhoids, leg cramps, and varicose veins. Still others have used it to treat swine flu, influenza, the common cold, fevers, throat diseases, muscle cramps, and enlarged spleens. That's not all: cinchona is also effective in eye lotions to numb pain and kill germs, and is used as an astringent. Even its extracts have found their way into treatments for baldness.

Like Cures Like

The movement known as homeopathy started as a result of experiments with cinchona bark. Samuel Hahnemann, considered the father of homeopathy, had been translating *Materia medica,* a famous book on botany and herbs by William Cullen, when he noticed a curious section on what was called "Peruvian bark" and its ability to reduce fever. Hahnemann then conducted experiments on himself, taking large daily doses of the bark. After two weeks he felt some symptoms similar to those of malaria, though when he reduced the quantity his fever reduced. This led to the premise on which homeopathy is based: "like cures like." In other words, treatments that cause a specific sort of illness in healthy people will cure the sick afflicted with the same disease.

RAGWEED
Ambrosia artemisiifolia
An American Allergen

Each year, millions of Americans develop ragweed allergy symptoms during the fall, when this plant is a literal pollen-producing mega-machine. One of the reasons for its widespread effects is the plant's great adaptability: it can grow nearly anywhere, and do so quickly. It grows along roadsides and riverbanks, and in other open spaces, which makes escaping from its vast, windborne pollen dispersal nearly impossible. Each plant boasts about a thousand male flowers, which can yield a billion pollen grains in total. If allergic, you can run, but you can't hide—the pollen will find you.

Ragweed is also known as common ragweed, of the genus *Ambrosia* and belonging to the sunflower family Asteraceae. Other names include *bloodweed* or *bitterweed*. The word *ambrosia* is believed to be derived from the ancient Greek term *ambrosia,* usually attributed to the special kind of drinks that the ancient gods on Mount Olympus sipped on their cloud cushions in the sky. Ragweed grows best in the temperate regions of South America and the Northern Hemisphere. It favors dry, sandy soils, or sunny, grassy plains, yet almost anywhere will do. There

Symptoms of ragweed allergy include watery eyes, sneezing, and swelling or itching of the tongue, the roof of the mouth, and the lips. However, these reactions can actually be avoided by eliminating the so-called trigger foods during ragweed pollination, including bananas, chamomile tea, cucumber, melons, and zucchini. The body thinks the proteins of the pollen are bad and kicks the immune system into action; these foods have similar proteins, and the combination can make one's immune system go into overdrive.

are 41 known varieties of ragweed throughout the world, many of them adapted to even arid climates and deserts. Most varieties are summer annual plants, 6 inches to 6 feet tall, and have egg-shaped long leaves. Its stems are green below the cotyledons—the first pair of leaves and seed clusters—after which the plant turns purple. Ragweed stems are straight and branched, with long, rough hairs, and they have a shallow taproot. Ragweed produces small green flowers, with both male and female flowers blooming on the same plant. Males usually bloom at the top, and then drop their pollen to the female flowers below. Its fruits are yellowish or reddish brown and less than $\frac{1}{10}$ inch long.

Although it causes many of us to wheeze and sneeze, ragweed is a great source of food and cover for different wildlife. Eastern cottontail rabbits love to munch on ragweed, as do a number of different species of grasshoppers. Birds such as the junco, meadow vole, brown-headed cowbird, purple finch, northern bobwhite, American goldfinch, mourning dove, and red-bellied woodpecker seek this plant for nourishment, thus making it a significant contributor to the ecosystem.

Double Trouble

Ragweed pollen is the subject of an interesting allegory. Some claim that while honey can help relieve allergy symptoms, certain types can actually make it worse. Although honeybees rarely visit ragweed, since its pollen is mostly dispersed by the wind, the bees do pick it up in their travels. Ragweed produces "clouds" of pollen around the area, and honeybees do get this abundant ragweed pollen attached to them. As such, honey produced during ragweed season can contain allergens that induce ragweed symptoms after ingestion.

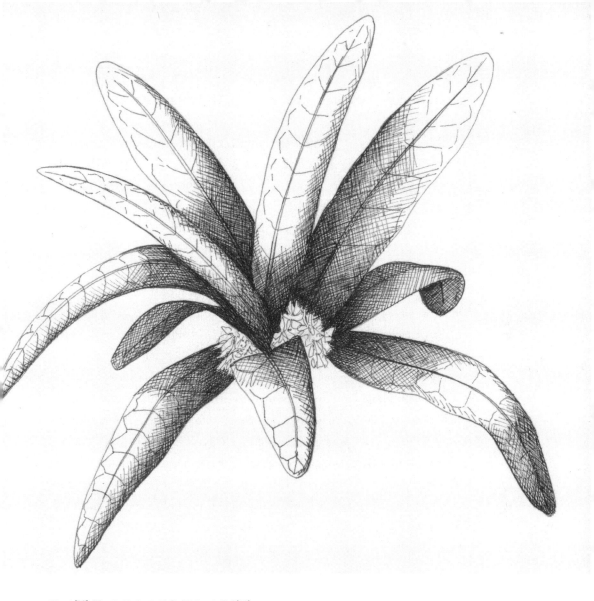

RAT POISON PLANT
Dichapetalum cymosum
Who's Killing the Cattle?

This dangerous little plant kills not only rats, but also much bigger animals. It is considered among the "big six" plants most toxic to cattle in Africa, and is concentrated the most in South Africa, where it originated. Statistically it's blamed for more than 8 percent of cases of poisoned cattle, most of which have occurred in Limpopo province. Sodium fluoroacetate is its main toxic element. The rat poison plant goes by many regional names—including *gifblaar* among Africans and *poison leaf* among Europeans.

On the surface, *Dichepetalum cymosum* (family Dichapetalaceae) appears like a small, dwarf woody shrub, no more than 6 to 10 inches tall. Despite its small size, its root system is huge, similar in length and span to that of much larger trees. Its leaves are bright green, alternately spaced, and simple, with fine hairs that later become glabrous, or smooth. The flowers are white and small and grow in dense clumps during the early spring. Its fruits are rare; the plants go for long periods bearing nothing. The fruits are orange and leathery when they do appear, and they are not toxic, at least to the San people of Africa. The rat poison plant is a perennial species, preferring plateau woodlands and shrub savannas with open, grassy vegetation and rocky and sandy soils. When mature, the plant's leaves appear to bulge.

Cymosum leaves are toxic not only to cattle, but to sheep and goats as well, though these animals consume the poison much less frequently than cows do. The only possible explanation is that cattle have bulk grazing habits, or a less selective style of eating, while sheep and goats are more selective, or perhaps they are simply smarter. Most poisonings occur during the late winter, before spring rains, when the plants sprout; however, poisoning can also occur during the late season, in autumn. There have been cases of poisoned carnivores, including dogs that ate meat from poisoned cattle carcasses.

Infected animals die from acute cardiac arrest, called chronic *gifblaar* poisoning. The poisoned animal first gets dyspnea (difficulty breathing) and arrhythmias, in addition to problematic neurological symptoms such as twitching, trembling, and convulsions. Death inevitably comes four to twenty-four hours after ingestion of *cymosum*. There are some rare cases in which animals initially survive eating *cymosum* leaves, but after a few months drop dead of heart failure.

Some Good with the Bad

There are a few mechanical methods of stopping the spread of these plants, but they are mostly ineffective because of the plant's phenomenal root system. Cut the plant at the base and it comes back. Even so, this cattle killer has some positive aspects: its roots are effective against diarrhea and some liver-associated problems, when given as a cooled infusion. In addition, according to a journal article published by the American Chemical Society, the rat poison plant could have some use in AIDS therapy. Nothing is ever black-and-white in the complex schematic of nature.

RATTAN
Calameae
Hard, Elastic, Useful, Punishing . . .

This plant provides material to make shelters, furniture, and a wide array of helpful products. One can also earn a living and run a business from cultivating it. Indeed many people do so, and trade in rattan products is estimated at $4 billion a year and growing. There are many village communities in Vietnam, Cambodia, and Laos whose entire economy is centered on rattan production and derived products. The plant belongs to the palm family Calameae (or Palmae) and grows between sea level and an altitude of 3,000 feet. There are 13 genera and more than 600 species of rattan, most of which are native to the tropical regions of Asia, Africa, and Australia. The commercially useful strains grow in hilly tropical areas, preferring an average temperature of 90 degrees Fahrenheit, with abundant rainfall. Consequently, the primary areas for rattan production are the tropical regions of South and Southeast Asia.

Rattan palms have different shapes, including high or low climbers,

and clustered or single-stemmed species. Some have very short and even underground stems, while some can reach 300 feet in length; however, all are only ½ inch in diameter, an elastic anatomical advantage that gives the palm its great versatility. Rattan is a very strong and adaptive species; its sheaths have spines for protection, along with "whip"-type shoots, which are also covered with spines. These are its hooks, of sorts, which play the main literally supporting role as the rattan grows and climbs and winds through and over trees and other plants in the jungle. In addition to lightness, durability, and flexibility, it's also very easy to harvest and transport in comparison to heavier timbers. Harvest and preparation are often done right where they grow; farmers dry those with small diameters in the sun, smoking them afterward with sulfur; they boil large ones in oil before drying, in order to protect the crop from insects.

Some species of rattan produce fruits that give a red resin called dragon's blood, used as a dye for violins and thought to have medical utility. In some Indian states, people treat the plant as a vegetable and prefer to eat it. Rattan is good for martial arts, too: long staves called *baston* are used for Filipino martial arts, such as *eskrima,* and also as striking weapons in some new and bloody full-contact combat sports. Other uses include (along with birch and bamboo) the handles in percussion mallets for vibraphones, marimbas, and xylophones, and for the stems used on high-end umbrellas.

However, as a result of over-exploitation, such as the harvesting of immature plants before they seed, forest degradation threatens to endanger many rattan species. The rush for immediate economic gain can affect the whole ecosystem in these tropical regions. Also, the pro-

Wooden Leg

Recent discoveries suggest rattan has spectacular potential as a bone replacement. Called "wood to bone," this process produces artificial bones for people by first placing small pieces of rattan in a furnace and then mixing them with calcium and carbon. This produces a close replica of bone material, which bodies do not seem to reject—a truly amazing feat. European Union countries plan to start using these "wood" implants in 2015.

cessing of rattan with toxic chemicals affects the soil, air, and water resources of its growing areas, which can seriously shrink these once-suitable habitats.

Rattan Punishments

Rattan sticks were once a tool for corporal punishment in English and Welsh schools. The infamous ritual that accompanied this act required the student to drop his trousers or lift her skirt, bend over a table, and receive the whacks from the rattan on his or her butt. Even today, some schools in Malaysia, Singapore, and a few African countries use rattan for this purpose. It's still a punishment employed by the Singapore armed forces, as well as a judicial corporal punishment allowed in Brunei, Singapore, and Malaysia. The greater the crime, the thicker the rattan used for castigation.

REDWOOD
Sequoioideae
Ambassador from Another Time

This redwood genera subfamily of the family Cupressaceae gives us the biggest, tallest, and most massive trees in the known history of the planet. The world record is held by a *Sequoiadendron giganteum,* measured at 311 feet tall and 56 feet in diameter. The oldest known living redwood (according to its ring counting) is 3,500 years old. Redwood is an ancient taxon: a *Sequoia jeholensis* has shown up in deposits dating from the Jurassic era. The fossils have shown that the genera originated in the northern parts of the globe, which conclusion is supported by genera of redwood found in the Arctic Circle, northern Europe, and North America, as well as throughout Asia and Japan. Its evolutionary

adaptation shows that as the climate was changing, the species migrated southward to survive. Could this impulse for life be attributed to an unfathomable type of consciousness among plants?

There are three known redwood species: the first two are *Sequoia sempervirens* and *Sequoiadendron giganteum,* from California and Oregon, which are the largest in the world; the third, *Metasequoia glyptostroboides,* found in China, is a much smaller species. All are endangered, which means we are on the verge of losing some of the oldest and tallest plant forms on the planet, purely as a result of humans—supposedly the most enlightened forms of consciousness ever to walk the planet. Actually, the Chinese *Metasequoia* is so rare, it was considered extinct until a forester found one in 1948, in the Hubei region; luckily he didn't cut it down. Attempts to reestablish it are under way.

There are two California redwood species, as well as the Chinese redwood from 1948, that people have successfully cultivated in habitats far beyond their native areas. These attempts were successful, so today some redwoods can be found in botanical gardens, public parks, and private lands within similar climates throughout the world, particularly in the northwestern and eastern United States and some areas in China, the United Kingdom, and Germany, all of which gives hope for further migration and adaptation of the species.

Redwoods reproduce both sexually and asexually through layering, sprouting buds, or lignotubers, which are woody burls or knobs that form on the root crown. The seeds appear after the tenth year of age, when large crops are frequent, although the feasibility of the tree producing seeds is very low. Redwoods reproduce primarily by burls, which occur as lignotubers appearing on the tree, usually 10 feet below the soil surface; burls sprout into new plants when detached from the mother tree, particularly after a forest fire, although botanists still do not fully understand the process. Redwoods actually benefit from flooding and flood deposits, which can result in rapid growth. Throughout its evolution, the species have obviously learned to use everything possible to survive.

Silence and Awe

The great John Steinbeck wrote about the redwood: "The redwoods, once seen, leave a mark or create a vision that stays with you always. No one has ever successfully painted or photographed a redwood tree. The feeling they produce is not transferable. From them comes silence and awe. It's not only their unbelievable stature, nor the color, which seems to shift and vary under your eyes, no, they are not like any trees we know, they are ambassadors from another time."

The Top 10

Here is a list of the largest known redwoods, with their name, height, diameter, volume, and location, as measured in 2009.

1. **The Lost Monarch:** 321 feet tall, 26.0 feet in diameter, 42,500 cubic feet, located in Jedediah Smith Redwoods State Park, Crescent City, California.
2. **Melkor:** 349 feet tall, 22.4 feet in diameter, 39,100 cubic feet, in Redwood National Park, Crescent City, California.
3. **Iluvatar:** 300 feet tall, 20.5 feet in diameter, 37,500 cubic feet, in Prairie Creek Redwoods State Park, Orick, California.
4. **Del Norte Titan:** 307 feet tall, 23.7 feet in diameter, 37,200 cubic feet, in Jedediah Smith Redwoods State Park.
5. **El Viejo del Norte:** 324 feet tall, 23.0 feet in diameter, 35,400 cubic feet, in Jedediah Smith Redwoods State Park.
6. **Howland Hill Giant:** 330 feet tall, 19.8 feet in diameter, 33,580 cubic feet, in Jedediah Smith Redwoods State Park.
7. **Sir Isaac Newton:** (strange name, as redwoods don't produce apples) 299 feet tall, 22.5 feet in diameter, 33,192 cubic feet, in Prairie Creek Redwoods State Park.
8. **Terex Titan:** 270 feet tall, 21.3 feet in diameter, 32,384 cubic feet, in Prairie Creek Redwoods State Park.
9. **Adventure Tree:** 334 feet tall, 16.5 feet in diameter, 32,140 cubic feet, in Prairie Creek Redwoods State Park.
10. **Bull Creek Giant:** 339 feet tall, 22.3 feet in diameter, 31,144 cubic feet, in Humboldt Redwood State Park, Weott, California.

RHODODENDRON

Rhododendron ferrugineum

"The Day We Were Lying Among the Rhododendrons"

The ancient Greek name for rhododendron means "rose tree," most probably arising from the Greeks' tendency to classify all beautiful flowers simply as "roses." The spectacular flowers of the rhododendron, however, deserve poetic descriptions all their own; theirs is a different kind of beauty, not as mysterious as the rose's, but gentler, purer, and more innocent. It is a genus with about 1,000 species of mostly woody plants of the heath or heather family, Ericaceae; some are evergreen or deciduous, but nearly all bear large flowers. There are also two subgenera of rhododendron, the more famous of which is *Azalea*, which botanically differs by containing more anthers per flower. Rhododendron is native to Asia, Europe, North America, and Australia, while the highest diversity is found in the Himalayas (it is the national flower of Nepal) and East Asia. Most people grow the tree for its flowers, which usually bloom in spring; the deciduous rhododendrons give flowers both in spring and autumn.

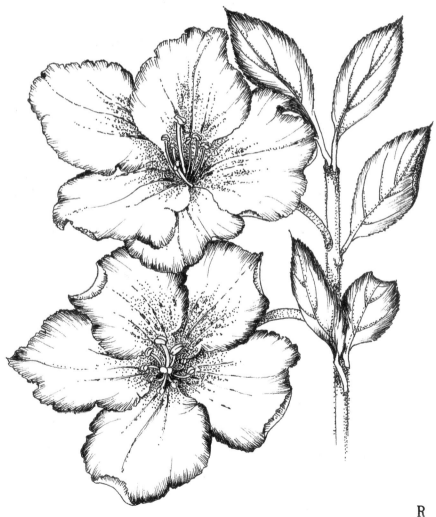

Some rhododendrons grow as shrubs of less than 5 feet tall, while some are large trees, such as the *Rhododendron protistum* var. *giganteum,* which soars up to 98 feet high. Generally, leaves appear in spirals, about ½ inch long in the small species, but can be as large as 23 inches long in some varieties—like the *Rhododendron sinogrande.* Some rhododendrons have their leaves covered with scales or hairs on the underside. The most valued species have many leaf clusters, bearing large flowers.

Sometimes, beauty isn't enough, and certain species of rhododendrons have earned the classification "invasive." *Rhododendron ponticum* in Great Britain is one such example; this variety dominates other plants because of its wide-spreading roots, which constantly give new shoots and out-compete other species for resources. Rhododendrons have fibrous roots and prefer well-drained, highly organic soils; cultivation requires mulching and careful watering before the plant is established. So much is the plant beloved that people have produced 28,000 hybrids of the species to date.

Some rhododendrons are even edible. In Nepal people use the flowers for their sour taste. Fresh or dried flowers have also found their way into fish curries, as many believe this combination makes their bones softer, more supple, and less likely to break. In the state of Uttarakhand, India, people make rhododendron juice called *buran,* which is also the Indian name for rhododendron.

The tree's flowers have significant cultural symbolism. Certain types serve as national flowers (or trees) in the Indian states of Kashmir and Sikkim, while in the United States the so-called mountain laurel, or *Kalmia latifolia,* is the state flower of Pennsylvania.

In the famous James Joyce novel *Ulysses,* the flower plays an important and symbolic role in Molly and Leopold's courtship. In a soliloquy, Molly remembers: "The sun shines for you he said the day we were lying among the rhododendrons on Howth head in the grey tweed suit and his straw hat the day I got him to propose to me." The rhododendrons' beautiful flowers have of course been the source of much inspiration in the world of literature. British author Jasper Fforde, for example, has used the rhododendron as a motif in most of his books.

Sherlock's Toxin

Despite its symbolism of innocent love and simple beauty, some rhododendrons have a toxic element. Their pollen and nectar contain grayanotoxin, poisonous to grazing animals and to humans. Xenophon, for example, describes a strange behavior of Greek soldiers who had consumed honey in a village surrounded by rhododendrons. The Pompeiian soldiers had similar problems from honey produced by bees feeding on rhododendron flowers. Such problems had been reported in Turkey in the 1980s. The most suspected species with this toxic nectar are *Rhododendron ponticum* and *Rhododendron luteum,* both from Asia Minor. This effect of rhododendron was mentioned in the 2009 film *Sherlock Holmes,* in which the master detective considers the plant's ability to help a person fake a death.

ROSE
Rosa
Beauty Itself

The rose is inspiration, legend, myth, divine scent, and transcendence, made all the more mysterious by its guard of thorns. There are 100 species in the genus *Rosa,* all bearing flowers of immense symbolic importance. This plant seems to require deeper speculation than other plants: What is beauty, the rose asks, and why does it exist? Can something truly beautiful be innocent? These reflections have permeated numerous cultures and made the rose a perfect symbol of beauty. Unlike other flowers, which may be merely pretty, roses seem to encapsulate the irony that all beauty is fleeting and often accompanied by thorns, or a terrible danger of some kind.

The rose belongs to the genus *Rosa* (Rosaceae family), which grow as shrubs or climbing (trailing) plants, with stems containing sharp thorns that are actually *prickles*. Its scientific name comes from the Latin *rosa,* derived from the Old Greek *rhodon*. Species vary in size, and their flowers

come in a spectrum of white, red, burgundy, yellow, and (rarely) lavender. There are now numerous hybrids that boast different color combinations, even a pure blue one. The plant is native to Asia, northwest Africa, Europe, and North America—the most characteristically rose-shaped variety is from a species commonly called *American Beauty*. Rose bushes can grow up to 21 feet tall. After the flowers bloom, the bush produces red fruits, called rose hips or rose hep, which are rich with vitamin C. Rose hips are food for some birds (thrushes, finches, waxwings), which aid in dispersing the seeds.

In addition to the flowers' beauty, roses have a sweet fragrance that has long been used as a perfume. Bulgaria and Iran produce what are considered the best rose perfumes; these usually employ the Damask rose (*Rosa damascena*), which originated in Syria. The perfumes are made from rose oil, also known as *attar.* The technique requires collecting a mixture of volatile essential oils from the stem and a distillation of the petals of roses. It takes about 2,000 flowers to yield only 1 gram of rose oil!

Roses are also sometimes used in foods and drinks. Hips are an ingredient in jelly, marmalade, tea, and syrup, as well as in rose hip seed oil, used for skin and makeup products. Syrup made from rose petal extract is widely popular in France; Americans use it to make marshmallows and scones. Rose flowers are also used for flavoring some meals. A traditional English confection is rose cream, which is a rose-flavored condiment, covered in chocolate and topped with crystallized petals. Medicinal applications are minor, though traditional Chinese medicine makes extensive use of *Rosa chinensis* for stomach problems.

Which Color Do You Prefer?

From a sociocultural and symbolic point of view, rose colors carry nearly universal meanings. The red rose represents love, romance, beauty, and perfection; the white one means innocence and purity; the burgundy rose symbolizes grace, elegance, admiration, appreciation, and joyfulness; the yellow rose expresses warmth, friendship, and happiness; orange is for desire, enthusiasm, passion, excitement, and fervent romance; while the amazing lavender rose is a symbol of enchantment and love at first sight.

SANDBOX TREE
Hura crepitans
Don't Mess with Me

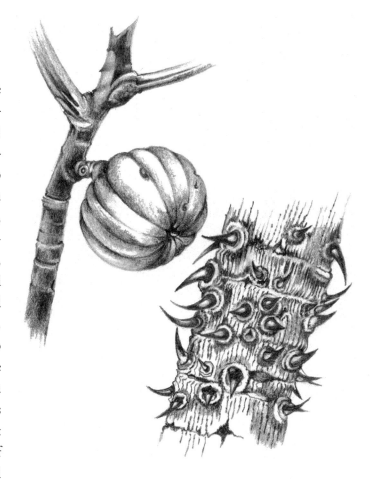

The sandbox tree is one of two species (*Hura crepitans* and *Hura polyandra*) of the large family *Euphorbiaceae*. It is native to tropical regions of South America, the Caribbean, Mesoamerica, the Amazon rain forest in Brazil, China, and Australia, and grows best in wet soil and partially shaded areas. Sandbox trees grow up to 195 feet and have ovate (egg-shaped) leaves, with shiny purple blossoms that are more than 2 feet in width. The trunk of the tree has dark, pointed thorns, which are 1 to 1½ inches wide at their base, and act as a sort of natural barbed wire. Because of this feature, many have come to call the trees "monkey no-climb trees."

Sandbox flowers are red in color, but have no petals. Female flowers blossom at the axil (the space between leaf and stem or branch), whereas the male flowers grow on the long spikes and also have no petals. Flower stalks are up to 5 inches long. The tree's fruit is a large, pumpkin-shaped seed capsule, which explodes violently when ripe. This launches the seeds all around at a speed of 160 miles per hour and to incredible distances of 300 feet. The fruit of this plant is literally a bomb! The shrapnel of this botanical capsule contains flattened, circular seeds, with dolphin-shaped sections. From its burstlike strategy of seed dispersal, the tree is sometimes also called *the dynamite tree.*

Known Properties

Sandbox trees were introduced as boulevard trees to decorate urban landscapes, since they are hardy enough to grow in polluted environs and between buildings. However, their poisonous leaves, bark, and exploding capsules frequently caused injury to humans and livestock, making the sandbox one of the most ferocious trees in existence. Serious stomachache, vomiting, diarrhea, temporary problems in vision, and rapid heartbeat result when humans ingest the seeds.

In some regions, people use sandbox wood to make furniture, called *hura.* Fishermen use its milky, caustic sap to poison fish. In the Caribbean, arrows dipped in its toxic sap, or latex, were once a staple of hunts. Before the advent of fountain pens, the unripe seedpods of the trees were cut in half, with each half used to make a pen, hence the name. In the past, people cultivated these trees for medicinal and ornamental purposes. The latex even proved useful for addressing decayed teeth; with a small dab of the latex, an aching tooth will fall out on its own within hours. The sap also proved useful in treating rheumatism and killing intestinal worms. The United States even uses the sap in the manufacture of tear gas shells. Others have used it to great effect as a treatment for leprosy, as it dries the lacerations caused by the disease. The plant can also cause a skin disease called dermatitis, however, when skin is exposed to the sap for only a short period of time. Lumberjacks who cut this tree must wear face masks to take extra care to cover their eyes because the sap can cause temporary blindness. This is one tree that employs serious warrior tactics, both chemical (sap) and physical (sharp thorns), to ensure its survival.

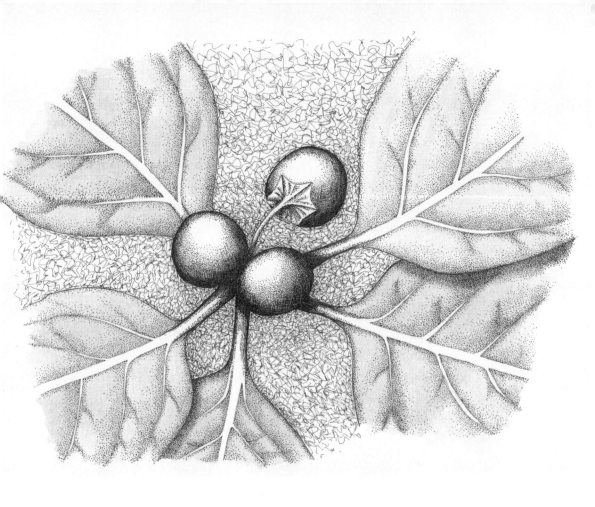

SATAN'S APPLE
Mandragora officinarum
Just One Bite

Mandragora officinarum is a species of plant native to central and southern Europe. Historically, people have associated the plant with a variety of superstitious practices. *Satan's apple,* or *mandrake,* is actually a common name that is given to plants that belong to the nightshade family. It is a very pretty plant, with attractive flowers that grow in the middle of huge, beautiful green leaves. These flowers remain in bloom for more than a month; the plant retains its leaves even during milder winters, an uncommon ability that adds to this plant's mystery. The tree can self-pollinate, since it has both the male and female parts (also known as a hermaphrodite or having hermaphroditic capabilities) that generally pollinate with the help of insects.

The plant has egg-shaped leaves that grow into a flowerlike pattern. The leaves can be very long, sometimes looking a lot like tobacco leaves. The color of the flowers can vary anywhere from white to purple, and the fruits look like small tomatoes and generally become ripe in the later months of summer. The plant needs almost no shade at all. The roots of the plant look similar to a human body, with a plump center, two lower roots (or legs), and two additional root extensions that look like arms.

Every part of the mandrake is poisonous. If eaten raw, the fruit will kill, but if it is cooked and boiled, the toxicity can be neutralized. The name *Satan's apple* arises from the fruit's edible appearance, which tempts one to pluck it right off the tree for a bite—a nasty deception for an unsuspecting person. Unless truly desperate for food, one should avoid consuming the plant at all costs. The roots are the most poisonous part, as they contain a combination of dangerous chemicals such as atropine, scopine, scopolamine, and hyoscyamine.

Satan's apple played a role in the treatment of certain medical conditions in ancient times. One such potential benefit comes from a chemical extracted from the mandrake, which is a useful topical ointment to treat warts.

Some people used the plant to enhance the libido, claiming it could cure impotency in low dosages. In reality, it is dangerous in any dosage and is not fit for human consumption. However, ancient physicians (especially Arabian) used the plant as an anesthetic before performing surgery. It was also a well-recognized painkiller at one time. Today even alternative medicine shies away from Satan's apple, due to its hazardous effects on humans. The root has narcotic and hallucinogenic effects as well—a possible explanation for the belief that the plant could cure impotency.

SKUNK CABBAGE
Symplocarpus foetidus
A Shrewd Stench

Skunk cabbage, also known as *meadow cabbage,* is a foul-smelling plant that grows in wet areas. The odor emanating from the plant, especially when the leaves are crushed or broken, bears a stark similarity to the smell emitted by skunks. This plant is native to eastern North America.

Skunk cabbage has large leaves, about 21 inches long and 16 inches wide. The plant first flowers in the spring and afterward grows its longer leaves throughout the summer. New cabbages appear as a small shoot or a spathe that emerges from the ground. The spathe is a brownish purple pod, which covers another part called a spadix that is covered with tiny yellow flowers. The plant is not poisonous to the touch, but its nasty odor gives a kick to the senses. The smell it generates is an effective adaptation to keep big animals away from foraging on it or damaging it in any way.

Stinks on Purpose

The skunk cabbage apparently realized that flies could survive better in the decaying wetlands than other types of insects. Hence it produced a chemical to imitate something dead to attract pollinators. In fact, the plant produces the same compounds, namely putrescine and cadavarine, found in rotting animal cadavers.

Habitat and Life Cycle

Skunk cabbage grows in freshwater wetlands, as well as near rivers and streams. It has an ability to generate temperatures up to 95 degrees Fahrenheit, which enables it to shoot out of the frozen ground. It is often the first flower that blooms during the late winter season. This unique ability to generate heat helps it to spread its odor in the air. The carrion-loving insects, which are also among the first to emerge in spring, are most attracted to the plant, fooled into thinking they have found something to eat and unaware the plant is duping them. Once successfully pollinated, the plant transfers its energies to its leaves. In autumn, these leaves fall to the ground and rot, but they do not dry up and crumble, like other leaves. They in fact dissolve into the soil, creating for the plant its own patch of fertilizer for next year's crop. The leaves are poisonous to mammals.

From midsummer to fall, an egg-shaped fruit, green in color, starts growing in the mud around the plant. This fruit turns black as it grows, with white flesh and seeds around the border. After growth, the roots contract, pulling the plant into the ground farther and making it sink deeper and deeper into the earth. They reproduce by hard seeds, which fall into the ground and are transported by animals or water—proving, perhaps, that this stinking plant is smarter than we think, having mastered every aspect of survival in its given environment.

Medicinal Uses

When boiled in oil, skunk cabbage leaves make an ointment useful in treating ringworm as well as sores and swelling. Tea made out of the roots and seeds can help improve the immune system by acting as an expectorant. Medicines made from the plant have proven useful in the treatment of arthritis, edema, and epilepsy.

Other Uses

The fallen leaves give shelter to ants and other insects. The heat generated by the flowers melts the snow in the soil and also gives warmth to other small animals around it. Birds such as the yellowthroat build their nests in the hollow of large skunk cabbage leaves. Native Americans have used skunk cabbage extensively—in medicinal remedies, as a talisman, and in their cooking. Today, some knowledgeable woodsfolk know how to dry out the leaves, boil off the toxins, and use the product in soups and stews.

SPHENOPHYLLUM
Reconstruction of a Fossil

Sphenophyllum is a genus of extinct plants believed to have flourished at end of the Devonian and the beginning of the Triassic period— estimated at about 360 to 251 million years ago. Today, the plant is known only through fossils, so we only have reconstructions to give us a picture of this prehistoric plant. It's now scientifically accepted that *Sphenophyllum* was a shrub or a creeping vine. It had node-internode architecture, meaning it had jointed stems, which has led current botanists to connect it to modern horsetails. Its branches and leaves were ordered in whorls at each node, similar to the later *calamites,* but it is obvious from the fossils that the *Sphenophyllum* leaves had a trian-

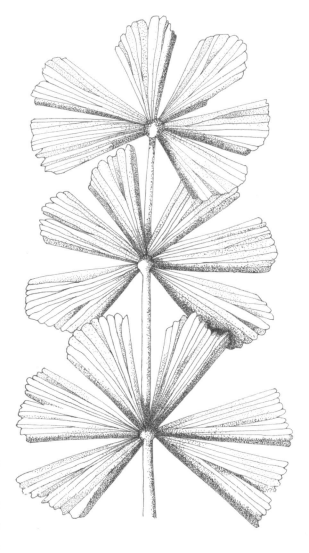

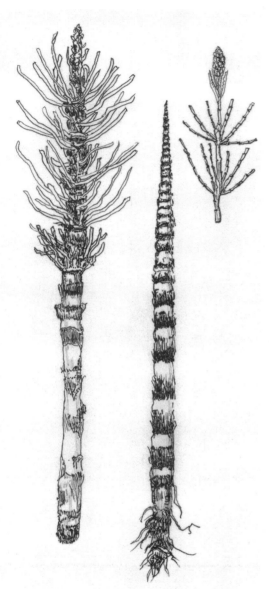

gular shape. The spore-bearing cones are also considered similar to those of calamites and horsetails.

Sphenophyllum lacked a central stem, which posed a handicap in transferring water to cells throughout the plant. Fossil reconstruction shows it probably grew in floodplains or swamps. These were small plants, growing to a maximum of 3 feet, with slender branches that were ribbed and joined by other stems, which gave it a vinelike or shrublike shape.

The anatomy of the stems was protostelic, or rootlike, with a solid main xylem core and additional or secondary xylem tissue—basically, it looked like a root system but one above the ground. The leaves were less than an inch long and were wedgelike, linear, forked, or fan shaped. Scientists believe the reproductive parts of *Sphenophyllum* were long terminal cones and reproduced by *strobili,* or spores. It is unknown what kind of animals ate it, though, due to its abundance, it likely was a kind of Triassic-Devonian salad for the epoch's many herbivores.

The first description of these prehistoric plants was made by the British geologist and botanist Albert Charles Seward in 1898. The word Sphenophylum *derives from the Greek* sphén, *meaning "wedge," and* phyllon, *meaning "leaf."*

STINKING ROGER

Tagetes minuta
Not All Sour

Stinking Roger is popularly known as *southern cone marigold,* or *black mint,* and belongs to the family Asteraceae. The plant is tall, growing upright to 3 feet tall. It is actually a variety of marigold and has small orange and yellow flowers. It is found in all parts of the world, playing a part in prayers and weddings in the Hindu culture, because of its healing properties. Many even consider it a blessing and an omen of good fortune. The plant grows in abundance in South America, where it has many more medicinal uses.

The plant gets its name from its seeds, which come from the flowers of the plant and do not smell very good. If accidentally harvested along with wheat or other grains, its seeds will contaminate the entire batch with an unpleasant odor. That's why many commercial growers consider the plant a weed. However, its roots provide the soil with beneficial extracts that are helpful to a number of important vegetables, such as corn.

As an herb, the plant has several uses: Its leaves, dried, are used as a seasoning; one can make a paste from an ingredient found in the plant, called *huacatay,* that is useful in making potato dishes; as a medicine, the plant can help treat colds and the flu very efficiently. It provides relief from respiratory inflammations and stomach difficulties. It is also used to produce an organic kind of dye. Stinking Roger is beneficial in loss of appetite, intestinal gas, colic or stomachache, and dysentery. Alternative medicine practitioners use it to treat intestinal worms, mumps, sore eyes, and sore breasts. Folk medicine employed the plant in the treatment of menstrual pain or cramps, and in pregnant women it is said to prevent miscarriage. However, pregnant women should always consult a professional herbalist or health-care provider before using the plant. Stinking Roger is considered safe as a food, but its side effects are not well studied. It's best to stay on the safe side and not use this plant before consultation with an expert. Stinking Roger may lead to an allergic reaction in people who are sensitive to plants in the Asteraceae or Compositae family.

SUNFLOWER
Helianthus annuus
Toward the Sun

Sunflower is one of the few crop species native to North America, histori-cally a kind of "camp follower" of some of the western Native American tribes who domesticated the crop in about 1000 B.C. They then spread it eastward and southward, taking the seeds with them as they traveled. Europeans first encountered the sunflower growing in Mexico, and intro-duced it to Spain in the sixteenth century. The plant was a gardening hit and a curiosity that had everyone desiring the seeds, even as far as Russia, where the plant readily adapted. Today the sunflower has high economic value, and is cultivated worldwide for its high-quality cooking oil.

Sunflowers tolerate both low and high temperatures; the seeds germinate at 39 degrees Fahrenheit and are unaffected by cold in their early germination stages. Cotyledon-stage seeds have survived temperatures as low as 23 degrees. Optimum temperatures for growth are 70 to 78 degrees, while extremely high temperatures lower the oil percentage, or seed fill, and germination. Sunflowers can grow in different soils, from sands to clays, which have significant levels of macronutrients and good soil drainage. One of the best-looking mass-produced crops, fields of sunflowers, with their dignified large, circular yellow heads and broad, rough leaves, are simply a touching sight. The sunflower is an annual plant, with a large inflorescence growing atop a broad stem that is rough and hairy. The heads have hundreds of small flowers that later mature into seeds.

Nature's Mathematics

There is a pure mathematic calculation concerning the pattern of florets in the sunflower head. In 1979 H. Vogel discovered that sunflowers follow a mathematical formula. Simply, sunflower patterns form what is known as a Fermat spiral, relating to ratios and angles. Leonardo da Vinci called it the golden ratio and used this calculation to add dimensions in painting compositions. Scientists have shown that most sunflower floret patterns have exactly 55 or 144 seeds. The mathematical principles exemplified in sunflower formations are used in computer science, proving further the kind of secrets nature still holds and has yet to reveal.

Helianthus annuus has rich historical, cultural, and symbolic importance. Some Native American peoples, including the Aztecs, Incas, and Otomi, interpreted it as a symbol of solar deities. In the eighteenth century, the sunflower became very popular in Russia, especially for the Russian Orthodox Church, whose members were permitted to consume the oil during Lent and other fasting periods. The medicine men of the Zuni people used fresh or dried roots of sunflower against snakebite, applying a poultice on wounds, as well as in religious ceremonies.

Other sociocultural aspects of the sunflower include its use as a symbol of "green" ideology, as well as by the Vegan Society. In the nineteenth century, the flower was a symbol of the aesthetic movement in art. The Spiritualist Church also used it as a symbol, mostly because they believed that sunflowers constantly turn toward the sun (proven only partially true by science, since the flower head can move slightly to face in the direction of the day's most intense sunlight, though it cannot twist about on its entire stalk); still, the plant is a fitting representation of the notion that "spiritualism turns toward the light of truth" for the organization. Even now, modern spiritualists often use stylized sunflower heads on their jewelry. The sunflower is the state flower of Kansas, the city flower of Kitakyushu, Japan, and the national flower of Ukraine. In art, possibly the best representation of the flower is Vincent van Gogh's series *Sunflowers*.

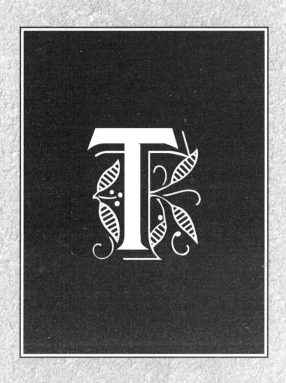

TOBACCO

Nicotiana tabacum
It Casts Its Spell

Christopher Columbus famously discovered the tobacco plant, *Nicotiana tabacum,* on his monumental journey to the Americas. On October 12, 1492, in the Bahamas, the crew of Columbus's ship brought reports of natives smoking dried tobacco leaves rolled in other leaves—the original cigar. According to historical sources, Columbus was initially unimpressed with the discovery (making him the first antismoking activist, too), but soon afterward, other Spanish and European sailors took up the practice, introducing it on their return to Spain and Portugal. The trend then caught on in France and Italy, as well. In Britain, after Sir Walter Raleigh demonstrated before the royal court the enjoyable taste of smoking the dried leaf, it wasn't long before the whole of Europe was under tobacco's spell. Always enterprising, the English immediately realized the potential dollar value of such an addictive plant. The scientific name of the plant—and the root of *nicotine,* its main psychoactive chemical—was bestowed in honor of the French ambassador Jean Nicot. He sent seeds to Catherine de Medici in 1559, praising the plant's medical properties. Early European cultivators even attempted to market tobacco medicinally, as a cure for nervousness. Tobacco was first popular not in cigars, but rather as snuff.

The history of tobacco smoking goes back more than five thousand years. Although the ultimate origins of the word *cigar* are unknown, some researchers argue it comes from *sikar,* a Mayan word for smoking. (Ancient Mayans considered tobacco a sacred plant.) The first truly for-profit tobacco plantations began in Virginia in 1612, followed by Maryland in 1631. American colonists smoked tobacco from pipes only, though cigars became more popular in 1762, when Israel Putnam, a British officer in Cuba, set up a cigar factory in Connecticut upon his return to the colonies. The first mass-produced cigarette, the French word meaning "small cigar," began in the 1880s.

Nicotiana tabacum is classified as a perennial herbaceous plant, originating in South America and the American subtropics, but today it's cultivated worldwide. It is very sensitive to temperature, soil humidity, air, and type of soil. The best temperature range for good yields is 68 to 86 degrees Fahrenheit, with an atmospheric humidity of 80 to 85 percent, and it prefers a soil with lower levels of nitrogen. Tobacco is a little branched, robust annual plant, about 3 feet tall, with green leaves and trumpetlike flowers. The tobacco leaves vary radically in size, 2 feet long at the lower end, while those toward the top of the plant are only 3 inches. Flowers bear a 1-inch tube and are predominantly white-pinkish in color, though some varieties have pale violet or yellowish flowers. The seeds are very small, kidney shaped, numerous, and brown.

Each part of *Nicotiana tabacum* contains the nicotine chemical, the concentrations of which will fluctuate based on the plant's age. The total nicotine distribution in the plant is: 64 percent in the leaves, 18 percent in the stem, 13 percent in the root, and 5 percent in the flowers. The tobacco plant also contains the chemicals anabasine, naphthylamine, glucosides, propionic acid, and anatabine. Some of the tobacco plant's ingredients have anesthetic, analgesic, antibacterial, anticonvulsant, antiglaucomic, and antioxidant qualities, as well as noted antistress effects. A rich, complex plant, tobacco suffers from the world's forceful fixation on the carcinogenic aspects of its use, rather than its other uses worldwide.

- In Colombia, fresh leaves are used over infected wounds.
- Brazilians heat leaves, squeeze out the juice, mix them with the *Theobroma* species, and make some intoxicating snuff.
- In Fiji, fresh roots are used orally against asthma; Fijians also use seeds for rheumatism and hoarseness.
- Ecuadorians use tobacco leaf juice to treat snakebites.
- In Haiti, dried leaves are taken orally to prevent and cure pneumonia and bronchitis.
- In India dried leaves in combination with other plants are used to ward off parasites.
- As a Mayan legacy, in traditional Mexico, the entire plant of *Nicotiana tabacum* is considered a basic medicine. People use tobacco leaves in combination with other herbs, preparing them for a variety of different cures.

The Coveted Cuban Cigar

In Cuba, tobacco is usually planted in flat fields. After the planting process, farmers cover the seedlings with special cloth or straw to protect them from the sun, removing it once the seedlings start to germinate. After thirty-five days of growth, usually in October, the plant is transplanted to vast tobacco fields. The watering process uses natural rains, dew, and artificial irrigation, if needed.

The all-important tobacco wrapper comes from the outer leaves, called the *corojos,* which farmers place under big sheets of gauze after harvest. For best effect, the plants should be strong, with broad leaves. This technique is called *tapado* (Spanish for "covering") and helps the leaves become smooth. Cubans always harvest their tobacco by hand—they trust no machine to do this delicate work. They collect the leaves for the wrappers in bundles of five, named *manojo.* The first section is never used while picking wrapper leaves. A week must pass between each phase of harvest. The best leaves for smoking come from the middle of the plant. The corona, or top leaves, are too oily, so they make poor wrappers. The whole cycle of harvesting takes about 120 days of hard work. Each individual plant gets visited about 170 times by farmers, so it's not surprising Cuban cigars are so expensive and considered the best among connoisseurs.

TOMATO
Lycopersicon esculentum
The Paradise Fruit

It's a well-known source of confusion—is a tomato a fruit or vegetable? Scientifically, as the ovary of the flower, a tomato is a fruit—actually a "berry," in the strictest botanical sense. In botanical terms, a berry is the part of the plant produced by a fertilized flower and contains a seed. Nevertheless, whatever you call it, the tomato is a remarkable food plant, providing nutritional value and flavor to cuisines around the world. It belongs to the family Solanaceae (also known as the nightshade family). Earlier, its Latin name was *Solanum lycopersicum*. The French call it *pomme d'amour,* meaning "love apple," while in Italy the tomato is sometimes named *pomodoro* or "golden apple," probably referring to varieties of the plant that bear orange-yellow-tangerine-colored fruits. In the Balkans, its local names speak to a "divine" aspect: Serbs call it *paradajz,* derived from the English *paradise,* while Croats call it *rajchica*—the word's root *raj* also means paradise. What a plant!

Since it is a native species to South America, many believe the name *tomato* originates from the Aztecan word *tomatl,* meaning "the swelling fruit." The plant was unknown to European populations until the Spanish colonizers transported its seeds from Mexico to Spain in the 1500s. Now there are about 7,500 varieties of tomato, which come in different sizes and shapes and for different uses. The nutritional and health benefits are spectacular: tomatoes support the cardiovascular system, strengthen bones, and help prevent cancer. It's also an antioxidant, and reduces the danger of neurological diseases such as Alzheimer's. The tomato keeps the prostate disease-free and reduces the risk of obesity—and on top of all this, it offers a delicious taste.

The plant grows 3 to 10 feet tall, with a weak stem that sprawls over the ground and can vine over other plants. Its stems are usually supported when cultivated. The tomato is a perennial in native habitats, but it is often grown outdoors as an annual in temperate climates; an average, nice red fruit weighs about 4 ounces, though there are species that can give fruits weighing as much as 2 pounds. The wild tomato cross-pollinates to reproduce, but after moving it from its native areas, the Spanish colonizers forgot to also take its traditional pollinator, the Halictid bee. In greenhouses, a tomato reproduces poorly on its own, so growers use an artificial wind and plant shaker (there is even a special vibrator for this purpose, called an "electric bee," which is used manually) to spread pollen. In large commercial fields, farmers count on a special breed of bumblebees for pollination. The tomato is one of the main subjects of efforts to produce new varieties by means of genetic modification. Scientists have taken to adding pesticide compounds to the plant's DNA, a move that has met with a backlash of resistance throughout the world, particularly since there are no long-range studies to prove these modification are not carcinogenic or cause some other unknown harm.

There is one new such species grown in greenhouses in Great Britain. The new variety has been dubbed "Moneymaker," which says everything about the motivation behind genetically modifying plants.

Frenki Goes to the Balkans

The Strumica region of Macedonia is considered to yield some of the world's best tomatoes. Urban (and rural) legends say that until World War I, people from the region consumed tomatoes while they were still green, a practice met with astonishment by the arriving French army, who insisted the fruits be harvested only when mature and red. The Macedonians, of course, were pleasantly surprised, so they gave the plant a new name: *frenki,* meaning Frenchmen. Still, Macedonians often use green tomatoes soaked in water with salt for winter storage—a delicious dish in its own right.

TULIP
Tulipa
Blooming Spectacle

In springtime, a special flower blooms, blessed with a nearly perfect shape. Its colors are so intense, one cannot help but conclude that nature is the greatest artist of all. It comes in virtually all hues: red, yellow, rose, deep purple, and even one that looks black. This beauty is the tulip, but act fast, since the plant blooms its splendid prime for no more than ten to twelve days a year.

Although associated mostly with the Netherlands, the cultivation of tulips began first in Persia, in the tenth century. During the rule of the Ottoman Empire, people spread the plant widely, calling it *lale* in Arabic, Turkish, Farsi, Macedonian, and Bulgarian. Its name comes from the word *Allah,* which is the reason tulips became a holy symbol in some Muslim countries. The tulip was originally known in Europe as *tulipa* or *tulipant,* which was taken from the French *tulipe.* The Persians called it *delband,* meaning "turban." The tulip's shape is similar to a turban's, and it was very fashionable in the Ottoman Empire as an ornament for people to place in the folds and wraps of their turbans. Allegedly, when marketplaces were filled with people wearing turbans, the mass looked like a moving garden.

Tulips are blooming perennials that grow from bulbs and, depending on the species, can grow up to 28 inches tall. Most tulips give only one flower per plant, although there are a few species, like the *Tulipa turkestanica,* that can produce multiple. The cup shapes and snowy flowers have three petals and three sepals, commonly called tepals. Colors are mostly different, depending on the variety, but there remains a global challenge to see who, if anyone, will be the first to produce a "pure blue" tulip, which no one has yet bred. The stems usually have few leaves, two to six, while some species have up to twelve; the leaf is strap-shaped, with a waxy coating and light green color.

Tulips reproduce by seeds, offseting, or what's called micropropagation, which is taking a tissue from the plant and basically cloning it. Offsetting is an asexual method that yields genetic clones, while seed propagation produces a bigger genetic variation, with subspecies or new hybrids. Most tulip species are able to be cross-pollinated with each other. However, commercial tulip cultivars are complex hybrids and are mostly sterile.

Culture and Art

In Old Persia, a gift of a yellow or red tulip was a declaration of love, and the plants retain a significant place in classical and modern Persian literature. The poet Musharrifu'd-din Saadi described paradise thus: "The murmur of a cool stream / bird song, ripe fruit in plenty / bright multi-colored tulips and fragrant roses." During the Ottoman Empire, the tulip held a double meaning, one of abundance and another (especially among the more religious) of frivolous indulgence.

Today there are numerous tulip festivals worldwide, with the grandest in Netherlands, England, and Switzerland. North America also has annual festivals that display the flowers' range of colorful beauty. The best U.S. shows are in Holland, Michigan; the Skagit Valley, Washington; and Pella, Iowa. Australia also celebrates tulips with festivals in September and October, springtime in the Southern Hemisphere.

Dutch Origins

It was Carolus Clusius who first planted tulips in Europe, at the Imperial Garden in Vienna in 1573. Twenty years later, he also planted tulips in the newly established Hortus Botanicus at Leiden University. The result is that 1594 is used as the official date of the first flowering tulips in the Netherlands, though there are reports of tulips being privately cultivated in Amsterdam and Antwerp three decades earlier. However, those first tulips at Leiden kicked off what is known as "Tulipmania" in the Netherlands, and there remains a significant tulip industry in that country to this day.

TUPELO TREE
Nyssa
The Nymph's Gifts

Have you ever tried tupelo honey? If not, know that sampling it may change your perception of how honey should taste. There are 10 species of tupelo trees inside the genus *Nyssa,* in the family Cornaceae; 5 of them are native to North America, while the others belong to East and South Asia. *Nyssa sylvatica* is grown for its beautiful foliage, especially in autumn, while *Nyssa aquatica* has some commercial uses. The name *Nyssa* is derived from the name in ancient Greek mythology for a water nymph, while the most common name, *tupelo,* comes from a Cree Indian phrase meaning "tree of the swamp." The city where Elvis Presley was born, Tupelo, Mississippi, is named after this tree.

Truly Golden

The most valuable and tasty tupelo honey comes from the *Nyssa ogeche* species, found in the southeastern United States and across the Gulf Coast area. The honey is very light and mild tasting; it's hard to abide any other type of honey after tasting this blend. In Florida, during the tupelo blooming season, beekeepers keep the hives near the river swamps and actually place the hives on floats or platforms to increase honey production. The monofloral honey from *Nyssa ogeche* has a very high ratio of glucose and fructose, so it doesn't crystallize, which is an additional quality that helps to produce its special blend of flavor. The Apalachicola River in Florida is often considered the center for the best tupelo honey. The most expensive honey originates from this region, certified by special pollen analysis. In a good year, a group of specialized beekeepers can earn up to $1 million from one tupelo honey crop.

And as a side note, listen to "Tupelo Honey," the song by Van Morrison, while tasting this honey for an equally sweet sensation.

These trees are sometimes called *pioneer's toothbrush,* since people used to break the brittle twigs off smaller tupelos and use the bundle of woody fibers within to clean their teeth. Another name is *bee gum,* because hollow trees will sometimes house beehives. Tupelo can grow from 30 to 50 feet high and 15 to 25 feet wide. Its leaves are dark green and glossy, most intense in summer, followed by brilliant autumn shades of yellow-orange, yellow, bright red, scarlet, or purple. The tree grows slowly and prefers moist, acidic soils, with partial or full sun. As a food, tupelos fall prey to the larvae of species of the Lepidoptera order, but the plant is resistant against most other pests.

Many have used the tupelo for artistic woodcarving and other commercial purposes, such as decorative furniture inlay, as well as for wood paneling and for making veneer. When pulped, tupelo wood makes for high-quality book and magazine papers. It's an elegant and gentle tree, used in only special products, so it's no surprise it was bestowed the name of the beautifully delicate Greek nymph.

UNICORN PLANT
Proboscidea louisianica
The Oily Devil

Though its precise place of origin is unknown, many consider the unicorn plant a native of the southwestern United States and Mexico. It now
grows in other regions, including South Africa, Australia, and Europe.
The unicorn tree has a special means of seed dispersal, since it produces

fruits with hooks on them that attach to the fur of passing animals. This so-called Velcro method helps the plant spread its seeds far and wide from the parent tree.

The unicorn plant's many other nicknames are pretty exotic as well, including *devil's claw, purple flower devil's claw, goat's head, ram's horn, aphid trap,* and *elephant tusks.* Clearly it's a very inspiring tree for creative minds! No matter what it's called, it belongs to the family Martyniaceae. Its stems reach up to 2½ feet long, opposed by leaves up to 1 foot long. The flowers are lavender, or purple-cream, or sometimes pinkish purple with yellowish nectar holders. Each plant yields about eighty fruits, which are dehiscent capsules (meaning they naturally split open) and feature long, curving, narrow beaks. When the fruit gets dry, it breaks in two horn-shaped parts. The seeds inside these pods are black or white, and are rich in oil—the same substance also present as oil droplets in the herb's glandular hairs gives the plant quite a slippery feel. As its oil vaporizes, the whole area around the plant is overcome with a strong, acrid odor.

The plant grows in diverse soil types and easily adapts to all kinds of habitats, even dumps. It's found in feedlots, pastures, and cultivated fields. It's detrimental to certain agricultural crops, particularly cotton, since its oil production can cause drastic changes to the content of surrounding soil. This "devil" of a plant can resist many herbicides, and the only way to eliminate it is by manually yanking it from the ground.

Even though it is very adaptable to varied soil types, including sandy, loamy, or clay, *Proboscidea louisianica* prefers well-drained landscapes with lots of moisture, and can't grow very well in shady areas. When there are no bees or other species particularly fond of its nectar to perform pollination, the unicorn plant simply self-pollinates. The plant perhaps has no special enemies, most likely because of its oily appearance and odor. More than most, the unicorn plant is a well-equipped survivor.

Uses

The "devil" is edible, and many pickle its young green fruits. Native Americans used its seeds for food, too. The plant has found its most prevalent use in basketry, particularly since its husks are suitable to shape the basket forms, and serve as good sewing implements. The plant was used traditionally for basket weaving by the Apache, Hopi, Kawaiisu, and Havasupai, and the Tohono Indians cultivated it as well—using its dark, dried fruits for basketry ornaments. In this context, people grow the unicorn plant not only for an ornament, and a garden novelty, but also for floral arrangements.

VANILLA
Vanilla planifolia
A Royal Flavor

Vanilla is certainly one of the most likable flavors worldwide, first used by ancient Aztecs (probably in Mexico, which is its place of origin) to flavor drinks made of cocoa and honey, named *xocolatl*. The plant grows wild in tropical forests and belongs to one of the largest and oldest families of flowering plants, Orchidaceae. It produces high amounts of vanillin and is the only one of the orchid species widely cultivated in agriculture. Nearly 95 percent of the traded vanilla comes from this very species, *Vanilla planifolia*. Today the plant grows wild mostly in Central America and the West Indies, as it prefers hot, tropical climates. The greatest harvest yields are from Mexico.

Like all other plants from the *Vanilla* genus, planifolia is a vine, using its fleshy roots to strongly support itself while growing. Its flowers are greenish yellow, 2 inches in diameter, and last only one day. Though twenty-four hours may seem a small window in which to reproduce, vanilla is a self-fertilizing plant, so pollination is achieved by simply transferring the pollen from anthers to stigmata. If not pollinated, for some reason the flower dies the next day and the parent plant has no hope of reproducing again. In the wild, vanilla flowers have less than 1 percent chance of pollination, yet the species has survived for countless eons. In commercial growing, farmers ensure reproduction by hand or with mechanical aid.

Vanilla fruits are pods 6 to 9 inches long, sometimes also called beans, though that term is scientifically erroneous. Nevertheless, fruits come only from mature plants, usually when the plant is at least 10 feet tall. Its fruit or bean pods mature after five months, before farmers harvest and cure them. The curing dries and ferments the pods in order to ensure minimum loss of their essential oils. They then make vanilla extract from this portion of the herb. Pods are useful whole or split into tiny pieces, which are then infused into a liquid.

Vanilla planifolia got its name in 1808, though Montezuma first introduced the plant to Cortez in 1520, after which the conquistador transported it to Europe, where it was immediately recognized as a highly valuable plant. The Spanish word *vainilla* represents a diminutive of *vaina,* meaning "sheath" or "pod," inspired by the sheathlike shape of vanilla fruits.

Best Vanilla

Vanilla from Madagascar and Réunion (also called *Bourbon vanilla*) is highly prized for its most intensive, balanced, and "dark" flavor. Mexican vanilla is a cheaper variety and has a fresher, softer flavor. Tahitian vanilla, which is very rare, stems from the species *Vanilla tahitensis* and boasts a more floral vanilla fragrance.

Have a Vanilla Smoke

The vanilla plant has some nonculinary uses, including aromatization of perfumes, liqueurs, and cigars. Europeans usually use the bean, while Americans prefer the extract. Some substances marketed as "vanilla flavor" do not contain any trace of the plant, but rather a mixture of synthesized clove oil (or eugenol), wastepaper pulp, and coumarin, which is found in tonka beans. So read the label to make sure you're getting the real thing!

VARNISH TREE
Toxicodendron vernicifluum
Poison Art

The varnish tree grows in China, Japan, Korea, and the Himalayas. Cultivated for its toxic sap, the varnish tree yields the base for a high-quality, durable lacquer or varnish. The sap contains the allergenic urushiol (from the Japanese word *urushi,* lacquer), which is also found in poison ivy and causes skin rashes if touched.

The varnish tree grows from 45 to 60 feet tall and has compound leaves, each of which has seven to thirteen leaflets, 4 to 7 inches long and half as broad. Its berries are ¼ inch in diameter and straw colored. The milky sap, or latex, turns black after only a few minutes of exposure to air, and harvesters collect the substance much like they would maple sap, usually by making a slash into the tree and allowing the sap to drain through a reed or tube into a bucket. Some use this latex for lacquer, which is highly prized for its extreme durability, most often as a coating on finer wood products, such as musical instruments, tableware, and bows; it also adds luster and protects delicate jewelry and even expensive fountain pens. In Kashmir and Nepal, in India, the varnish tree grows at altitudes of 5,000 to 8,000 feet—practically in the clouds.

Here's how the varnish is produced: First, five to ten horizontal lines are made into the trunks of trees, which must be at least ten years old. Once the yellow or grayish sap is collected and filtered, it is heat-treated and colored. Then the sap is dried in humid and warm chambers for twelve to twenty-four hours, which allows the urushiol to polymerize. At this point, the mix forms into a hard, clear, and waterproof liquid and is ready for application.

Various types of lacquerware can be produced by using sap from different trees and by adding tints of color. Probably the best regarded is the cinnabar-red variety, which has iron added to it for pigmentation. Uncolored lacquer, which is naturally dark

Buddhist Self-Mummification

Buddhist monks once practiced a ritual called *sokushinbutsu,* a spectacular use of the varnish tree's sap. The monks applied the lacquer to their skin, adding layer upon layer until they achieved death and self-mummification! Members of a Japanese school of Buddhism known as Shingon, meaning "true word," were the primary practitioners of this ceremony between the eleventh and nineteenth centuries. These monks considered Shingon not an act of suicide, but rather one of austerity and enlightenment. Not everyone who tried it succeeded, but even those who failed to complete it were still much respected. According to records, among the hundreds of monks who tried it, only twenty-four succeeded in actual self-mummification. Today it is not practiced by any Buddhist sect, and Japan has outlawed the practice. One can't help but wonder: what might Buddha have said about such a thing?

brown, is applied with brushes. The process is very time-consuming, and requires many repetitive layers. The creation of what's known as *urushi* art is a slow process that adds the thinnest layers of varnish, taking weeks or months to complete. An *urushi* lacquered bowl, for example, might take three months to finish properly. In addition to being made into varnish, the resin of the tree, as well as the leaves and seeds, plays a role in traditional Chinese medicine, where it is prescribed to treat certain internal parasites and to stop bleeding.

VENUS FLYTRAP
Dionaea muscipula
Botanical Jaws

The Venus flytrap seeks insects, as all plants do, although not for pollination; they are for the plant to feed on. When the plant opens its "jaws-flowers," its color invites insects to enter. The bug's movement touches the tiny hairs in the plant's inner structure, which triggers the plant to close its "mouth." The insect becomes trapped, though it will take ten slow days until the creature is fully digested. Venus flytraps get nutrients from the insect that it cannot get from the soil. These plants aren't exotic tropicals, as many believe, but are actually native to North America. The plant only grows naturally along the coast of North and South Carolina.

Venus flytraps are carnivorous plants, primarily thriving in bogs and brackish water environments. The plant forms as a rosette with four to seven leaves, arising from a short, subterranean, bulblike stem of about 4 inches in length. The robust traps form after the plant flowers. The traps are triggered by trichomes on their upper surfaces, but the mechanism kicks in only if two hairs are touched within twenty seconds. The closing speed of the "jaws" depends on the amount of light, humidity, the size of prey, and general growing conditions, and is also an indicator of

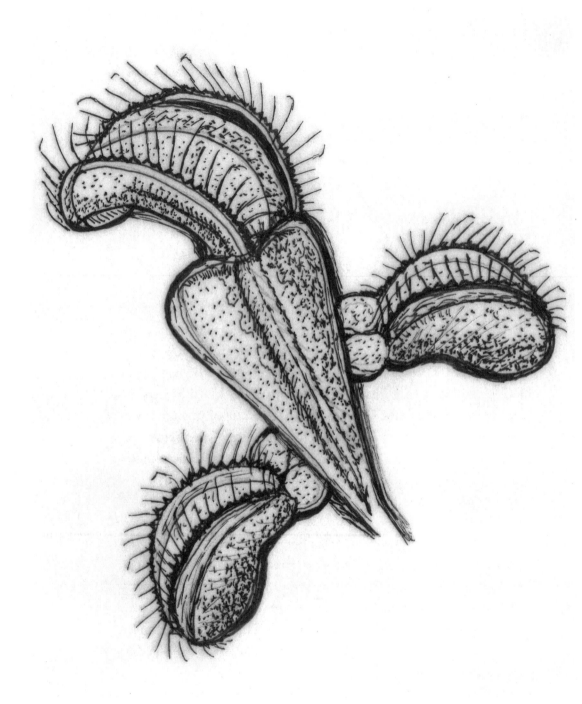

the plant's health. When cultivated, the plants are propagated by division during spring and summer; they can reproduce by seeds, although it takes four or five years for these plants to mature. Once rooted in an ideal environment, the plant can live for twenty to thirty years.

However, the Venus flytrap doesn't eat meat, such as a piece of hamburger or sausage, and it primarily seeks only insects (though in some cases they have been known to capture and digest small frogs). Each of the plant's traps works efficiently for only four to six catches, after which the mouth-shaped part turns brown, withers, and falls off. After it has the nutrients it needs, the plant becomes dormant for about five months, from October through March. Each trap has six hairy triggers, three on each lobe. The plant needs about fourteen hours of full sun exposure every day and can grow in nutrient-deficient soil. Indoors, potted Venus flytraps will die if given fertilizer.

The plant's common name of course pays tribute to Venus, the Roman goddess of love. The genus name, *Dionaea*, means "daughter of Dione," the Greek goddess Aphrodite, while its Latin species name *muscipula* means "mousetrap."

The Evolution Process

The following is the most commonly accepted scenario on how Venus flytrap evolved in the distant past: Instead of attracting flying insects, it adapted to lure larger ones that could walk over the plant. The plant, having been faced with a situation of living in bogs, where soil pH might change and stable nutrient supplies become scarce, gradually transformed its leaves into traps. As these traps became a successful modification, the plant needed the energy and the anatomy to "wrap" its leaves around its prey, in addition to having the ability to differentiate insects from pieces of worthless debris. This is why it needed the inner tentacles that evolved into "jaws" with inner trigger hairs. Finally, at some point, the plant developed the digestive glands found inside its leaf-modified traps and no longer relied on its stalk to send nutrients to its upper parts—proving, perhaps, how function, in nature, dictates design.

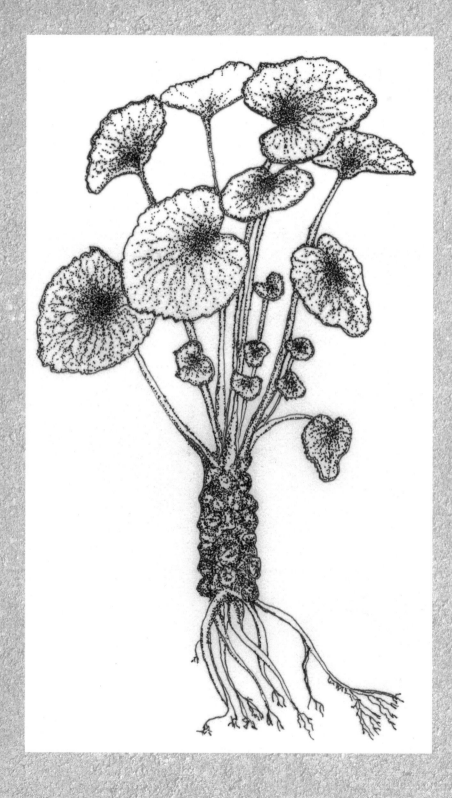

WASABI
Wasabia japonica
Wild Ginger

Wasabia japonica (or *Eutrema japonica,* or *Eutrema wasabi*), also known as *Japanese horseradish,* is a native condiment crop of Japan. It isn't known when people first took to cultivating the plant, but most believe the Japanese have done so for at least a thousand years. A Japanese medical encyclopedia called *Honzo-wamyo,* published in A.D. 918, states the plant's original name means "wild ginger." Records indicate that wasabi farms were primarily located in southern coastal provinces, and wasabi was long considered a delicacy. During the fifteenth and sixteenth centuries, laws were passed that forbade commoners from using it, allowing only the ruling classes to consume it. Today, the plant is grown throughout Japan, prized as a valuable economic crop, and anyone who can tolerate its bold flavor can consume it.

It is a member of the Cruciferae family and related to broccoli, cabbage, and radishes. Wasabi roots are used to make the popular condiment that has a notable strong flavor and "heat," more similar to hot mustard than chili pepper. The reason some people begin to cry when eating too much wasabi is that the vapor it produces affects the nasal passages more than it does the taste buds.

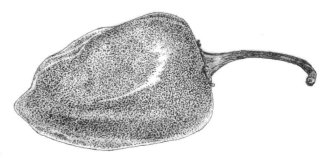

Wasabia is a perennial, glabrous (smooth) and glossy-leafed plant, growing up to 2 feet in height. It bears white flowers and is cross-pollinated by insects. Depending on the variety, wasabi roots can have one or more main rhizomes. The length of these rhizomes varies from 10 to 20 inches, and they weigh about 4 ounces. However, the biggest wasabi root ever known was grown in New Zealand and tipped the scale at 2½ pounds— quite a lot of the hot green mustard.

At markets, wasabi is sold as a root, as a dried powder, or as a paste in small tubes. Japanese restaurants make the paste only after a customer orders it; its hot flavor lasts for only fifteen minutes once prepared. For sushi, it is traditionally put between the fish and rice, in order not to cover its flavor. Wasabi leaves also can be eaten and have the same flavor, though less intense. Roasted or fried peanuts, peas, or soybeans may be coated with wasabi powder, mixed with salt, sugar, or oil, and then eaten as a crunchy snack. The specific flavor of wasabi comes from the complex chemical mixtures found in the root's cells, particularly a compound called isothiocyanate, which inhibits microbe growth.

Traditionally, there are two methods of growing commercial wasabi in Japan, either in soil (*oka* wasabi) or in water (*sawa* wasabi). Most Japanese wasabi farms are family-run and rarely change hands. Since there are limited areas in which the plant can thrive, the last wasabi bed was planted alongside a mountain stream in Japan some two hundred years ago.

Nobel Prize for Wasabi

Inhaling the vapor of wasabi results in effects similar to those of smelling salts. Some researchers have even created a wasabi smoke alarm for deaf people; one subject of their test awoke from a deep sleep only ten seconds after the vapor was sprayed in the room. In 2001, the Nobel Prize in Chemistry was awarded to the researchers who determined the ideal combination of airborne wasabi to alert people in cases of emergency.

WATER HYACINTH
Eichhornia crassipes
Aggressive Upstart

Eichhornia crassipes, an aquatic plant, is one of the seven species constituting the genus *Eichhornia.* Commonly known as the water hyacinth, this free-floating perennial plant is indigenous to the Amazon Basin in Brazil. An invasive species, water hyacinth is highly problematic outside its native range as it infests the water bodies, lakes, rivers, dams, and irrigation

channels on every continent except Antarctica. Once removed from its natural environment, where there is an established ecological system of checks and balances, the plant can become an aggressive invader. It forms thick mats and envelops entire pond surfaces, for example, leading to oxygen depletion and destruction of other native aquatic life-forms. Billions of dollars are spent every year around the world to regulate the devastating effects of these "water weeds."

The silky, lustrous, round, dark green leaves of the water hyacinth are attached to spongy, inflated petioles, and can be as wide as 6 inches in diameter, rising up to 3 feet high above the water surface. The floating plant has a feathery, black to purple root system that dangles 2 feet in the water below it. The erect stalk of *Eichhornia crassipes* bears a single spike of eight to fifteen noticeably alluring blossoms, mostly from light blue to violet in color, with a yellowish center. The six showy petals of the flower are joined at the base to form short tubules. The fruit of the water hyacinth is a three-celled capsule, which is only about ½ inch long, but which contains as many as three hundred tiny, egg-shaped, ribbed seeds.

Water hyacinths breed over an extensive diversity of wetlands, ranging from lakes, ponds, and streams to ditches, waterways, and backwater seas.

> *Water hyacinths cannot tolerate extreme temperatures; they wither in water temperatures above 94 degrees Fahrenheit or if the water gets near the freezing point. They grow best in freshwater or in a diluted estuary, since highly salty waters can also prove fatal for the plant.*

Once Removed

Most sources trace the plant's U.S. debut to the World's Industrial and Cotton Centennial Exposition, held in New Orleans, Louisiana, in 1884. A visitor from Florida picked up a cluster of water hyacinth plants on exhibit and upon returning to Florida released them into the St. Johns River. It flourished and spread rapidly to neighboring states.

The plant prefers and grows effectively in waters that have high amounts of bacterial sediment or nutrition content, and it favors slow-moving water currents. Water hyacinth, because of its gaudy flowers and leaves, is popular in garden ponds and as an ornamental plant.

Water hyacinth grows leisurely during the cooler winter months, but as soon as the temperature rises, the pace picks up considerably. Although it grows from seeds, vegetative reproduction is the plant's main means of propagation, meaning that parts of the parent plant fall off and take root. Flowers begin to bloom as early as October and unusually, unlike most blooming plants, continue to flourish throughout winter. A fully grown flower begins to wither within two days. The empty stalk then bends and dips itself into the water body, and after a period of eighteen days, the nourished seeds are released from the capsules of the dead flower, which then sink to the mucky bottom of the water source.

Limited Uses

Considered the world's worst "pest" aquatic plant, water hyacinth is a serious environmental pollutant in the Gulf Coast states. Its highly invasive nature makes it a drain on nations' economies, regardless of its beauty. However, the plant does produce plentiful nitrogen content and does substantial good in the regions where it originally evolved. The roots can also assist in wastewater treatment, as they naturally absorb environmental pollutants. In some regions of Africa water hyacinth is even used to make handbags and ropes, while in other regions its flowers are used to medicate the skin of horses.

WATER LILY
Victoria amazonica
Floating Wonder

Nature's work rivals that of even the most endlessly imaginative artist. How amazing some plant forms can be! One is led to question whether

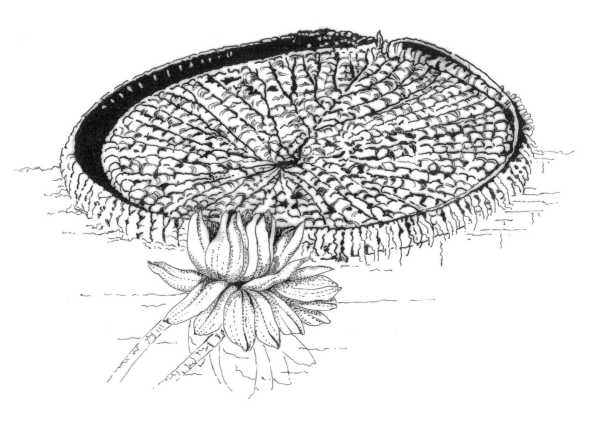

such beauty exists by coincidence or through an evolutionary fluke. Perhaps you've seen old photos of people floating on amazingly large water lily leaves? If so, you must surely have thought the image was Photoshopped, or accomplished through some trick photography. While there is a "trick," it may not be what you think.

This floating miracle is the plant *Victoria amazonica,* from the family Nymphaeaceae. First discovered in 1801, it caused a big stir when introduced to Europe in the 1800s, where it was touted as the *giant water platter.* Its first scientific name was *Victoria regia* in honor of Britain's queen, but this was later emended, possibly by the queen herself. Native only to equatorial Brazil, *amazonica* grows in calm waters along the Amazon River, in placid lagoons, or in former river channels. Its unbelievable glossy green leaves grow up to 7 feet in diameter, with a pronounced maroon lip around the circumference. This lip is very practically notched in two places to get rid of accumulated rainwater, and naturally prevents the plant from sinking. Except for the roots, flowers, and the upper sides of the leaves, most of the *Victoria amazonica* is covered with flesh-piercing spines. The submerged, strong, elastic stalks of the leaves are "tied" or anchored to the bottom and can be 21 feet long.

Its gigantic leaves are what make *Victoria* so visually striking, though there are some other equally interesting properties that create the "trick" of people being able to float upon them like inflatable rafts. First, the surface of the leaf has a quilted texture that almost feels like touching a wet balloon. The real engineering is on the underside of the leaf: the bottom is purple and covered with a spiderweb of spongy ribs, all covered in spines. Its tall ribs create pockets, which trap air, giving the leaf tremendous buoyancy. Still, the leaves are fragile and could be easily punctured by hand. People who ride them usually place a thin mat to evenly distribute their weight and not cause this leafy float to sink.

From White to Pink

The whole of *Victoria amazonica*'s appearance is impressive, particularly its nocturnal flowers, which are 12 inches wide. On the first night that they bloom, the flowers are pure white and emit a strong, sweet, pineapple-like scent. These first blooms are classified as females, and they attract one special pollinator, a scarab beetle (*Cylocephata castaneal*). With the coming of daybreak, the beautiful flowers close their lattices and trap the beetle inside. During the day, the *Victoria* flowers transform themselves into functional males, indicated by the maturation of the anthers and the releasing of pollen. This covers the beetle with pollen, though the flowers cannot pollinate while still in the male state. So on the second evening, these clever plants open their flowers once again, having transformed them to pink. The beetle is finally released and ready to fall for the scent of another fragrant, white flower on another lily pad, unknowingly depositing the collected pollen to achieve fertilization. Among plants, it's hard to beat this flowering deception or the unique design that allows it to remain buoyant.

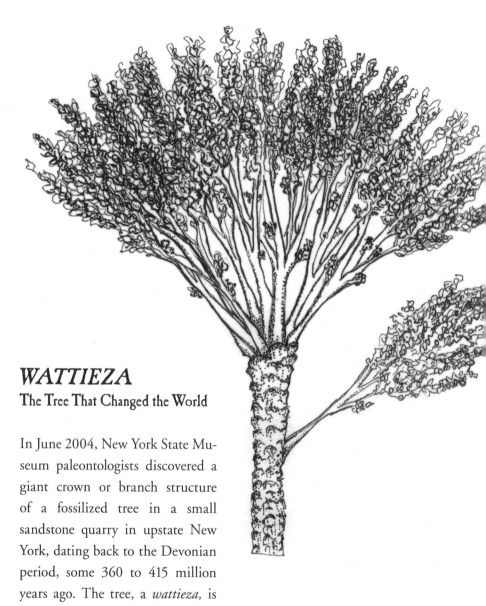

WATTIEZA
The Tree That Changed the World

In June 2004, New York State Museum paleontologists discovered a giant crown or branch structure of a fossilized tree in a small sandstone quarry in upstate New York, dating back to the Devonian period, some 360 to 415 million years ago. The tree, a *wattieza,* is officially the first and oldest known tree to have thrived on the planet. It transformed the environment more significantly than any other plant before it, paving the way for more complex life-forms, including land animals and eventually humans, to exist. You likely wouldn't be holding this book or reading device if not for the *wattieza.*

From this decisive discovery of a full *wattieza* fossil, it seems a critical and unique prehistoric evolutionary event occurred in upstate New York's Catskill Mountains, considered one of the oldest mountain ranges on the planet. The *wattieza* appears to be the precursor of all the forests now growing on earth. These trees preceded the dinosaurs by 140 million years, meaning that when this fossil of *wattieza* was alive, terrestrial life in the area was limited to arthropods, or insects, spiders, and crustaceans. There was nothing else—no reptiles, no amphibians, and no flying creatures.

The recent finding of *wattieza* also solved a century-old mystery: In 1870, a "forest" of fossil stumps was unearthed a few miles away, and they perplexed generations of botanists ever since. Without the upper sections of the trees, experts were unable to precisely identify the species. After the discovery of *wattieza* branches, a match was found and the mystery was solved.

The tree stood with an erect trunk about 24 feet in height and bore branches only at the crown, with leaves that were fernlike. *Wattieza* belonged to a genus of prehistoric species living in the mid-Devonian period that are related to current-day horsetails and ferns. It was in this period, scientists estimate, that the first seed-bearing plants spread on dry land, forming forests similar to ones today. However, *wattieza* itself didn't have seeds, but rather reproduced by spores, similar to ferns. Until this new discovery, the oldest known entire tree was believed to be the *Archaeopteris*, a close relative of seed-bearing plants flourishing in the late Devonian period. The *wattieza* tree differs from this later species with its smaller trunk, fully developed leaves, lack of horizontal branches, and more limited root system.

Although the reconstruction of such a fossil is a very difficult process, and though it may take many years to fully understand the structure and habits of early plants, it appears *wattieza* was the first of its kind—a lifeform that literally changed the world.

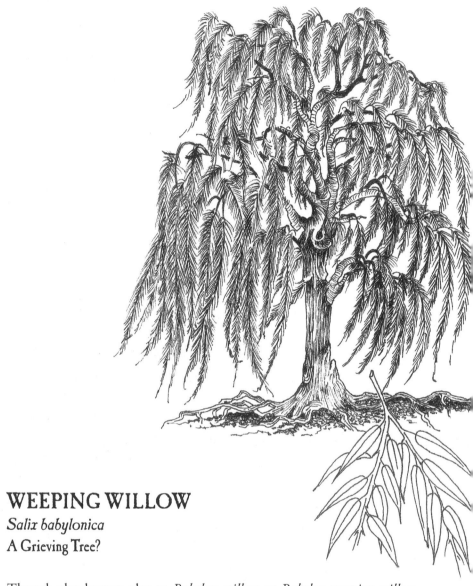

WEEPING WILLOW
Salix babylonica
A Grieving Tree?

Though also known also as *Babylon willow* or *Babylon weeping willow,* the weeping willow is native to China, not ancient Babylon. Throughout history, people have grown the tree ornamentally and for lumber. The Chinese preferred to plant willow to create shelterbelts, especially around oases in the Gobi Desert, protecting cultivated plants from desert winds. Later, the plant spread worldwide (the plant was traded along the Silk Road), giving rise to many hybrid species, particularly in Europe and the United States.

Willows are deciduous trees, medium to large in size, growing 66 to 82 feet tall. *Salix babylonica* has one of the most rapid growths among all trees (6 to 8 feet per year) and can live from forty to seventy-five years. It has a unique beauty with its falling, pendulous, or "weeping" branches. Its shoots are yellowish brown with small buds, while the leaves are alternate, narrow, and spirally arranged, with a light green color, about 6 inches long. In autumn the leaves turn gold-yellow, an equally beautiful sight. Flowers come in catkins, or as a slim flower cluster early in the spring. The tree is dioecious, growing male and female catkins on separate trees.

The weeping willow is an aggressive water seeker; its roots, while searching for moisture, can break through iron pipes and overturn sidewalks. This is the reason willows are most often planted in open areas near water sources and not close to a home or building. Still, roots can be helpful if placed in the right setting to help with soil drainage and prevent erosion.

Medical uses of weeping willows date back to ancient times. A Chinese reference dated to 400 B.C. recommends chewing the bark as an effective cure for inflammation and fever. How correct the ancients were—willow's bark does indeed contain a chemical ingredient (acetylsalicylic acid) that is now used in aspirin. Some recent studies suggest that its bark also contains additional antioxidants and has antiseptic and immune system–boosting properties.

Willow tree wood is also useful in arts and crafts, traditionally for wickerwork and basketry. Before the invention of plastic, willow wickerwork proved useful in the construction of many types of containers; many houses and furniture were also once made from the wood. The wood from weeping willows has also been used for charcoal manufacturing, for cricket bats, and in a dye to tan leather. In more humid European climates, as well as in eastern North America, a canker disease named willow anthracnose, or *Marssonina salicicola,* can drastically shorten a willow tree's life.

Not So Sad

Many different symbolic meanings are attributed to weeping willows. The most common, perhaps, is one of grief. This probably originates from a Bible passage: "By the rivers of Babylon we sat down and wept when we remembered Zion. There on the willow trees we hung up our harps" (Psalm 137). Historians, however, generally agree that the trees referred to in the psalm aren't actually willows, but are more likely poplars. Ironically, in other parts of the world, including China, the willow symbolizes growth, vitality, rebirth, and even immortality. This symbolism is born from the plant's ability to grow easily from simply cut branches. Nevertheless, the association between weeping willows and grief and sadness has persisted throughout history, and people frequently planted the tree in graveyards during the nineteenth century.

Carl Linnaeus first described the tree in 1736, although he named it incorrectly. He thought it was native to old Babylon, perhaps persuaded by the biblical verse, and did not know it was native to China.

WELWITSCHIA MIRABILIS
Life Comes from the Fog

Welwitschia is a peculiar, weird, strange, bizarre, unique, but nevertheless fascinating and beautiful plant. No other plant is similar, so it is not easy to categorize *welwitschia*, though it is surely a monotypic, dioecious (separate male and female plants) plant of the gymnosperm group. Unlike any other herb, the tip of its stem stops growing straight at an early stage, and instead turns downward, resulting in an asymmetric and obconical shape. The plant bunches up and lies on the ground, looking like a dumped pile of old landscaping—a wholly unique growth pattern. *Welwitschia* is a cone-bearing plant with naked seeds, though the male flowers (microstroboli) are similar to flowering herb plants.

The adult *welwitschia* has roots, a stem base, and a few leaves, and that's all! These leaves are unique in the plant kingdom: they are original from when the herb was a seedling, but they simply continue growing, never being shed. They are broad and leathery, and lie on the ground, and in this way become torn to ribbons and tattered as they mature. The stem is woody, low, hollow, sturdy, and cone-shaped, growing up to 20 inches high. The largest known specimen was found in the Messum complex of the Gobobose Mountains, in Namibia, Africa, and was 5 feet tall. These odd plants can live five hundred to six hundred years, although some larger examples are considered to be two thousand years old. Growth occurs only during the summer months.

Welwitschia mirabilis lives in strictly isolated communities in the Namib Desert, in a narrow strip, 600 miles long, up the coast from the Kuiseb River to Mossamedes in southern Angola. The plant shows variability, a sign it is far from going extinct. *Welwitschia* aren't rare or endangered, but are still protected by law, which is wise because of their originality. Ecologically, this is a highly specialized plant, preferring to grow under arid conditions. It thrives off the regular, dense fog formed when the cold, north-moving Benguela Current meets the Namib Desert's hot air, a radical contrast instrumental in the rise of the plant. Rainfall in the region is extremely low and erratic, so *welwitschias* developed an ability to reach underground waters with their long taproots. Other environmental adaptations are equally spectacular: the largest plants are growing to the south, with poor rainfall, while plants of much smaller size grow in the north, where the rains are more intense. The reason for the size difference is that the northern plants have to compete with other savanna vegetation, while those in the south have practically no competition.

Welwitschia is not wind-pollinated, as it produces a small amount of pollen, but flowers are open in an extended period that encourages cross-pollination by beetles and some wasps. Female cones mature in spring, nine months after fertilization. Seeds are large, with papery wings that take flight with the spring winds, after the female cones disintegrate. The seeds have a limited time to germinate, only several days. Once established, the seedlings depend on the fog until the next rain. They are a determined species, that is for sure, and the plant survives some very unique environmental conditions.

A Prehistoric Relic

In earlier times, people used the core of the female plant as food; it is supposedly very tasty, and the reason for its original name, *onyanga,* meaning "desert onion." The rest of the world was introduced to *Welwitschia mirabilis* by Austrian explorer and medical doctor Friedrich Welwitsch in 1859, who found it in southern Angola. The legend says that when he saw the plant, he was so excited that he knelt next to it and stared, speechless. Later, he sent the plant to Joseph Dalton Hooker, the director of the Royal Botanic Gardens, Kew, in England, who then officially described it and named it in honor of its discoverer, even though Welwitsch had recommended the native Angolan name *tumboa* be used. The Latin name for the species, *mirabilis,* means "wonderful" or "marvelous." The *welwitschia* is a kind of relic from the Jurassic period, which partially explains many of its unique qualities.

WINTERGREEN
Gaultheria procumbens
Minty Cover

Gaulteria procumbens, also known as American wintergreen, is a woody, rhizomatous, creeping, evergreen ground cover in the heath family of Ericaceae. It's native to woodlands in eastern North America, from Georgia and Tennessee to Newfoundland and other parts of Canada. Its erect stem can grow up from the rhizomes to be 3 to 6 inches tall, while the glossy, elliptic, leathery, dark green leaves usually grow about 2 inches in length. It makes an attractive ground cover that bears comparatively large, waxy, white flowers approximately 3 to 4 inches long. The flowers bloom in early summer, forming between the leaf axis, and then produce bright red berries. The berries are edible and can persist on the plant along with its green leaves throughout the winter, from which comes the name *wintergreen*. Both the leaves and fruits have a minty taste and aroma. The essential oil extracted from wintergreen's foliage has stimulating, astringent, and diuretic effects when consumed. Berries possess a minty flavor all their own, and many make herbal teas from the leaves and branches. Wintergreen is also a popular ice cream flavor in regions where the plant grows.

Wintergreen grows best in organically rich and slightly acidic soil. It likes an even amount of moisture and must be in areas with drainage, although well-established plants may tolerate drier soils. The plant requires full to partial shade and withers quickly in full sun. However, the herb does best in climates with cool summers. Wintergreen regenerates primarily by spread of its rhizomes, which lie close to the surface. While it can't survive forest fires, a brief fire will not kill it off completely, as its shallow rhizomes allow it to rejuvenate even if its leaves have been destroyed or consumed. *Gaultheria procumbens* is a food for many animals, and for some it is the only source of food through winter. The survival of berries in winter is very important, as it is one of the rare green foods animals can eat when nothing else is available.

A Plant of Many Names

The genus name of wintergreen, *Gaultheria,* was given in honor of Jean-Francois Gaultier, who was a special king's physician for the French colony of Quebec during the period from 1742 until 1756. He was also an avid plant collector and botanist. There are also many other common names given to this plant, depending on the region: *American mountain tea, Canada tea, boxberry, canterberry, chickenberry, creeping wintergreen, deerberry, gingerberry, partridge berry, squaw vine, teaberry,* and *spiceberry,* to name but a few.

WITCH HAZEL
Hamamelis
Exploding Seeds

Witch hazel has about fifteen medical uses, each proven useful in treating a number of different problems. Native Americans knew of its many health benefits and treated the plant with great respect. Also known as *Hamamelis,* witch hazel is a genus of flowering plants from the family Hamamelidaceae. Three species are known in North America, one in China, and one in Japan. North American species are also known as *winterblooms.*

The plant typically grows as a deciduous shrub, reaching 9 to 26 feet tall. It has oval, alternately arranged leaves, 1½ to 6 inches long and 1 to 4 inches wide. The leaves are wavy in the center, with a smooth margin. The plant's genus name means "together with fruit," which refers to the blooming of its flowers alongside the previous year's maturing fruits. Most of the species bloom during January to March, except for *Hamamelis virginiana*, which produces flowers from September to November. The flowers have four slender petals, with pale to dark yellow, red, or orange colors, and comprise two-part capsules, less than ½ inch long, each half of which contains only one black seed. The capsules split in two when mature. The opening of the pod, however, is violent, such that it literally combusts with an explosive sound as loud as a firecracker. This causes the seeds to be ejected to distances of more than 30 feet from the mother plant. This process has led to another nickname, *snapping hazel.*

The *witch* part of the plant's name actually comes from the Old English word *wiche,* or *wice,* meaning both "pliant" and "bendable." The name *witch hazel* was used in England as a synonym for *wych elm,* or *Ulmus glabra,* but Americans have simply extended the familiar name to the newfound plant. Witch hazels are very popular ornamental plants, mostly grown for their rich-colored clusters.

The Plant as Medicine

Witch hazel contains the chemical tannin, which is partly amorphous and partly crystal. It also has gallic acid, physterol, fat, resin, and other bitter and odorous elements that make it widely used in medicine, both traditional and modern. The plant provides many health benefits:

- Controls blemishes and spots
- Shrinks bags under the eyes
- Heals and soothes diaper rash
- Relieves varicose veins
- Reduces and soothes external hemorrhoids
- Soothes poison oak and poison ivy
- Treats chicken pox blisters
- Soothes and treats bad sunburns
- Soothes and in some instances prevents razor burn
- Heals bruises
- Moisturizes dry skin
- Heals and soothes various bruises and cuts
- Heals bug bites
- Refreshes tired eyes
- Serves as a natural (and pleasurable) deodorant

WOLFFIA ANGUSTA
Big Potential in a Small Package

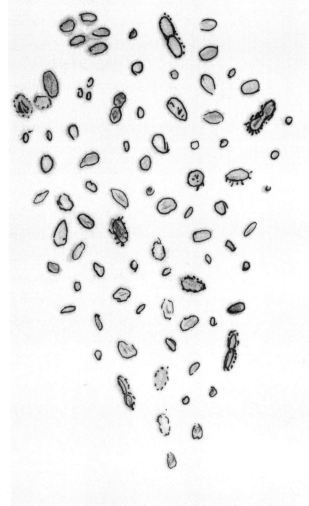

The only way to identify the species of a *Wolffia* flower is to look at it with a microscope; otherwise you will see only small green spots on the water surface where they grow. Scientists consider the *Wolffia* the smallest flower in the world. Its fruit, called utricle, is also the smallest known, with an average weight of .00007 grams. The microscopic plant is composed of 40 percent protein, similar to soybeans. The people of Thailand, Burma, and Laos use it as a food supplement, although it takes a forest of it to make one meal.

Wolffia is a rootless, freely floating water plant, preferring freshwater. It's shaped like a blob, and its size says everything: 0.01 inch long and a fraction of that wide. Native to Southeast Asia, Australia, and the Pacific, this amazing specimen of life belongs to the family Araceae (or Lamnaceae), and is a perennial, with round-edged green leaves. It blooms in summer, with flowers weighing only as much as two grains of sand. In addition to its flowers being speck-size, they are even harder to notice because they are nearly the same green color as the plants' leaves—and it would take somewhere around five thousand of its tiny flowers to fill one thimble. *Wolffia angusta* belongs to a genus of about 10 species, commonly named aquatic plants or *thalli*.

Wolffia often grows in colonies, forming a dense mat on the water's surface. They are angiosperms and reproduce vegetatively. Each plant (or frond) is able to reproduce several times before dying. Its tiny seeds are freeze-resistant. *Wolffia angusta* is often referred to as a *watermeal,* and many have wrongly identified it as duckweed. It is rich with proteins, and nearly all aquatic animals and fish prey on the plant.

Solving the World's Problems

The significance of *Wolffia* is much larger than its size. Some recent studies show that *Wolffia angusta* has a great potential to help solve some serious problems, including the bioremediation or filtering of polluted waters, since the plant can absorb a number of known harmful chemicals and covert them into nutrients. Some have even identified the plant as an excellent source of biofuel, which could hopefully reduce our dependence on oil. The plant grows fast, and people have begun trials to find an efficient means to mass produce it for its protein and inexpensively help end world hunger. Who knows? The world's smallest flower might prove to be nature's solution to one of the world's biggest problems.

YERBA
Ilex paraguariensis
The Miracle Tea

What has the health benefits of tea, the strength of coffee, and the euphoria of chocolate, all in one? Yerba leaves contain theophylline, caffeine, and theobromine, all of which are present in coffee, tea, and chocolate. However, unlike tea, drinks made from yerba have much lower levels of tannin, lessening the bitter taste; unlike coffee, it's not very acidic and oily, so you won't get jitters or stomach woes.

A species belonging to the family Aquifoliaceae and native to subtropical South America, yerba is traditionally consumed as the beverage *maté*. The Guarani people of Paraguay were the first to use and cultivate the plant prior to colonization. Yerba starts its life as a shrub and then, as it matures, grows into a tree up to 49 feet tall. Its leaves are evergreen, with serrated margins, 2 to 4 inches long. Its flowers are greenish white and small, and have four petals each. The fruits or drupes are red, and less than ¼ inch in diameter. The original name comes from the Spanish *yerba* and Portuguese *erba,* both meaning "herb," and refers mostly to the leaves that contain mateine, which remain the only part of the plant harvested commercially.

Historically, a broader consumption of yerba started in the sixteenth century, when Spanish colonizers cultivated it in Argentina, Bolivia, Chile, Brazil, and Peru. In the seventeenth century, Jesuits established the first plantations in Argentina, which is now the largest producer of yerba.

Multivitamin Tree
Yerba tea is also often called a "miracle tea," as the plant's leaves contain twenty-four vitamins and minerals, lots of antioxidants, and fifteen amino acids. According to the results of a study conducted by the Pasteur Institute, "It is difficult to find a plant in any area in the world equal to mate in nutritional value." Yerba has "practically all of the vitamins necessary to sustain life." In addition, the plant is very versatile, and people can prepare the tea in many different ways, using tea infusions, French presses, coffee

machines, and even espresso makers. Yerba drinks can be consumed cold or hot, served with honey and milk, or with mint and lemon.

Some of the most common health benefits include an enhancement in the ability to focus, strengthened physical endurance, aid to the digestion process, weight control, and significant support of the cardiovascular system. A yerba a day (instead of the traditional apple) might truly keep the doctor away.

YEW
Taxus baccata
A Secret Poison

Yew is a plant rich in myths, legends, folklore—and toxins, which are disguised by its intensely beautiful greenery. A conifer, yew is found in Europe, North America, northwestern Africa, northern Iran, and Southwest Asia. Its other common names are *European yew* and *English yew*. Yews usually live for four hundred to six hundred years, though several specimens in Britain are thought to be from the tenth century B.C. and are more than nine thousand years old. It is the longest-living species in Europe, thanks to its slow growth, ability to resist pests and disease, and the process by which its drooping branches take hold in the soil and form new trunks.

Belonging to the family Taxaceae, yews are evergreen trees, 33 to 66 feet high (in rare, extreme cases up to 92 feet!), with trunks 6 feet in diameter. Leaves are lanceolate, dark green and flat, 1½ inches long, and are spirally arranged on the stem—not to mention very poisonous. Each cone produced contains a single seed, surrounded by a modified scale that later develops into a red, berry-shaped structure called an aril. Arils mature about seven to nine months after pollination and are the only part of the tree that is not toxic, and as such are a food for different birds.

The oldest yew tree is in Bermiego, Asturia, Spain, and is 45 feet tall at the crown. In 1995, the Spanish government declared it a national monument, and it is now protected by law. The oldest wooden artifact made of yew is a Clactonian spear, found in 1911 in Essex, England, and estimated to be 450,000 years old. Celts believed the tree magical. Its wood was used for divining rods to find water and was considered the best wood to make bows. William Tell, who shot an arrow through an apple on his son's head, had a yew bow. People took to planting the tree near graveyards to ward off evil spirits or as a border around towns to bring good luck.

Ancient peoples considered the yew a symbol of transcendence of death and reincarnation. *The Canon of Medicine*, written in 1021, describes the plant as a cardiac remedy. In some regions of the central Himalayas, people use yew to treat breast and ovarian cancer.

The yew's toxic qualities have also been well-known through history. When the Cantabrians were under siege by the Roman Gaius Furnius, many in the walled compound committed suicide by yew poisoning, rather than face humiliating defeat.

Toxicity and Incidents

All parts of the yew (except the berries) contain taxin, which is a complex alkaloid, as well as ephedrine, cyanogenic glycoside, and a volatile oil. When poisoned, animals and humans may not display symptoms of illness but will die nonetheless in as little as a few hours. Although the berry's flesh isn't poisonous, the seed inside is toxic. Only three seeds are enough to kill a person.

YOPO
Anadenanthera peregrina
Spiritual Snuff

Anadenanthera peregrina and *Piptadenia peregrina* are two names for the same plant, which has many other common names, such as *yopo, nopo, mopo, jopo, cohoba, jungle juice, calcium tree,* or *parica.* Whatever you call it, if you use its beans or seeds (or sometimes its dried leaves) as a snuff, you may forget not only its name, but also your own. Yopo is a hallucinogenic plant with psychoactive properties.

A perennial tree, *yopo* is native to South America and the Caribbean, growing up to 60 feet high. Its flowers come in colors ranging from white to pale yellow and have a spherical shape. Although people have smoked and sought after its leaves since ancient times, *yopo* isn't a threatened species. Many consider the plant an entheogen, meaning "generating the divine within," and it has found its way into many different rituals and ceremonies. Beyond the realm of spirituality, many know the plant as a good source of dietary calcium.

The plant has a rich ethnobotanical history and was once a valuable religious component of at least fifty-five indigenous tribes from its native regions. The snuff made from its bean was called *cohoba,* used in Chile, Brazil, Colombia, Peru, the Dominican Republic, Haiti, and Puerto Rico. Archeologists have discovered many artifacts, including long tubes, usually made of bamboo or bird bones, used for blowing *cohoba* into the nostril of another person. Not many people from modern cultures know about *yopo* snuffing, but it was (and still is) very popular among indigenous South Americans and Mexicans. Records indicate that as much as 20 percent of the ancient Mayan population used *yopo* snuff regularly.

Psychedelic *yopo* snuff is prepared by roasting the black beans until they break out of their husks, similar to popcorn popping. The husks are then removed, and the beans are ground into a powder, after which calcium hydroxide or limestone, or calcium oxide from ashes or crushed seashells, is added. The mix becomes similar to bread dough by adding just a bit of water, and after moistening, it gets shaped as a ball. After a few days, it's ready to use. Some indigenous tribes from the Orinoco basin in Venezuela and Colombia, as well as some across the Amazon River in Brazil, still use the snuff for spiritual healing. The beans and falling leaves of *yopo* trees are hallucinogenic to cattle, too, as well as toxic.

The Effects

Yopo contains the hallucinogen DMT; while sniffing, the user may feel a significant pain in the nostrils, although it is quickly replaced by the psychedelic effects. Physical effects include numbness and tingling throughout the whole body, as well as an increased heart rate. The hallucinatory effects start with colors becoming more vivid, while shapes take on altered dimensions. Effects usually intensify quickly, but last only briefly, quickly giving way to nausea and general unease.

ZUBROWKA
Hierochloe odorata
Vodka, and Much More . . .

Widely known as the plant that makes the best Polish vodka, *zubrowka* has many traditional uses in other regions. Its names include *sweetgrass, holly grass, Mary's grass, Seneca grass,* or even *vanilla grass,* probably because it is an aromatic plant growing natively across northern Eurasia and also in North America. Its sweet scent comes from coumarin, a chemical compound found in the plant that is used in herbal medicine.

Zubrowka is a perennial, hairless, slender plant with tufted underground stems or rhizomes. It belongs to the family Poaceae. Its leaf blades are aromatic, and grow 7 to 11 inches long, with slightly rough edges. Flowering parts come in open panicles—a branched flowering structure of about the same length as the leaves. The fertile spikelets, or the structures on which the flowers are held, arise from two sterile florets and one fertile floret. The *zubrowka's* fruits are small, dry, thin walled, with only one seed inside that is fused to an ovary wall. This seed combination is called caryopsis. The herb grows with full or partial sun exposure. The seeds aren't very viable since it takes a young plant two to three years to develop a strong root system. The easiest way to propagate is by cutting plugs from well-established herbs.

Uses for *zubrowka* include traditional basketry, in which the dry and brittle stems are soaked in warm water to make them pliable. Other European uses include its treatment as holy grass to be posted on church doors on specific saints' days, but also in honor of the Virgin Mary. The French use *zubrowka* to flavor tobacco, candy, soft drinks, and some perfumes. Russians use it to make vodka and as an additive to flavor certain teas. *Zubrowka* has a mellow, calming effect and is used by some people for entering a meditative state, although it is not known to have any psychotropic effects.

American Traditions

Native Americans used *zubrowka,* or sweetgrass, primarily for basketry. Some tribes, including the Dakota, Cheyenne, Lakota, Kiowa, and others, used it as a protection from evil spirits and to honor ancestors in numerous ritual practices. Native Americans also used it in cosmetics and as an aromatic hair shampoo. Teas made from the plant proved useful in fighting coughs and sore throats in the Blackfoot and Flathead tribes. The Kiowas used its fragrant leaves for mattresses and pillows. The Cheyenne tribe smoked it in pipes during their Sacred Arrow and Sun Dance ceremonies.

ACKNOWLEDGMENTS

Once again, foremost thanks to Peter Hubbard, now Senior Executive Editor at William Morrow. His steadfast encouragement harks back to the days when editors nurtured writers, not only doing the job of redlining, but taking time to listen to a writer's particular tales of woe. Peter retains that special love of books and writing—no small feat in our current world of bottom lines and corporate power. Big thanks to editorial assistant Cole Hager for his insightful comments, and to all those at HarperCollins and William Morrow for their much-appreciated efforts.

Also, another tip of the hat to my agent, Frank Weimann of Folio Management, who remains a longtime and loyal supporter of yours truly. Much thanks to botanists and researchers Dr. Jagdev Singh, Dr. Manish Goyal, and Krum Velkov, who helped me navigate through this complex science. And last but not least, sincere gratitude to the talented artists of the Tropical Botanic Artists Collective. I thank them for their enthusiasm and diligence in providing original art to accompany my passages.

CREDITS

All of the original drawings in this book were created by the artists of the Tropical Botanic Artists Collective. The group was established in Miami, Florida, in 2006 to pursue the beauty of tropical plants through art. Its members come from all walks of life and each brings a unique viewpoint to his or her work. They share a love of the natural world and it is reflected in their admiration for botanical subjects. They hope that their viewers will take a moment to observe the wonders of minute detail in plants and bring these new powers of observation into everyday life. If you would like to obtain prints, contact them through their website, http://www.tropicalbotanicartists.com.

MARGIE BAUER: *Mimosa pudica.*

KRISTI BETTENDORF: *(Caesalpina pulcherrima); Sphenophyllum;* Wintergreen *(Gaultheria procumbens).*

BEVERLY BORLAND: Castor Oil Bush; Anise Hyssop (*Agastache foeniculum*); Black-eyed Susan (*Rudbekia hirta*); Diviner's Sage (*Salvia divinorum*); Lavender (*Lavandula*); Licorice *(Glycyrrhiza glabra)*; Ragweed; Red Tide Algae.

SILVIA BOTA: Absinthe (*Artemisia absinthium*); Artichoke; Azalea; Bird of Paradise (*Strelitzia regina*); Broccoli; Calla Lily; Dahlia;

Dragonwort; Elderflower (*Sambucus*); Ginkgos; Khat (*Catha edulis*); Kiwi; Magnolia; Nepenthe; Nettle; Rhododendron; Rose; Sandbox Tree (*Hura crepitans*); St. John's Wort; Water Hyacinth; Weeping Willow; *Victoria amazonica;* Witch Hazel.

MARGE BROWN: Carrot; Foxglove; Ferns; Hydrilla (*Hydrilla verticillata*); Palms.

MARIE CHANEY: Bad Woman (*Cnidoscolus angustidens*); Bamboo; Blue Algae (*Cyanobacteria*); Fungi; Hemlock; Marigold; Venus Flytrap; *Wolffia angusta.*

SUSAN CUMINS: Bleeding Heart (*Dicentra*); Buttercup; Cannabis; Cyanide Grass (Johnson Grass); Eucalyptus; Fig; Giant Hogweed; Horsetails; Mistletoe; Paprika; Tupelo Tree; Varnish Tree (*Taxicodendron verniciiluum*); Wasabi (Wasabia japonica); Wattieza.

JEANIE DUCK: Death Cap; Doll's Eyes; Jasmine flowers (*Jasminum* spp.); Juniper; Kumquat.

JULIO FIGUEROA: Aloe vera; Amorphophallus titanium; Avocado (Persea Americana); Beech (*Fagus grandifolia*); Birch (*Betula alleghaniensis*); Birch; Cashew; Coconut; Conifers; Garlic (*Allium sativum*); Hot Peppers (*Red savina*); Jackfruit; Mango; Oak (*Quercus alba);* Philodendron; Potato; Sugar Maple; Tomato.

BOBBI GARBER: Eggplant; Opium Poppy (*Papaver somniferum*); Sunflower.

PAULINE GOLDSMITH: Agave (*Agave tequilana*); Beer Plant (*Humulus lupulus*); Belladonna; Betel Palm; Blister Bush (*Peucedanum galbanum*); Blue Bell (*Hyacinthoides non-scripta*); Burning Bush (*Dictamnus albus*); Chrysanthemum; Dumb Cane (*Diffenbachia*); Indonesian Bay Leaf; Kudzu (*Pueraria lobata*); Leaf of God (*Tabernanthe iboga*); Lie Detector Bean (Calabar); Mace (*Myristica fragrans*); Poison Ivy; Poison Leaf Plant (*Dichapetalum cymosum*); Quinine (bark of cinchona tree); Rattan Palm; Satan's Apple (*Mandragora officinarum*); Snakeroot (Death Camas); St. Anthony's Fire (Ergot); Stinking Roger (*Hyoscyamus niger*); Yerba (*Ilex paraguariensis*); Yew (*Taxus baccata*); Zubrowka (*Hyerochloe odorata*); Monkey Tree; Mustard.

LEO HERNANDEZ: Ant Plant (*Hydnophytum formicarum*); Corn; *Hydnora africane*; Peyote (*Lohophora williamsii*); Skunk Cabbage; Vanilla; *Welwitschia mirabilis.*

ANDRES KELICH: Coffee.

CAROL ANN LANE: Angel Trumpet; Be-Still Tree (*Nerium oleander*); Hot Lips Plant (*Psychotria elata*); *Lithops julii.*

ELSA NADAL: Alfalfa Sprouts; Celery; Chinese Juniper; Cypress; Cordaites; *Drakaea glyptodon* (Australian endangered orchid); Fennel (*Foeniculum vulgare*); Horseradish; Lepidodendron; Olive Tree; Oregano (*Origanum vulgare*); Maple (*Acer palmatum*); Onion; Redwood; Water Lily; White Pine.

CAROL ONSTAD: Cucumber.

JOE PULLEN: Elm.

DONNA TORRES: Ayahuasca; Cigarette Plant (*Nicotiana tabacum*); Coca; Mystical Mushrooms; Tulip; Yopo (*Anadenanthera peregrina*).

SOURCES

Andrews, H. N., Jr. 1961. *Studies in Paleobotany.* Wiley.

Arnold, C. A. 1947. *Introduction to Paleobotany.* McGraw-Hill.

Atkinson, M. D. "*Betula pendula* Roth (*B. verrucosa* Ehrh.) and *B. pubescens* Ehrh." *Journal of Ecology* 80(4): 837–70.

Bailey, L. H. 1949. *Manual of Cultivated Plants.* 2nd ed. Macmillan Co.

Baker, H. G. 1947. "Biological Flora of the British Isles (series): *Melandrium dioicum* (L. emend.) Coss and Germ." *Journal of Ecology* 35: 283–92.

Barkley, T. M., ed. 1991. *Flora of the Great Plains.* University Press of Kansas.

Barnaby, Conrad, III. 1988. *Absinthe: History in a Bottle.* Chronicle Books.

Baskin, J. M., and C. C. Baskin. 1983. "Germination Ecology of *Veronica arvensis.*" *Journal of Ecology* 71: 57–68.

———. 1994. "Germination Requirement of *Oenothera biennis* Seed During Burial Under Natural Seasonal Temperature Cycles." *Canadian Journal of Botany* 22: 779–82.

———. 1986. "Temperature Requirements for After-Ripening in Seeds of Nine Winter Annuals." *Weed Research* 26: 375–80.

———. 1995. "Variation in the Annual Dormancy Cycle in Buried Seeds of the Weedy Winter Annual *Viola arvensis.*" *Weed Research* 35: 353–62.

Beltz, R. C., and D. F. Bertelson. 1990. *Distribution Maps for Mid South Tree Species.* U.S. Department of Agriculture, National Forest Service.

Bisacre, M., R. Carlisle, D. Robertson, and J. Ruck. 1984. *The Illustrated Encyclopedia of Plants*. Exeter Books.

Brown, Tom, Jr. 1983. *Tom Brown's Guide to Wild Edible & Medicinal Plants*. Berkeley Books.

Clewell, A. F. 1990. *Guide to the Vascular Plants of the Florida Panhandle*. University Presses of Florida.

Coker, W. C., and H. R. Totten. 1945. *Trees of the Southeastern States, Including Virginia, North Carolina, South Carolina, Georgia, and Northern Florida*. University of North Carolina Press.

Cronquist, A. 1980. *Vascular Flora of the Southeastern United States*. Vol. 1. University of North Carolina Press.

Cullina, William. 2000. *The New England Wild Flower Society Guide to Growing and Propagating Wildflowers of the United States and Canada*. Edited by Nancy Beaubaire. Houghton Mifflin Company.

Daubenmire, R. F. 1947. *Plants and Environment*. Wiley.

Dean, B. E. 1961. *Trees and Shrubs in the Heart of Dixie, Including Some Cultivated Plants and Common Vines*. Coxe Publishing Company.

————. 1988. *Trees and Shrubs of the Southeast*. Birmingham Audubon Society Press.

Denny, Guy L. 1990. *Ohio's Trees*. Ohio Department of Natural Resources Press.

Druse, Ken. 1994. *The Natural Habitat Garden*. Clarkson Potter.

Duncan, W. H. 1975. *Woody Vines of the Southeastern United States*. University of Georgia Press.

Duncan, W. H., and M. B. Duncan. 1988. *Trees of the Southeastern United States*. University of Georgia Press.

Edwards, D. 1980. *Early Land Floras*. Academic Press.

Elias, J. 1984. Geological Society of America, Special Paper. pp. 1–176.

Foote, L. E., and S. B. Jones Jr. 1989. *Native Shrubs and Woody Vines of the Southeast*. Timber Press.

Franks, J. 1979. *The Encyclopedia of Prehistoric Life*. McGraw-Hill.

Gentry, Howard Scott. 1982. *Agaves of Continental North America*. University of Arizona Press.

Gilmore, Melvin R. 1978. *Uses of Plants by the Indians of the Missouri River Region*. University of Nebraska Press.

Godfrey, R. K. 1988. *Trees, Shrubs, and Woody Vines of Northern Florida and Adjacent Georgia and Alabama*. University of Georgia Press.

Green, C. H. 1939. *Trees of the South*. University of North Carolina Press.

Harrar, E. S., and J. G. Harrar. 1946. *Guide to Southern Trees*. McGraw-Hill.

Harstad, Carolyn. 1997. *Go Native! Gardening with Native Plants and Wildflowers*. Indiana University Press.

Hutchens, Alma R. 1992. *A Handbook of Native American Herbs*. Shambhala Publications.

Isley, D. 1990. *Vascular Flora of the Southeastern United States*. University of North Carolina Press.

Joyce, Christopher. 1994. *Earthly Goods*. Little, Brown & Company.

Kay, Margarita Artschwage. 1996. *Healing with Plants in the American and Mexican West*. University of Arizona Press.

Lambeth, W. A. 1911. *Trees, and How to Know Them: A manual with analytical and dichotomous keys of the principal forest trees of the South*. B. F. Johnson.

Loewer, Peter. 2000. *The Wild Gardener: On Flowers and Foliage for the Natural Border*. Stackpole Books.

Lounsberry, A. 1901. *Southern Wild Flowers and Trees*. F. A. Stokes Company.

Maisenhelder, Louis C. 1969. *Identifying Juvenile Seedlings in Southern Hardwood Forests*. U.S. Department of Agriculture, National Forest Service.

Marinelli, Janet. 1998. *Stalking the Wild Amaranth: Gardening in the Age of Extinction*. Henry Holt & Company.

May, D. M., J. S. Vissage, and D. V. Few. 1990. "New Tree-Classification System Used by the Southern Forest Inventory and Analysis Unit." U.S. Department of Agriculture, National Forest Service.

Mayes, Vernon O., and Barbara Bayles Lacy. 1989. *Nanise', A Navajo Herbal*. Navajo Community College Press.

Moore, Michael. 1990. *Los Remedios: Traditional Herbal Remedies of the Southwest*. Red Crane Books.

————. 1989. *Medicinal Plants of the Desert & Canyon West*. Museum of New Mexico Press.

Murray, Michael T. 1992. *The Healing Power of Herbs*. Pima Publishing.

Nabhan, Gary Paul. 1985. *Gathering the Desert*. University of Arizona Press.

Ody, Penelope. 1993. *The Complete Medicinal Herbal*. Dorling Kindersley, Inc.

Otteson, Carole. 1995. *The Native Plant Primer*. Harmony Books.

Phillips, Kathryn. 1998. *Paradise by Design: Native Plants and the New American Landscape.* Farrar, Straus & Giroux.

Preston, R. J., Jr., and V. G. Wright. 1981. *Identification of Southeastern Trees in Winter.* North Carolina Agricultural Extension Service.

Robinette, G. O. 1985. *Trees of the South.* Van Nostrand Reinhold.

Rose, Cassandra, and Mary Ann Rose. 1988. *The Native Plants of Ohio.* Department of Horticulture, Ohio State University.

About the Author

© by Lisa Lee

MICHAEL LARGO is the author of *The Big, Bad Book of Beasts, God's Lunatics, Genius and Heroin, The Portable Obituary,* the Bram Stoker Award–winning *Final Exits: The Illustrated Encyclopedia of How We Die,* and three novels. He is the former editor of *New York Poetry* and the researcher and archivist for the film company Allied Artists. He and his family live in Florida with a dog, two turtles, a parrot, two canaries, and a tank of fish.